The Schaubühne Berlin under Thomas Ostermeier

Methuen Drama Engage offers original reflections about key practitioners, movements and genres in the fields of modern theatre and performance. Each volume in the series seeks to challenge mainstream critical thought through original and interdisciplinary perspectives on the body of work under examination. By questioning existing critical paradigms, it is hoped that each volume will open up fresh approaches and suggest avenues for further exploration.

Series Editors
Mark Taylor-Batty, University of Leeds, UK
Enoch Brater, University of Michigan, USA

Titles
Performing the Unstageable, Karen Quigley
ISBN 978-1-3500-5545-2

Contemporary Drag Practices and Performers, edited by Mark Edward
and Stephen Farrier
ISBN 978-1-3500-8294-6

Authenticity in Contemporary Theatre and Performance,Daniel Schulze
ISBN 978-1-3500-0096-4

Drama and Digital Arts Cultures, David Cameron, Michael Anderson
and Rebecca Wotzko
ISBN 978-1-472-59219-4

Social and Political Theatre in 21st-Century Britain: Staging Crisis,
Vicky Angelaki
ISBN 978-1-474-21316-5
Watching War on the Twenty-First-Century Stage: Spectacles of Conflict,
Clare Finburgh
ISBN 978-1-472-59866-0

Fiery Temporalities in Theatre and Performance: The Initiation of History,
Maurya Wickstrom
ISBN 978-1-4742-8169-0

*Ecologies of Precarity in Twenty-First Century Theatre: Politics, Affect,
Responsibility*, Marissia Fragkou
ISBN 978-1-4742-6714-4

Robert Lepage/Ex Machina: Revolutions in Theatrical Space, James Reynolds
ISBN 978-1-4742-7609-2

The Schaubühne Berlin under Thomas Ostermeier

Reinventing Realism

Edited by Peter M. Boenisch

Series Editors: Mark Taylor-Batty and Enoch Brater

methuen | drama

LONDON • NEW YORK • OXFORD • NEW DELHI • SYDNEY

METHUEN DRAMA
Bloomsbury Publishing Plc
50 Bedford Square, London, WC1B 3DP, UK
1385 Broadway, New York, NY 10018, USA
29 Earlsfort Terrace, Dublin 2, Ireland

BLOOMSBURY, METHUEN DRAMA and the Methuen Drama logo
are trademarks of Bloomsbury Publishing Plc

First published in Great Britain 2021
This paperback edition published in 2022

Copyright © Peter M. Boenisch and contributors, 2021

Peter M. Boenisch and contributors have asserted their right under
the Copyright, Designs and Patents Act, 1988, to be identified as
authors of this work.

For legal purposes the Acknowledgements on p. xxiii constitute an extension
of this copyright page.

Cover design: Charlotte Daniels
Cover image © Gianmarco Bresadola/Schaubühne

All rights reserved. No part of this publication may be reproduced or transmitted
in any form or by any means, electronic or mechanical, including photocopying,
recording, or any information storage or retrieval system, without prior
permission in writing from the publishers.

Bloomsbury Publishing Plc does not have any control over, or responsibility for,
any third-party websites referred to or in this book. All internet addresses
given in this book were correct at the time of going to press. The author
and publisher regret any inconvenience caused if addresses have
changed or sites have ceased to exist, but can accept no
responsibility for any such changes.

A catalogue record for this book is available from the British Library.

A catalog record for this book is available from the Library of Congress.

ISBN: HB: 978-1-350-16579-3
PB: 978-1-350-19070-2
ePDF: 978-1-350-16582-3
eBook: 978-1-350-16580-9

Series: Engage

Typeset by RefineCatch Limited, Bungay, Suffolk

To find out more about our authors and books visit www.bloomsbury.com and
sign up for our newsletters.

Contents

List of Illustrations	vii
Notes on Contributors	ix
Preface: Twenty Years of the Schaubühne Berlin under Thomas Ostermeier: Ambitions, Achievements, Transformations	xiii
Acknowledgements	xxiii

Part One   The Schaubühne Berlin under Thomas Ostermeier: Reinventing an Institution

1	The First Season: The Mission (1999) *Thomas Ostermeier, Jens Hillje, Sasha Waltz and Jochen Sandig*	3
2	Between Philosophical and Sociological Theatre: The Political *Regietheater* of Peter Stein and Thomas Ostermeier at the Schaubühne Berlin *Erika Fischer-Lichte*	7
3	The Schaubühne's Civic Mission in the Age of Globalization: An Imaginary Island that Probes Society *Ramona Mosse*	22
4	'Audiences Know Their Cause will be Treated': Making Political Theatre at the Schaubühne *Thomas Ostermeier in Conversation with Clare Finburgh Delijani*	39

Part Two   Thomas Ostermeier at the Schaubühne: Reinventing 'Directors' Theatre'

5	Socialist Realism, Capitalist Realism, Ostermeier Realism *Marvin Carlson*	53
6	Thomas Ostermeier's Shakespeare Productions: The *Mise en Action* of Canonical Plays *Jitka Goriaux Pelechová*	66
7	*Hamlet* Out of Joint: Variations on a Theme in Thomas Ostermeier's Production, 2008–20 *Elisa Leroy*	81
8	Sensing the North: Thomas Ostermeier and the Schaubühne in Brazil *Igor de Almeida Silva*	95

vi *Contents*

9   Confronting the Present: Thomas Ostermeier's Post-conceptual
     Regietheater   *Peter M. Boenisch*   105

Part Three   The Schaubühne's Experiments Across Forms and Borders:
Towards a New Realism

10   Theatre Towards the Liberation of Thinking: Experimenting
     with Realism(s) at the Schaubühne, 2000–10   *Jens Hillje*   123
11   Re-scripting Realism: Katie Mitchell and Thomas Ostermeier
     at the Schaubühne   *Benjamin Fowler*   141
12   Encountering the Rage from the South: Latin American Theatre
     at the Schaubühne's FIND Festival   *Marina Ceppi*   159
13   Performing Bodies as a Scenic Playground of Social Realities:
     Choreographic Theatre at the Schaubühne Berlin
     Sabine Huschka   173
14   REST/less EXHAUSTION, SEMI-CALM: Some Notes on
     Falk Richter and Anouk van Dijk's *Trust*   *Hans-Thies Lehmann*   191

Index   202

List of Illustrations

Cover Designed by architect Erich Mendelsohn in 1927 as a cinema, the Schaubühne am Lehniner Platz is based in a huge horseshoe-shaped modernist building on the old West Berlin shopping street, the Kurfürstendamm. It is part of an ensemble of buildings set to model progressive city life, combining culture, living, sports and shopping facilities.

1 In the summer of 1999, the Schaubühne's co-founder and long-term managing director Jürgen Schitthelm presented the theatre's new, young team of artistic directors: Thomas Ostermeier, Jens Hillje, Sasha Waltz and Jochen Sandig. xv

2 In Thomas Ostermeier's production of Ibsen's *Ein Volksfeind* (*An Enemy of the People*, 2012), characters and audience met for a joint debate that reflects the Schaubühne's civic mission far beyond its theatre productions: David Ruland as newspaper publisher Aslaksen, and Stefan Stern as Ibsen's Doctor Stockmann, during the discussion scene in the performance on 8 September 2012. 29

3 Maja Zade's *Status Quo* (dir. Marius von Mayenburg, 2019) lambasted misogynistic power dynamics in the contemporary work place, including the theatre, by flipping the gender hierarchies: Jenny König, Jule Böwe and Carolin Haupt gave a juicy parody of rehearsal room practices. 34

4 In contrast to the lavish realism of their Ibsen sets, Jan Pappelbaum's stage designs for Thomas Ostermeier's Shakespeare productions were characterized by their minimalistic simplicity of form in an empty, unchanging space. Here, the director's regular Shakespeare protagonists Jenny König and Lars Eidinger play Isabella and Angelo in *Mass für Mass* (*Measure for Measure*, 2011). 71

5 Showing dancing bodies against the Schaubühne's gigantic concrete walls, Sasha Waltz's *Körper* (2000) found a productive relationship with the theatre's architectural space. 126

6 As the Schaubühne's associate director, Flemish Luk Perceval introduced a new aesthetic where acting and performing were no longer considered as different approaches between which one needed to decide. His work at the theatre peaked with *Molière* (2007), featuring Thomas Thieme, amid Katrin Brack's economic scenography that gradually filled the stage with snow. 134

viii   *List of Illustrations*

7   In Thomas Ostermeier's 2003 production of Franz Xaver Kroetz's
    silent play *Wunschkonzert*, conceived as companion piece to his
    staging of Ibsen's *Nora*, Anne Tismer played Fräulein Rasch as a
    woman performed by (rather than performing) a movement score
    of habitual acts that structure her 'leisure' time.   146

8   Katie Mitchell's *Ophelias Zimmer* (2015) examined *Hamlet* from
    the fixed perspective of Ophelia's bedroom. Allowing water to seep
    in, Chloe Lamford's set visualized Ophelia's loosening grip on
    reality, under forced medication in her prison-like room.   151

9   Bringing dance and drama together, *Trust* (2009), by Falk Richter
    and Anouk van Dijk, portrayed the disorientation and loneliness
    in contemporary society. The dancing bodies made viscerally
    palpable the inner state of an utter loss of trust in our dominant
    way of life.   187

Notes on Contributors

Igor de Almeida Silva is Assistant Professor of Theatre Studies at the Universidade Federal de Pernambuco, Brazil. He graduated with his PhD in performing arts from Universidade de São Paulo and Université Sorbonne Nouvelle in 2014. He is the author of *Réquiem à Infância: um Estudo sobre Um Sábado em 30 e Viva o Cordão Encarnado de Luiz Marinho* (2009). Most recently, he was awarded a research grant by the Capes-Humboldt Research Fellowship Program to carry out postdoctoral research on Thomas Ostermeier's theatre at the Universität Hildesheim (2019/2020).

Peter M. Boenisch is Professor of Dramaturgy at Aarhus University, and a part-time Professor of European Theatre at the Royal Central School of Speech and Drama, University of London. His research areas are theatre direction and the intersections of theatre and politics, as they become manifest in aspects such as spectatorship, the institutional conditions of theatre production and transcultural performance in a globalized Europe. His books include *Directing Scenes and Senses: The Thinking of Regie* (2015), *The Theatre of Thomas Ostermeier* (co-authored with the German director, 2016) and, as editor, the volume *Littlewood – Strehler – Planchon* in the Methuen series *The Great European Stage Directors* (with Clare Finburgh, 2018), as well as the thirtieth anniversary new edition of David Bradby and David Williams's seminal study *Directors' Theatre* (2019).

Marvin Carlson is Sidney E. Cohn Distinguished Professor of Theatre, Comparative Literature and Middle Eastern Studies at City University of New York and Director of the Marvin Carlson Theatre Center at the Shanghai Theatre Academy. His many influential books include *Performance: A Critical Introduction* (1980), *The Haunted Stage: The Theatre as Memory Machine* (2003), *Speaking in Tongues: Languages at Play in the Theatre* (2009) and *Shattering Hamlet's Mirror: Theatre and Reality* (2016). A major chronicler of contemporary theatre and passionate theatre aficionado, he has spent most evenings in the theatre since obtaining his PhD from Cornell University in 1961, regularly seeing productions not only in New York, but also in Paris, Berlin, Moscow, Milan and many other places around the world.

Marina Ceppi started acting when she was twelve years old. She has worked in several plays on Buenos Aires's independent theatre circuit, not only acting but also playwriting and as assistant director. She has also acted in cinema, in both long and short films. She studied arts at the University of Buenos Aires and holds a teaching degree from the same institution. Besides her acting activity, she works as a language and theatre teacher in bilingual schools. Based in Berlin, she writes theatre and film reviews in specialized magazines, and researches about theatre and politics.

Clare Finburgh Delijani is Professor in the Department of Theatre and Performance at Goldsmiths University of London. She has published widely on modern and contemporary European theatre, and has co-authored and co-edited volumes include *Jean Genet* (2012), *Contemporary French Theatre and Performance* (2011) and *Jean Genet: Performance and Politics* (2006). Her recent research engages with the pressing political and social issues of the ecological crisis and global conflict. She has co-edited a volume of eco-critical essays, *Rethinking the Theatre of the Absurd: Ecology, the Environment and the Greening of the Modern Stage* (2015), and written a monograph on representations of war in recent British theatre, *Watching War: Spectacles of Conflict on the Twenty-First-Century Stage* (2017). Clare has also translated several plays from French into English, notably by Noëlle Renaude.

Erika Fischer-Lichte is Professor Emeritus and director of the International Research Centre *Interweaving Performance Cultures* at Freie Universität Berlin. One of Germany's most distinguished theatre scholars, she has held visiting professorships in China, India, Japan, Russia, Norway, USA, Sweden, Portugal, Spain, Brazil and Cuba. She has published widely in the fields of aesthetics, history and theory of theatre, in particular on semiotics and performativity, contemporary theatre and interweaving performance cultures. Recent book publications include *The Transformative Power of Performance: A New Aesthetics* (2008), *Tragedy's Endurance: Performances of Greek Tragedies and Cultural Identity in Germany Since 1800* (2017), and *The Politics of Interweaving Performance Cultures* (2014).

Benjamin Fowler is a lecturer in Drama, Theatre and Performance at the University of Sussex. He researches directorial practice in contemporary European theatre, focusing on directors who circulate between translocal hubs such as the Schaubühne or the International Theatre Amsterdam. He has published in journals including *Contemporary Theatre Review* and *Shakespeare Bulletin*. His work on Katie Mitchell includes an in-depth monograph on her career thus far (2021) as well as an edited collection of essays and practitioner interviews, featuring Alex Eales and Leo Warner, in *The Theatre of Katie Mitchell* (2019), also available as a series of films on Digital Theatre+.

Jitka Goriaux Pelechová is currently a Research Fellow and Associate Professor at the Drama Department of the Academy of Performing Arts in

Prague. She has authored a monograph on Thomas Ostermeier's theatre published by *Études théâtrales* (no. 58, 2013) in French, and by KANT, in Czech (awarded Best Book on Theatre by *Divadelní noviny* in 2014). Since 2006, she has been teaching at theatre studies departments of the universities of Paris Nanterre, Poitiers and Lille 3. A particular, but not exclusive, focus of her research is on contemporary European stage directing and its major figures (Thomas Ostermeier, Luc Bondy, Antoine Vitez, Einar Schleef and others). Along with her research activities, Jitka Goriaux is also a dramaturg and translator. In 2016, a collection of texts by Thomas Ostermeier, *Le Théâtre et la peur* (Actes Sud), which she co-edited with Georges Banu, and also translated into French, received the Best Book on Theatre award by the French Association of Art Critics.

Jens Hillje was, from 1999 to 2009, head dramaturg and a member of the artistic direction at Schaubühne Berlin. Having graduated in cultural studies from the universities of Hildesheim, Perugia and Berlin, he worked as freelance actor, author and director before being a co-founder, with Thomas Ostermeier, of the Baracke at Deutsches Theater in 1996. From 2013 to 2019, he was artistic co-director, with Shermin Langhoff, of Maxim-Gorki-Theater Berlin, where he now continues as a member of the Artistic Advisory Board. For almost two decades, he has collaborated as dramaturg with the German author-director Falk Richter, and for some years now has been a curator of the annual Radikal Jung (Radically Young) festival for emerging theatre directors that takes place in Munich every year. In 2019, he was awarded the Golden Lion of the Venice Biennale for his life achievement.

Sabine Huschka is a dance and theatre scholar living in Berlin. From 2015 to 2020, she headed the DFG research project *Transgressions* at the Inter-University Centre for Dance Berlin (HZT), and currently works as a fellow of the research training group 'Knowledge in the Arts' at the University of Arts (UdK) Berlin. She has held various national and international assistant professorships for performance studies, theatre and dance studies. Her publications include *Energy and Forces as Aesthetic Interventions: Politics of Bodily Scenarios* (2019), *Wissenskultur Tanz: Historische und zeitgenössische Vermittlungsakte zwischen Praktiken und Diskursen* (2009), *Choreographierte Körper im Theatron: Auftritte und Theorie ästhetischen Wissens* (2020) and *Moderner Tanz: Konzepte – Stile – Utopien* (2002/2012).

Hans-Thies Lehmann was from 1988 to 2010 Professor of Theatre Studies at Johann Wolfgang Goethe-Universität in Frankfurt. He published widely on contemporary theatre, the theory of theatre, theatre aesthetics and not least on the works of Bertolt Brecht and Heiner Müller. His most widely read books are *Postdramatic Theatre* (1999) and *Tragedy and Dramatic Theatre* (2013). For many years, he was president of the International Brecht Society. In 2017, he became a member of the Berlin Academy of Arts. In addition to his academic work, he devised numerous scenic projects, and worked as a dramaturg, most recently on Jan Fabre's epic 24-hour project *Mount Olympus*.

Elisa Leroy is a French-German dramaturg and Shakespeare scholar working in Berlin, Munich and Paris. She is currently completing her PhD on text and performance in contemporary German productions of Shakespeare's *Hamlet* at Ludwig-Maximilians-University Munich. After graduating in comparative literature in Munich and Berkeley, she worked as an assistant director on Thomas Ostermeier's francophone productions *Les revenants* by Henrik Ibsen (Théâtre de Vidy-Lausanne, 2013) and *La mouette* by Anton Chekhov (Théâtre de Vidy-Lausanne, 2016), and was assistant to the artistic director at Schaubühne Berlin from 2014 to 2016. Most recently, she worked as Thomas Ostermeier's dramaturg for *La nuit des rois ou Tout ce que vous voulez* by William Shakespeare at the Comédie-Française in Paris (2018), and as producer on *Qui a tué mon père?* by Édouard Louis (FIND, Schaubühne am Lehniner Platz, 2020).

Ramona Mosse is a Visiting Lecturer in English Literature at Bard College Berlin and a former Fellow of the Institute of Interweaving Performance Cultures at the Free University Berlin, who has also taught at the Free University Berlin, the Goethe University Frankfurt, as well as at Columbia University and Barnard College in the US. She has published widely on topics in contemporary European and American theatre, including the legacies of political theatre since Bertolt Brecht, modern tragedy, hip hop performance and aurally based dramaturgies. Ramona holds a PhD in English and Comparative Literature from Columbia University. She is a core convenor of the Performance Philosophy Network and also works as a dramaturg and translator.

Preface

Twenty Years of the Schaubühne Berlin under Thomas Ostermeier: Ambitions, Achievements, Transformations

In the early summer of 1999, Jürgen Schitthelm, one of the original founders of the Berlin Schaubühne back in 1962, and for half a century, until 2012, the theatre's managing director, informed the public about a veritable *coup de théâtre*: with the start of the new millennium, theatre director Thomas Ostermeier and choreographer Sasha Waltz, together with their respective dramaturgs Jens Hillje and Jochen Sandig, would become the Schaubühne's new artistic directors (see Figure 1). Following half a year of preparation, this new team opened its joint tenure in January 2000, with the double premiere of Waltz's by now classic choreography *Körper* (*Bodies*), followed two days later by Ostermeier's production of Lars Norén's social drama *Human Circle 3.1*, which brought his hard-hitting social realism to the stage at Lehniner Platz, directly on Kurfürstendamm, the major shopping and nightlife avenue of the old West Berlin. Just a few weeks earlier, spectators had been able to bid their farewell to the theatre's 'old guard' with the final premiere before the change in direction, a production of Shakespeare's *Hamlet* by the other great pioneer of the German *Regietheater* of the 1970s and 1980s, Peter Zadek. Together with Peter Stein, the Schaubühne's legendary artistic director between 1970 and 1985, Zadek belonged to the main protagonists of the political German *Regietheater* in the second half of the twentieth century. In the critical, politicized spirit of the 1960s, they had interrogated, deconstructed and reappropriated the plays from the classical bourgeois canon for their own post-war generation, thereby defining the (West) German trademark style of director-led theatre. Despite their often aggressive political critique against the establishment, their work was widely politically supported, since it produced a strong aesthetic signature for West German theatre to catch up and compete with its communist sibling in the East, thus finally healing the wound caused by the decision of Bertolt Brecht and other exiled artists to eventually return to the communist German Democratic Republic (GDR) rather than to the 'free' capitalist Western part of the divided German country.

The Schaubühne itself had been very much a direct result of the cultural Cold War between the two systems that accompanied the political and

xiv *Preface*

military competition between 1945 and 1989. As the East German government had cut off the sectors of the three Western allies by building the Berlin Wall on 13 August 1961, West Berlin had become an isolated exclave within the communist East. There was, from one day to the next, barely any theatre available in the West: the Deutsches Theater, the Berliner Ensemble, the Volksbühne – all major Berlin stages, with the sole exception of the Schillertheater, were located in the city's cordoned off East, and hence now beyond the reach of West Berlin audiences. In this unique historical moment, a group of theatre students (some of them, like Schitthelm, themselves originally hailing from the East) founded a theatre company; among them also was Dieter Sturm, who would become Peter Stein's celebrated dramaturg. They were able to move with their grassroots theatre project into the space of a worker union's assembly hall in Kreuzberg, which had become available since most of its members now lived on the other side of the wall that suddenly cut through the city on the street behind the theatre. This hall became the 'Schaubühne am Halleschen Ufer', where the company would reside until 1980. To convince the city's government, in 1969, to provide the funding to attract the aspiring theatre radical Peter Stein to join and lead them as artistic director, and to bring with him the company of actors he had gathered around him with his previous work at Bremen and Zürich, was the first time that these former theatre students, who never actually completed their degrees, wrote theatre history.

The change that Schitthelm, by then the only original founder remaining in the company's management, proposed thirty years later, was as radical, and even more of a surprise, since it looked beyond the founders' own taste and generation. Thomas Ostermeier and Sasha Waltz, at the time both barely in their thirties, represented not only a different aesthetic – not least with their proposed experimental interdisciplinary marriage of dance and theatre – but most of all they stood for a new, and different life experience. Those who had taken to the streets in 1968, like Stein, Zadek and the Schaubühne founders, protested for political freedom and against war, and, especially in Germany, critiqued their parents' generation's refusal to speak about their personal involvement in the disavowed barbarities of the Nazi regime. Yet those like Ostermeier and Waltz, who were born around that same time in the late 1960s into mildly affluent (West German) middle-class families, felt as if their own parents' generation, who had been active in these political protests of the 1960s and 1970s, somewhat monopolized the right to political critique. They themselves had now become 'the system', a biographical trajectory embodied by the erstwhile leader of the 1960s street protests, Joschka Fischer, who by then, in the 1990s, had become German foreign minister for the Green party, taking the country, for the first time since 1945,

Figure 1 In the summer of 1999, the Schaubühne's co-founder and long-term managing director Jürgen Schitthelm (back row, left) presented the theatre's new, young team of artistic directors: Thomas Ostermeier, Jens Hillje, Sasha Waltz and Jochen Sandig (clockwise). © Ullstein.

into a war, in Kosovo. Those in their twenties and thirties, who had hoped in vain that the country's reunification in 1989 might offer a chance to find a new, 'third way' beyond communism and capitalism alike, felt stifled in their chance to voice critique, let alone rebellion. The older generation no longer represented any of their political concerns.

More locally, Waltz and Ostermeier also represented a new, once more rapidly changing Berlin. Since 1990, the newly reunited city had become not only the capital of the Bundesrepublik again, but it attracted a young generation of artists and creatives, like Waltz and Ostermeier, as well as emerging entrepreneurs of the last pre-digital start-up generation. Rents in the city were cheap, space was available in abundance, especially in the former East with its many run-down houses that had seen little if any maintenance since the 1930s, many still bearing testimony of the deadly final weeks of the Second World War that had been fought out here street by street. Soon, a vibrant and creative alternative subcultural scene centred around the Mitte and Prenzlauer Berg districts of the former East Berlin, spearheaded by theatre director Frank Castorf and his dramaturg Matthias Lilienthal at their Volksbühne theatre. It was in this environment where both Ostermeier and Waltz started their

xvi   *Preface*

respective careers. Still in the final year of his directing degree at the prestigious Ernst Busch Theatre Academy, Ostermeier had been offered, in 1996, the chance to lead the new Baracke, a small experimental stage attached to Berlin's Deutsches Theater, Germany's unofficial 'national theatre'. In the following three years, Ostermeier and his dramaturg Jens Hillje made their names in particular by introducing the British 'in yer face' playwrights, such as Mark Ravenhill and Sarah Kane, to German audiences. Waltz, meanwhile, had returned from years of training and dancing in Amsterdam and New York (where she had somewhat 'missed' reunification overseas), setting herself up in Berlin, initially at Künstlerhaus Bethanien in Kreuzberg, where she created an immediate national success with her *Travelogue* trilogy. She then co-founded the Sophiensäle, also in 1996, with her partner Sandig and other fellow artists, such as the choreographer Jo Fabian and producer Holger Zebo Kluth, today's rector of the Ernst Busch academy. Ostermeier's and Waltz's stage work was aesthetically quite different, yet it shared a recognizable realism with explicit political undertones, which in very obvious ways directly related their stage work to the current lives of their peers in this very city, and with their concerns and problems. As they expressed in their joint mission statement for the Schaubühne, they articulated a new political critique that refreshed in its very attack the societal interrogations and provocations that Stein and Zadek had undertaken three decades prior. Furthermore, neither of them aspired for their work to be 'high art' for an educated, erudite audience alone, but a popular theatre happening for everyone – or at least, everyone of their generation, who would frequent the underground bars, concert halls and clubs, and the alternative cinemas in the city.

Schitthelm and his small group of shareholders of the private theatre cooperative certainly took a gamble to introduce such a radical shift at their Schaubühne. They had the right intuition, though – and, above all, they allowed the new project to mature over a number of years, supporting it steadfastly through initial periods of uncertainty, varied experimentation and outright mistakes. The reward was all the bigger. Straight away, however, Waltz's premiere piece *Körper* became a huge success with the public. The 'drama department' around Ostermeier, meanwhile, lagged behind, finding it difficult to continue, on the Schaubühne's big stage and in front of a larger audience from a different, much more affluent district of the German capital, the success they had celebrated at the Baracke with their intimate, rough and alternative 'in yer face' chamber aesthetics. After a few seasons, though, Ostermeier caught up with his own productions, as he turned to classics by Büchner and Ibsen. After just three years, Waltz withdrew partly – and from 2005 entirely – from their joint venture, which in reality had remained throughout two parallel projects with limited mutual exposure. Thus, a

Preface   xvii

second phase began, in which the 'new' Schaubühne continued to intensify its aesthetic explorations into the area of contemporary directing approaches: Falk Richter, already affiliated with the theatre since its inaugural season, and Flemish director Luk Perceval joined Ostermeier as associate directors for a number of years, exposing the ensemble of actors to three rather different directorial styles and working methods. Ten years into the 'new' Schaubühne, their directorial triumvirate dissolved, while at the same time head dramaturg Jens Hillje, until then remaining artistic co-director alongside Ostermeier, left the company to focus on the diversification of German theatre. He joined forces with Shermin Langhoff, first being involved in her postmigrant theatre work at the small Ballhaus Naunynstrasse, to eventually become, from 2013, joint artistic director again, with Langhoff, now at the city's Maxim Gorki Theater.

For the second decade, Ostermeier thus remained as sole artistic director and, eventually, also became a *Gesellschafter* (shareholder) in the cooperative company. By this time, the Schaubühne had managed to transform its audience; in notable contrast to other Berlin stages (with the exception of the like-minded Volksbühne and HAU), the theatre now attracted both a young and a very international audience, playing today to an otherwise unheard of capacity of 97 per cent, with tickets for almost every evening's show much sought after rarities and difficult to get hold of. Throughout its intense first decade, the 'new' Schaubühne had also forged together once again an ensemble of actors which eventually became at least as recognized as the protagonists of Peter Stein's theatre work had been. Many of the new Schaubühne performers, from Lars Eidinger, Jörg Hartmann and Mark Waschke to Ursina Lardi and Nina Hoss, became celebrated actors on national as well as international cinema and television screens as well. Regularly, they would also perform abroad with their stage work, as the Schaubühne has maintained a busy international touring schedule right from the early years of Ostermeier's tenure, initially mainly to France, soon to the US, and eventually performing around the globe. The theatre's productions, by Ostermeier himself, but equally by other acclaimed directors who would soon regularly work with his ensemble, from Katie Mitchell to Romeo Castellucci, Simon McBurney and Milo Rau, have become a regular presence beyond (yet of course certainly very much also within) the usual festival circuit of transnational contemporary Western theatre, yet also visiting Latin America, the West Bank, Iran and China.

Over the now twenty theatre seasons under his artistic (co-)tenure, Ostermeier has thus been able to consolidate, once more, the firm reputation of the Schaubühne Berlin as an international flagship of German theatre. At the same time, the company's work tends to be widely perceived, especially abroad, through the prism of Ostermeier's own work and aesthetics alone. For international audiences from beyond Berlin, and even for the many regular international visitors who frequent the theatre's four stages at Lehniner Platz on their visits to the city, little is known about this peculiar and – within the German theatre landscape – rather unique institution, its position and situation, and the transformations that Ostermeier and his various co-directors have instigated here over the past twenty years. The anniversary therefore has been an excellent occasion to bring together for this volume senior and emerging theatre scholars from Germany and beyond, as well as some key collaborators over that period, to discuss some of these aesthetic as well as institutional paradigm shifts that have taken place at the Berlin Schaubühne under Ostermeier's tenure. These achievements go far beyond singular productions or specific aesthetics, on which theatre research usually tends to focus. Today, the hegemony of neoliberal thought has long infiltrated the field of the arts as well, and the provision of art (just like that of education and health services) in many places has become perceived as a business, and no longer as a 'public service' for the community in the spirit of the post-1945 consensus that had somewhat still united the European cultural sphere of Eastern and Western Europe. While some may find it extraordinary that the city-state of Berlin supports the Schaubühne – not even a state theatre in its statute, but a private cooperative – with an annual budget of around 13 million euro, Ostermeier does not tire in pointing out that a cumulative arts budget, including all other funded Berlin stages, of 0.7 percent of the city's annual expenditure can hardly be considered a luxury, but rather a bare minimum. At the same time, the public funding – geared towards providing the Schaubühne with its building and 230 staff members, not contributing to actual production work – comes with the obligation to, for instance, train in-house apprentices in otherwise extinct specialist theatre professions, as well as to offer education for school classes and adults, provide affordable tickets for students as well as less privileged groups, and make a contribution to the city's intellectual infrastructure. As such, engaging with the Schaubühne's work of the past twenty years from an institutional perspective, we here see concrete evidence of what a 'sustainable' contemporary arts institution may look like: how such an institutional organization may foster, curate and progress aesthetic developments, while also reflecting and intervening in societal debates and contributing to global supra-cultural exchange.

Our volume addresses and unpacks the Schaubühne's work over the last two decades from three distinct perspectives. Part One concentrates on introducing and elaborating on the theatre's institutional context as well as its history, which has been briefly sketched above. The section begins, somewhat as a natural starting point for this volume, with 'The Mission', the programmatic manifesto published by the Schaubühne's new four co-directors in 1999, ahead of the beginning of their tenure, in the booklet that promoted their debut season. This key historiographical document is here, in Chapter 1, made available for the first time in full in English translation. Erika Fischer-Lichte, prominent professor emeritus of FU Berlin's Institute for *Theaterwissenschaft*, has been able to follow both of the stellar artistic enterprises at the Schaubühne since the 1970s. She is therefore ideally placed to trace, in Chapter 2, some of the key continuities and differences in the explicitly political theatre work of Peter Stein and Thomas Ostermeier, nuancing their variant approaches as 'philosophical' and 'sociological' political *Regietheater* respectively. Fischer-Lichte also emphasizes that to understand the work of these directors as well as their efforts in leading the theatre, we must consider them as interacting with the political and sociological contexts of their (very different) historical eras. Ramona Mosse first encountered the 'new' Schaubühne as it toured to New York in 2004, where our author studied theatre, some time before she would continue her career as a theatre scholar in Germany. Her Chapter 3 therefore draws on her illuminating dual vision of an 'insider's view from without', as Mosse positions the Schaubühne as an institution. Her attention is given both to the wider cultural fabric of Berlin, and to the theatre's institutional profile, in order to outline what she describes as the 'civic mission' to which the Schaubühne from its very beginning in 1962, and with a new dynamic since 2000, has remained committed over almost sixty years of theatre-making. The section then concludes with Thomas Ostermeier himself, as he responds in Chapter 4 to questions by English theatre scholar Clare Finburgh Delijani. He takes us from his personal perspective on the legacy of his famous predecessor Stein to his disappointment about the failure of establishing a model of institutional 'co-determination' among his actors and staff, while also discussing current issues such as the need to diversify the ensemble of actors.

Part Two of the book is then, somewhat inevitably, dedicated to Ostermeier's own directorial work, which – especially in the second decade of his tenure – has become the pivotal cornerstone of the Schaubühne's repertoire, at Berlin as well as in the theatre's international touring. Marvin Carlson, who personally embodies the vital link between Brecht, Stein and Ostermeier as a theatre spectator, who has paid annual visits to Berlin over more than half a century now, starts off this analysis. In Chapter 5, he outlines and contextualizes the trademark 'Ostermeier realism', from its beginnings at the Baracke in 1996, via the director's turn to classics from the European and US repertoire in the first years of the new millennium, to then arrive at his pivotal productions, beginning in particular with his 2008 *Hamlet*, which will remain a key reference point for most of the contributions in this section, and beyond, as well. Ostermeier's series of Shakespeare productions as a quite distinct 'œuvre' within the œuvre' is then more fully explored by Jitka Goriaux Pelechová in Chapter 6. The Ostermeier expert and editor of his writings in French demonstrates how the director here managed to fully develop his original approach of a collaborative *mise en action* of canonical playtexts. Elisa Leroy, herself an assistant of Ostermeier's for many years, continues this analysis with a specific case study: her Chapter 7 takes into view the ongoing, organic and erratic development of *Hamlet*, Ostermeier's signature production, from its premiere in the summer of 2008 until its 330th (and counting) performance in 2020. This view from within is then complemented in Chapter 8 by Igor de Almeida Silva's perspective from the outside, from far beyond Berlin. The Brazilian theatre scholar and director explores how Ostermeier's aesthetics resonate as well as irritate in the global south, as he exemplarily meditates on the director's antagonistic reception in Brazil; there, Ostermeier's materialist realism seems ambiguously close to as well as distant from a local horizon of expectations. The section on Ostermeier's work concludes in Chapter 9 with my own attempt to trace his 'post-conceptual' *Regietheater*, focusing on some of his recent work, in particular his stage adaptations of Didier Eribon's *Returning to Reims* (2017) and of Édouard Louis's novel *A History of Violence* (2018).

The contributions in Part Three engage with the Schaubühne's various aesthetic experiments towards a new realism, across a number of forms and genres, and (largely) beyond Ostermeier's own prominent work. The section begins, in Chapter 10, with the insightful reflections by Ostermeier's long-term co-artistic director, and head dramaturg, Jens Hillje. He contextualizes their approach to theatre within a Brechtian commitment to use theatre as a means for analysing the socio-political reality – through both content and the aesthetic form of theatre production. Hillje takes us through some of the key stages of his work alongside Ostermeier, from the difficult early years after their transition to the Schaubühne and the initial focus on defining a new dramatic repertoire to the period of the directing trio Ostermeier, Richter and Perceval. He also points us towards the indispensable impulses that the annual international festival – FIND – offered to their continuous development of the theatre's artistic programme. Benjamin Fowler, expert on Katie Mitchell's work as theatre director, scrutinizes in Chapter 11 the variant concepts of realism at work in Ostermeier and Mitchell. Comparing their re-scriptions of realist aesthetics for a twenty-first-century context, he demonstrates in rich detail how both directors employ different strategies to reclaim the political efficacy of realist aesthetics; at the same time, he argues, Mitchell manages to offer an important feminist correction to some blindspots in Ostermeier's work. The Argentinian actress and theatre critic

Preface xxi

Marina Ceppi, who first saw the Schaubühne's work in Buenos Aires before relocating to Berlin, returns to the FIND festival. Her Chapter 12 offers a case study of some recent Latin American productions, as these have featured particularly strongly within the annual festival under the curation of Florian Borchmeyer, the Schaubühne's head dramaturg from 2011 to 2019. Ceppi shows how the political 'rage' that is tangible in these productions from the south within the comparative context of the festival overcomes national perspectives. It resonates with and extends the political impetus of the Schaubühne's own work, while at the same time confronting the northern audiences with their own implications in a global economic world order whose local effects are directly confronted in these productions.

Senior German dance scholar Sabine Huschka then turns to an artistic achievement of the 'new' Schaubühne, which has so far found only limited attention in the international debate: the numerous productions created at the theatre, especially between 2000 and the early 2010s, which in a unique artistic space brought together dance and drama. In Chapter 13, Huschka offers detailed analyses of the most significant productions, and respective aesthetics, of the three choreographers associated with the Schaubühne during this period: Sasha Waltz, the theatre's co-artistic director between 2000 and 2005, who was followed by Argentinian Constanza Macras and eventually by Dutch Anouk van Dijk. Especially the choreographic work of the latter two, like the Schaubühne's dramatic productions, explicitly reflected social realities, albeit in their choreographic arrangements of movement and physical action. The final chapter continues the discussion of this aspect, and completes this volume with an analysis of one of the major coproductions of a choreographer, van Dijk, with the Schaubühne's then resident associate playwright-director, Falk Richter, on *Trust* (2009). German doyen of postdramatic theatre, Hans-Thies Lehmann, has contributed his detailed notes on seeing this production, which combine his intricate observations, associations and astute critical reflection of this interdisciplinary (post-)postdramatic theatre piece.

I am grateful to all contributors for coming on board this exploration of Thomas Ostermeier's tenure as the Schaubühne's artistic director; for taking us with their essays from production analysis and minute details to the bigger picture of this institution's intervention into the contemporary theatre world and beyond; and for helping in bringing together such a rich picture of various entry points that will allow theatre students and researchers alike to engage with the Schaubühne's unique theatre practice. It was perturbing to see that, on the very day I was writing this preface, for the first time in almost sixty years the Schaubühne had to cancel its performances and close its doors as a result of the coronavirus situation, like most, if not all, theatres around the globe. As I am following the daily news of these unprecedented developments, I hope that this theatre, and theatres everywhere, will come out of this situation and continue their important cultural work for us, their audiences.

Peter M. Boenisch
Aarhus and Berlin, March 2020

Acknowledgements

This book would not have come into existence without the inspired contributions of the chapter authors credited in the previous section. Special thanks to Jens Hillje for accepting the request to look back at his work alongside Thomas Ostermeier at the Schaubühne, and to Christopher-Fares Köhler for helping to bring his chapter into being. Thanks to the Schaubühne's team of photographers, who have granted their permissions to include the images in this volume. Furthermore, I am particularly indebted to the team at the Schaubühne's offices who have reliably supported this project alongside their busy daily schedules, in particular Dietmar Böck, assistant to Thomas Ostermeier, and Rachel-Sophie Dries, deputy head of the theatre's communications department. Lastly, thanks to Thomas Ostermeier himself, for engaging in the conversation with Clare Finburgh Delijani, and for seeing through my translation of the 'Mission' manifesto as well as granting permission to translate and make available this important historical document in full.

I am especially grateful to Mark Taylor-Batty and Enoch Brater, the series editors of Methuen's *Engage* catalogue, for including this volume under their banner. Thanks are also due to the team at Methuen, in particular to Mark Dudgeon, Meredith Benson and Anna Brewer, for patiently bearing with me while this project eventually took its shape, and for being helpful throughout the production process. Furthermore, I am in many ways indebted to the Research Department at the Royal Central School of Speech and Drama, University of London, especially to Maria Delgado and Dan Hetherington. The conference on (and with) Thomas Ostermeier, which we co-organised back in September 2014, was the original starting point for this book project. Since then, Central have generously supported my work and research for this book, as well as taken over the copyright fees so we were able to include some illustrations in this volume. And lastly, at home, Johanna has always kept me motivated and going forward, whereever this home had been, and no longer been, in the tumultuous years that now lie behind us.

Part One

The Schaubühne Berlin under Thomas Ostermeier: Reinventing an Institution

1

The First Season: The Mission (1999)

Thomas Ostermeier, Jens Hillje, Sasha Waltz and Jochen Sandig

This manifesto was originally published in the Autumn of 1999, in the programme brochure introducing the Schaubühne's first season under its new artistic directors Thomas Ostermeier, Jens Hillje, Sasha Waltz and Jochen Sandig. They opened their joint artistic tenure with a double premiere of Sasha Waltz's choreography Körper *(Bodies) on 22 January 2000, followed by Lars Norén's* Personenkreis 3.1 *(Human Circle 3.1), in Thomas Ostermeier's direction, on 24 January 2000. This document is here published for the first time, in its full version, in English, with kind permission from Schaubühne am Lehniner Platz.*

Theatre-makers in Germany have lost their mission. After two hundred years at the spearhead of enlightenment, theatre today bemoans the loss of its importance as a critical public theatre situated at the centre of German states and cities, a role it had once more regained in the wake of 1968. Nowadays, it finds itself within a society that is entirely apolitical, from the remote pub to the Kanzler's office. The context of clear ideological frontlines and the thinking in alternatives has given way to an encompassing loss of orientation. An excitable polemic that suits media headlines cannot hide the fact that we are living in a diffuse unease, without any political consciousness.

We have got to start all over again.

The wish for a different life – to live together in true liberty beyond the laws and values of economic efficiency dictated by neoliberal capitalism – does still exist. Without a consciousness of the possibility and the necessity to live a different life than this – both as individuals, and as a society – the conditions cannot be changed. Theatre can be one of these places where attempts to comprehend the world in a new way intensify into a shared, common view of the world, and into an attitude. Theatre can therefore be the place of realization, and thus of repoliticization.

For this purpose, we need a theatre that is properly contemporary, that makes the attempt to tell stories about the individual and the existential as well as the wider social conflicts of human beings who live in this world. Dramatic conflicts that spring from present-day reality, and not from the class society as in Schiller's *Luise Miller*. In the present historical situation of maximum freedom of the individual within a system of total submission under the laws of the market, this is the only chance for theatre in order to continue to be able to ask the question: how should we really live in our world?

We need a new realism, because realism works against a 'wrong consciousness', which today tends to be a comatose un-consciousness. Realism is not the simple depiction of the world as it looks. It is the view onto the world through an attitude that demands for change, born from pain and injury, which become the reason for making art in order to take revenge on the world for its blindness and stupidity. It attempts to comprehend and to express these realities, and to refigure them. In the very recognition of the familiar, realism wants to provoke surprise and astonishment, and it wants to tell stories, and that means insisting on the fact that actions have a consequence. This is the relentlessness of human life, and when this relentlessness is brought on stage, drama comes into being.

Theatre is connected to the world through the authors. In a time when the German drama of ideas keeps revolving around exhausted ideas and our fathers' anti-modern excrescences keep flourishing, or when it remains plainly tame in its intellectual self-reflection and its narcissistic love of language that lacks any idea or concern, we need authors who open their eyes and ears for the world and for its incredible stories. The explosion of many different realities, which results from the collapse of the great ideologies and of the old political camps, can only be reflected by the different ways of seeing and imagining the world offered by a diverse range of different authors, both in dance and in drama.

The ensemble

Under the artistic direction of Sasha Waltz, Thomas Ostermeier, Jochen Sandig and Jens Hillje, the Schaubühne aims to be a contemporary theatre.

For us, the utopian moment of theatre is the idea of the ensemble. Almost forty actors and dancers have agreed to reject, for an initial period of two years, any other jobs for film, radio and television, in order to work, with choreographers, directors, playwrights, musicians, set and costume designers, dramaturgs, assistants, prompters and stage managers, for equal and transparent pay, developing a shared idea of theatre and bringing it to life on stage. This is the starting point and the aim of co-determination

The First Season: The Mission (1999) 5

[*Mitbestimmung*]. The Schaubühne repertoire will be created through a constant, issue-based debate between the artistic direction, the dramaturgy department and the ensemble, and in an exchange between dance and drama. The Schaubühne sees itself as a laboratory, which works on the development of a new theatre language in dialogue with other disciplines such as architecture, visual arts, music, literature and film.

Dance and drama

The decision to bring together dance and drama as equal partners in one theatre is unique in the German theatre system. Contemporary dance, which has established itself over the past decades across the world as innovative and trendsetting theatre form, will now play a leading artistic role at the Schaubühne.

Attempts to appropriately represent on stage the complex perception of our present reality hit their aesthetic limit in the form of straight drama. A physical and sensory theatre – whether drama or dance – is able to approximate this reality more closely. By telling its stories through the body, dance manages to make palpable a world of experience beyond language, which defies the dominant logic of the Logos.

A new generation of artists have started to go beyond a hermetic, aesthetically highly developed, yet with regards to its content, empty style of dance. They want to tell stories, which bring to light the abyss of human existence, and which tackle existential questions of life.

The research

The co-determination of programme contents is based on an aesthetic and sociological research, which is undertaken by the entire ensemble, in order to confront through art one's own life and the reality of today's society. New writing and contemporary forms of narrating are the principal interests of the new Schaubühne. We start by commissioning playwrights, and jointly develop plays with dramaturgs, authors and actors. In addition, *all* submitted plays are read and discussed.

The dramaturgy department introduces the plays and projects to the ensemble. They are then read and discussed together. The ensemble has the right to reject an idea for a production proposed by the artistic direction, thus to reject a play, a playwright or a director. The ensemble has the duty to present an alternative proposal. This right to a constructive veto has been formally introduced in order to function as an 'emergency brake', and as a positive catalyst for a focused and engaged discussion about the development of the programme for a theatre season.

Thereby, after three heated meetings of the ensemble and after controversial debates, the ensemble fully shares the risky decision to open the new Schaubühne with Lars Norén's *Personenkreis 3.1* as its first drama premiere. Thomas Ostermeier's suggestion to stage a Feydeau piece was rejected following a read-through and discussion. Instead, the ensemble tasked the dramaturgy department with finding a contemporary comedy of equal calibre to Feydeau's, or to commission the writing of one. Another risk.

The objective

All this serves the aim of attracting, in addition to the traditional Schaubühne spectators, new audiences who no longer attend the theatre because of their commitment to the bourgeois value of education and erudition [*Bildung*], but who instinctively look out for well-presented stories, and therefore mostly decide to go to the cinema. It has got to be the ideal objective of every contemporary theatre to attract this audience for the strange experience of a theatre evening, and to connect them to the social space of theatre. If these different groups of spectators, old and new, were to mix and mingle in the auditorium without conflict, in order to watch together new plays – then we would have achieved, not only for Berlin, a small revolution.

Translated by Peter M. Boenisch

2

Between Philosophical and Sociological Theatre: The Political *Regietheater* of Peter Stein and Thomas Ostermeier at the Schaubühne Berlin

Erika Fischer-Lichte

Having served as artistic director of Berlin's Schaubühne theatre for twenty years in 2020, Thomas Ostermeier exceeded the time his most famous predecessor spent in office: Peter Stein held this position only for fourteen years, from 1970 until he left after the 1983/84 season. During their respective artistic directorships, and not least with their own productions, both directors have won the Schaubühne much international fame. The company came to be regarded in many parts of the world as the epitome of contemporary German theatre. While this might suggest a certain continuity of their approaches, such a claim, even if not outright wrong, must remain debatable and call for further substantiation. Theatre is an ephemeral art – as Schiller already pointed out in his preface to *Wallenstein*, 'Posterity will weave no wreaths for actors' – and a performance comes into being here and now, emerging out of the encounter between actors and spectators. Therefore, it can only be experienced in this very presence, however well documented it might be on film, video or in another medium. This means that any theatre production remains inextricably linked to the time of its coming into being, in all possible respects. Therefore, it would be pointless to discuss the theatre aesthetics of different directors without taking into consideration the overall historical, political, cultural, ideological and artistic conditions in which their productions were embedded – without, of course, suggesting that this context alone determines the work. Yet, to relate Thomas Ostermeier's work at the Schaubühne to that of Peter Stein only makes sense when keeping in mind these differences. In this chapter, it will be shown how they each developed a very different theatre aesthetic, and, even more importantly, how their work was embedded in such distinct historical, political and cultural contexts.

Peter Stein: New theatre for a time of transformation

Peter Stein (b. 1937) was appointed artistic director of the Schaubühne at Hallesches Ufer at the end of the 1960s – a crucial period for the German Federal Republic, marked by radical changes within as well as by an increasingly tense relationship between the two German states. On 13 August 1961, the wall separating West from East Berlin was built; the so-called *Antifaschistischer Schutzwall* (Anti-Fascist Protection Rampart) that cut right through Germany, restricting mobility between the two states and establishing the separation into two distinct countries as new status quo. In Berlin, former capital of Germany and since 1945 divided into four sectors governed by the US, British, French and Soviet allied forces, the Soviet sector was shut off by the wall. It was suddenly no longer possible for Berliners, who until then had often visited the other sectors of the city, to continue this habit famously portrayed in Billy Wilder's 1961 film *One – Two – Three* (a movie mostly shot in Munich due to the political tension). Now, only passport holders from the Federal Republic (i.e. non-Berliners) were still permitted to enter East Berlin with a special visa that required the exchange of 25 Deutschmark into 25 Eastmark.

Not least this growing tension between West and East led to a momentous change in the political constellation in the Federal Republic. Since the state had been founded in 1949, a coalition between the conservative Christian Democrats (CDU) and the much smaller Liberal Party (FDP) was in government, with the centre-left Social Democrats (SPD) serving as a strong opposition. Yet in 1966, the so-called 'Grand Coalition' was formed between the two major parliamentary parties, CDU and SPD, led by the conservative Kanzler Kurt Georg Kiesinger, who had been a member of the National Socialist Party and served as a judge during the Third Reich. The opposition was meanwhile reduced to the Liberal Party's few MPs. This situation led to the emergence of a widely supported movement of the so-called 'extra-parliamentary opposition' (APO), which soon partly merged with the student movement of the time.

The latter had come together to fight for a number of goals, including changes in the hierarchical university system; one of their popular slogans went, 'Unter den Talaren Muff von 1000 Jahren': 'Under the professors' gowns the mustiness of a thousand years'. These 'thousand years' not only referred to the professors' obsolescence but above all cited the Nazi propaganda proclaiming that their rule would last that many years. The slogan indicated that, like Chancellor Kiesinger, many of the university teachers had a Nazi past that was not publicly discussed. The younger generation of the student movement now attacked their parents for not having resisted the Nazis and their crimes, or for having collaborated and been complicit in committing these crimes themselves. They exposed former Nazis holding government and other public offices. At the same time, German students became engaged in the international protest movement against the Vietnam War and, more widely, against all forms of imperialism, supporting the liberation movements in the so-called 'Third World', and celebrating their prominent protagonists such as Che Guevara, Fidel Castro and, in particular, the leader of the Vietnam revolution and founder of the Vietnam Communist Party, Ho Chi Minh. Moreover, the students invented new forms of political protest and action that were steeped in theatricality.

Protesting against any form of violence the older generations exercised on them or on any revolutionaries at the hands of those in power – the old fascists holding on to power as well as those claiming authority over them because of their age and social status – the young protestors' experience of violence soon became very immediate. On 2 June 1967, during the Shah of Iran's visit to Berlin, students of the Freie Universität organized a large-scale demonstration against his dictatorial reign. Outside the West Berlin opera house, which the Shah visited with his wife, the protesters were confronted by a huge number of policemen who tried to push them back. In this tense situation, Benno Ohnesorg, a student who had done nothing to provoke the police, was shot dead. The police officer, who as we know today worked for the Stasi, the East German Secret Service, was taken to court but was acquitted of all charges. This caused an uproar among young people in Berlin and across West Germany. The event marked the beginning of the student rebellion led by Rudi Dutschke – who less than a year later survived an attempt on his life, but suffered from its consequences until his untimely death in 1979. Meanwhile, a small group of activists emerged from within the APO movement, led by the students Andreas Baader and Gudrun Ensslin as well as the journalist Ulrike Meinhof; during the 1970s, their group turned into the 'Red Army Faction' (RAF) terrorist movement. Baader, Ensslin and Meinhof were all raised in the educated middle class; they had experienced violence as the sole means of the authorities in defending the status quo and, in turn, saw violence as the only 'language' their opponents would understand. They first targeted large department stores with arson attacks, then carried out bank robberies and kidnapped prominent figures from the world of business and finance, publicly humiliating and then killing them. By the mid-1970s, the Republic was eventually on the verge of disintegrating.

This was the highly charged political situation at the time Peter Stein took over the Schaubühne in 1970. At the time, it was still a rather small, leftist, experimental theatre. Stein, meanwhile, at the young age of thirty-three, was already quite established. He had worked at the Kammerspiele in Munich, the Bremen theatre and the Zurich Schauspielhaus, and three of his productions had been invited to the prestigious Theatertreffen in Berlin.[1] During these early years, Stein considered himself as a leftist, asserting that theatre should have a political impact. At the end of a performance of Peter Weiss's *Vietnam Diskurs* (Vietnam Discourse) at the Werkraum studio of the Munich Kammerspiele, which Stein had directed, the actors descended into the auditorium and the lobby in order to ask for donations for the Vietcong. The theatre's *Intendant* at the time, August Everding, sacked Stein with immediate effect and did not allow him to set foot in the theatre after that.[2]

As Stein took on his new position at the Schaubühne, a decade had come to an end that had not only seen the drastic political developments mentioned above, but also a thorough transformation of the West German theatre landscape. Most of the directors in charge of West German theatre after the Second World War had begun their work in the 1920s. They preferred to stage classical plays, focusing on their perceived universal values, stressing humanism in particular. In the period of the German *Wirtschaftswunder*, the 'economic miracle' of the 1950s and early 1960s, controversial topics such as the Third Reich, the War and the Holocaust remained anathema. In 1962, Erwin Piscator was appointed artistic director of the Freie Volksbühne in West Berlin. The protagonist of the new 'Epic Theatre' in the 1920s, who had pioneered new forms of engaged, political theatre, had emigrated to the US in the 1930s, where he founded the legendary 'Dramatic Workshop', affiliated to the New York New School for Social Research. It was famously attended by, amongst others, Arthur Miller, Tennessee Williams, Judith Malina and Julian Beck. Following his appointment at the Freie Volksbühne, he supported the development of another novel theatre form: documentary theatre. It was devoted precisely to the taboo subjects ignored by other theatre-makers, and it was meant to address and come to terms with the recent past, and to force the spectators to engage with it and to take a clear political stand. Piscator staged Rolf Hochhuth's *Der Stellvertreter* (*The Deputy*), addressing the attitude of the Vatican and particularly that of Pope Pius XII towards the Nazi persecution of Jews, and he directed Peter Weiss's *Die Ermittlung* (*The Investigation*, 1965), based on the Frankfurt Auschwitz Trials between 1963 and 1965. Piscator's productions realized political theatre in this novel aesthetics of the documentary form, thereby also attributing a new function and purpose to theatre. At the same time, the fine arts underwent developments that also had significant repercussions for the theatre. Of particular importance in this context was the work of the Vienna actionists and the FLUXUS group, among them Joseph Beuys, Bazon Brock and Wolf Vostell. Their performances became notorious – as, for instance, Beuys's *How to Explain Pictures to a Dead Hare* (1965), Bazon Brock's *Theater der Position*

(*Theatre of Position*, Experimenta, Frankfurt 1965) or the happening *In Ulm, um Ulm, und um Ulm herum* (*In Ulm, at Ulm, and around Ulm*) organized by Wolf Vostell and the Municipal Theatre in Ulm in 1964.

In the very same year that Piscator arrived in Berlin, a group of students at the Institute for Theatre Studies at the Freie Universität, who had already worked rather successfully at the students' theatre for some years, decided to found a theatre of their own – the Schaubühne, which in a subtitle they explicitly labelled 'Contemporary Theatre'. Jürgen Schitthelm, Klaus Weiffenbach and the dramaturg Dieter Sturm served as its artistic directors. They were granted permission to use a building of the Arbeiterwohlfahrt (Workers' Welfare Association) in Berlin's Kreuzberg district, which marked the birth of the 'Schaubühne at Halleschen Ufer'. They chose Ariano Suassuna's *Das Testament des Hundes oder die Geschichte der Barmherzigkeit* (*The Dog's Testament or the History of Mercy*) as their first production, winning Polish director Konrad Swinarski to stage the project, who would, two years later, premiere Peter Weiss's then new *Marat/Sade* at the Schillertheater to much acclaim. The Schaubühne thus began its work as a leftist theatre without restricting its productions to contemporary plays, although these formed the core of its repertoire.

While the 1960s, not only in retrospect but even at that time itself, were felt as a time in search of new theatre forms that would be able to respond to the changing political, social and cultural situation discussed earlier, what would soon become known as *Regietheater* (directors' theatre) did not yet exist.[3] It only began to emerge in the second half of the decade, as Kurt Hübner, the artistic director of Bremen's theatre, invited Peter Zadek, Klaus Michael Grüber and Peter Stein, following his Munich dismissal, to work there. Simultaneously, Claus Peymann emerged as further protagonist of the new aesthetic approach to directing. He had staged Brecht's *Antigone Model* at the Schaubühne in 1965 and, a year later, put Peter Handke's *Publikumsbeschimpfung* (*Offending the Audience*) on stage at the Frankfurt Experimenta, seeking to create a new theatre out of the interaction of actors and spectators and causing a considerable scandal. As Peter Stein took over the Schaubühne, he brought with him numerous actors from Bremen such as Jutta Lampe, Edith Clever and Bruno Ganz. It was generally expected that something new, innovative and ground-breaking would take place there. Yet, contrary to expectations, Stein abandoned explicitly political actions in the style of his collection for the Vietcong – and was severely criticized by fellow leftists. Still, he introduced new organizational structures at the theatre that could be seen as concrete political action; above all, *Mitbestimmung*, the collective decision-making of all the employees of the theatre. While the *Direktorium* (management committee), consisting of the two licensees Schitthelm and Weiffenbach as permanent members along with three other members elected by a general meeting of the entire staff (initially these were Peter Stein, Claus Peymann and Dieter Sturm) took the day-to-day decisions, the final authority remained with the *Vollversammlung*, the general assembly. It usually met once a month, sometimes even more often, having the power to veto any decision taken by the *Direktorium*.[4] The *Vollversammlung* took its mandate very seriously in what frequently resulted in debates that lasted long into the night. The Schaubühne thus became the first truly democratic theatre in Germany.

Thomas Ostermeier: Theatre, neoliberalism and individualism

When Thomas Ostermeier was appointed, identifying as a leftist and deeply believing in the participation of everyone involved, he attempted to revive the tradition of *Mitbestimmung*. However, this did not work, as actors as well as the staff members experienced the many meetings as a burden. Ostermeier gave up the idea and henceforth took sole charge.[5] This failure to revive earlier forms is an obvious symptom of the completely different conditions at the turn of the millennium. Ostermeier took over as artistic director under very different political and ideological conditions than Peter Stein thirty years earlier. The situation had changed radically, not least politically, with the major turning point of 1989. Already at the beginning of the 1980s, an active peace movement emerged in the GDR. Deeply concerned about the development of the Cold War and the escalating threat of a nuclear confrontation between East and West, with Germany in the very frontline, their movement expressed its protest not least through weekly 'prayers for peace', first launched at Leipzig's Nikolai Church. These prayers started every Monday at 5pm, and were soon followed by a weekly protest march through the streets. By September 1989, these demonstrations happened each Monday, all over the GDR. Known as the Monday demonstrations, they finally resulted in the peaceful revolution that led to the opening of the Berlin Wall on 9 November 1989. The two German states were formally reunited on 3 October 1990, a major political transformation which brought about a number of changes in all spheres of life, not only in the five new (formerly East German) states – although, as a matter of fact, they were most momentous there. The 1990s were characterized by an upsurge in neoliberalism, new economics and a new ideology of individualism. Moreover, this was the decade when digital media began to pervade daily life and the process of globalization proceeded at an irrevocable pace.

The situation in German theatres was equally a world apart from that of 1970. German-speaking theatre had in its forms and aesthetics become more diverse. To begin with, it had become common practice for directors to leave the theatre buildings and have their productions performed in all kinds of other spaces, be it former factories, tramway depots, pavilions on fairgrounds, former slaughterhouses, even on the streets of a city, as was the case with the 'audio tours' of Hygiene Heute, the 1990s precursor of Rimini Protokoll. The aesthetics of performance art had meanwhile entered the state and municipal theatres, even merging with more conventional stage aesthetics in the production of the plays.[6] It was not just *Regietheater* that had spread all over the German-speaking theatre world but also new types of postdramatic theatre, devised theatre and participatory theatre. Moreover, new media technologies made their impact on stage aesthetics. The use of video cameras, with or without the camera operator visibly present on stage, had turned into a commonplace device. In the 1990s, different forms of choric theatre had also come into vogue, including huge choruses of amateurs mainly hailing from marginalized groups such as the unemployed or migrants. Here, the claim was to give the underprivileged a voice, to make those who usually remain invisible to mainstream society, publicly visible: by exposing them to the gaze of the well-to-do, middle-class theatre spectators, on the theatre stage. The underlying ideas and ideologies as well as the aims and proclaimed purposes were as diverse as the forms and aesthetics employed.

Despite this changing context, there is, however, a certain continuity from Stein's to Ostermeier's artistic directorship. Both contributed to the theatre's immense acclaim, also internationally, with their productions touring across the world. While at the time of Stein's directorship such foreign tours still remained an exception, in Ostermeier's time they had become the new norm; some of his productions even premiered abroad before being shown at the Schaubühne. Stein's work from as early as 1972 onwards travelled almost exclusively within Europe – notably his productions of *Fegefeuer in Ingolstadt* to Warsaw, *Prinz Friedrich von Homburg* to Vienna, Zurich, Paris, Warsaw, Gothenburg and Oslo. The performances of the *Oresteia* (1980), which was invited to Caracas, and of *Klassenfeind* (1981), performed in Mexico City, remained an exception. Ostermeier's productions, meanwhile, have been regularly shown, from Australia, China, Japan, Hong Kong, the US and Canada, to Latin America; so far, only the African continent remains absent from the theatre's busy touring record of the past two decades under his directorship. Undeniably, this far wider circulation is a result of present-day globalization and the widespread 'festivalization' that goes with it in the theatre sector. Still, despite the differences in range, in both cases it is a clear

14   *The Schaubühne Berlin under Thomas Ostermeier*

indicator that outside of Germany, the work of these two directors was and continues to be regarded as the most fascinating in German theatre.

At the same time, Stein and Ostermeier not only showcased their own work at the Schaubühne, but they also both invited other prominent directors to work at the theatre, thereby turning it, very literally, into a 'directors' theatre'. Among the most important of these directors was, during Stein's time, Klaus Michael Grüber, in particular. Stein and Grüber most famously collaborated on the first *Antiquity Project* (1974), when Stein directed the introductory *Exercises for Actors*, followed by Grüber's *The Bacchae*. Grüber, in fact, proved to be Stein's crucial counterpart in many respects, not least in terms of his working methods, as well as the (largely non-theatre) spaces he used for his productions. He chose some of Berlin's most 'mythical places' as venues, such as the Olympic Stadium for his *Winterreise* (1977), or the former Grand Hotel Esplanade, whose ruins were directly located in the 'no man's land' of the Berlin Wall (*Rudi*, 1979) near the (at the time no longer existing) Potsdamer Platz. It was also during Stein's directorship that Robert Wilson staged his first German production, *Death, Destruction and Detroit*, at the Schaubühne (also in 1979). Other directors who worked at Stein's Schaubühne included Claus Peymann, Wilfried Minks, Frank-Patrick Steckel and the late Luc Bondy, who would eventually succeed Stein as artistic director. The number of directors who have worked at the 'new' Schaubühne since 2000 is even larger, and also more international. Among them are, for instance, Ivo van Hove, Alvis Hermanis, Katie Mitchell, Luk Perceval, Volker Lösch, Jossi Wieler, Yael Ronen, Barbara Frey, Sebastian Nübling, Grzegorz Jarzyna, Michael Thalheimer and Herbert Fritsch. The diversity of styles, already a trademark of Peter Stein's Schaubühne, has increased even further.

Another continuity concerns the theatre's engagement with applied theatre that aims at particular groups, such as children, workers or apprentices. Since the names of Peter Stein and Thomas Ostermeier usually only call to mind their own great productions on the large stage, it seems important to emphasize that both took great care to open their theatre to marginalized groups, and to create productions that could address some of their concerns. In the 1972/3 and 1974/5 seasons, an extremely successful production of *Gilgamesch and Engidu* was collectively mounted for children, performed on the Schaubühne's main stage. Further productions addressing workers, such as Stein's staging of Gerhard Kelling's *Die Auseinandersetzung* (*The Altercation*, 1971) or the collective production of Johannes Schenk's *Transportarbeiter Jakob Kuhn* (*Transport Worker Jakob Kuhn*, 1972), were presented in industrial units, trade union centres, juvenile detention centres and vocational schools. Moreover, Stein invited Turkish 'guest workers', as they were called at the time, to stage plays of their own. From the 1979/80

Between Philosophical and Sociological Theatre 15

season until Stein's departure in 1984, between two and five productions by Turkish artists in Turkish were mounted each season. They travelled to other centres of expat-Turkish life in the Federal Republic, such as Essen, Duisburg, Mühlheim, Recklinghausen and Cologne; two of them even made it to Stockholm. At the 'new' Schaubühne, long term theatre pedagogue Uta Plate, who worked at the theatre from 2000 until 2014, established a youth theatre group called Die Zwiefachen (The Twofold). It revived similar efforts under Ostermeier's directorship. Composed of young people between the ages of fourteen and twenty-six, many hailing from less privileged social milieus, they develop their own performances as writers, choreographers, co-directors and performers, presenting their work at the Schaubühne and at venues such as the Jugendvollzugsanstalt (youth correction facility) in Berlin Plötzensee, as well as at national and international festivals.

Political *Regietheater*: From a critique of bourgeois culture to a critique of globalization

The most striking commonality between Stein and Ostermeier, however, is their understanding of their own work. Both regarded it as and called it political theatre. This shared label, however, hides the extreme differences between them that result from their divergent understanding of the very notion of political theatre. In each case, this understanding is closely linked to the different political, social and cultural conditions that met in their work as well as to the completely different climate prevalent in the German theatre scene that was sketched above. It seems plausible in retrospect to place Peter Stein's political theatre at the philosophical end of the spectrum, while Thomas Ostermeier's could be described as sociological – although such tags inevitably rely on a certain degree of simplification and generalization.

Stein's political approach, developed in the 1960s, manifested itself in his interrogation of the history of the bourgeoisie, searching for the reasons why all the revolutionary impulses of the eighteenth century, all the attempts to create a better life had ultimately failed. He used theatre as a means to unearth the contradictions inherent in bourgeois ideology that lay at the root of this failure. This approach entailed not only a particular method of working but also a novel aesthetics. Extensive research regarding the dramatic text and the historical circumstances at the time of its genesis became imperative. The particular reading of the text resulting from the joint efforts of Stein and the company then functioned as the guideline for the staging process, stimulating ideas for the acting style, the space, the lighting and other aspects. When Stein staged Goethe's *Torquato Tasso* in 1969 while still at Bremen (the production

16   *The Schaubühne Berlin under Thomas Ostermeier*

would later transfer to the Schaubühne), he and his actors found Goethe's view on the artist's (and his own) role in the society of his time reflected in their own contemporary situation. The programme notes read:

> What courtly society expected from their poet is similar to what bourgeois society expects from their theatre. We know that we are satisfying their expectations with this production: in this we are behaving as Goethe's Tasso and as Goethe himself. We are fulfilling the ready-made role and delighting the gaze of the mighty with elaborate contortions and inhibitions.[7]

These 'elaborate contortions and inhibitions' ('kunstvollen Verrenkungen und Verkrampfungen') were shown on stage in the artificiality of gestures and movements, which was further complemented by a way of speaking that came close to singing. This acting style was 'beautiful' in its artificiality, and so was the space created by Wilfried Minks. The beauty of Stein's productions, which is so often emphasized,[8] here however served the purpose of questioning the social value of the artistic beauty.

Typically, Stein's productions were preceded by – or even included – long phases of research. The already mentioned first *Antiquity Project* of 1974, for instance, began with the entire company travelling to Greece during the summer vacation, and their extensive study of research on ancient Greek theatre, mythology and rituals. They engaged with their own historical research by visiting sites of particular interest, reviewing the work of philologists, anthropologists, historians and others relevant to their own project. Excerpts from the most important works they consulted were assembled in the voluminous, eighty-page programme notes, which allowed the spectators to follow their trajectory. Among the works cited were Walter Burkert's study *Homo Necans: The Anthropology of Ancient Greek Sacrificial Ritual* (1972; Engl. 1983), René Girard's *Violence and the Sacred* (1972, Engl. 1977), Jan Kott's *The Eating of the Gods: An Interpretation of Greek Tragedy* (1970, Engl. 1973). Also included were excerpts from Eric Dodd's writings on *The Bacchae* to which Kott refers, Arnold van Gennep's classic *Rites of Passage* (1909), George Thomson's *Aeschylus and Athens* (1947) as well as Gilbert Murray's book *Euripides and His Age* (1913). The range of works consulted suggests that the company intended to focus on the relationship between tragedy and ritual on the one hand, and between tragedy and the *polis* on the other, i.e. on tragedy's place and function at that particular historical time. Bearing in mind the pivotal role that Greek tragedies played in the development of the cultural identity of the German educated middle class, the *Bildungsbürgertum*, during the eighteenth and nineteenth centuries, it

Between Philosophical and Sociological Theatre

becomes obvious that the Schaubühne's *Antiquity Project* was related to the history of the bourgeoisie that it questioned.[9] For the second *Antiquity Project*, Stein's *Oresteia* of 1980, the company not only engaged in more extensive research, but this time they set out to prepare the audience, too. A series of preparatory workshops began half a year before the premiere. They were led by Peter Stein and involved some of the actors. Amongst other activities, Hesiod's cosmogony was read and discussed, and problems relating to the text, its construction, genealogy and translation were debated. Even in this respect, the preparatory process was exhaustive.[10]

When the company decided to stage Shakespeare for the first time they once more felt the need to thoroughly prepare themselves and the spectators, not least taking into account the enormous impact his plays have had on German theatre. Meticulous research was undertaken on Shakespeare's time, including the study of writings on astrology, geography and other subjects. This research resulted in the project entitled *Shakespeare's Memory*, performed in the CCC Film Studios on 22 and 23 December 1976. The evening presented the results of the research in different parts of the vast space. The spectators could walk around as in a museum. As there were so many places where fascinating things were going on, no spectator was able to witness everything presented. Although this was criticized in some reviews, it prepared the spectators for the insight that it is impossible to have a comprehensive 'overview' of an entire era, and that one's knowledge must necessarily remain fragmented – a situation that will always affect the staging of a play from the past, particularly one of Shakespeare's works.

One might be tempted to think that such a learned approach resulted in somewhat dull and 'academic' performances. However, the opposite was the case. Stein's productions were admired for the clarity with which the narrative of a play was told and the characters' behaviour was explained, as well as for their beauty and general lightness of style. The Schaubühne – literally meaning 'stage where something is shown' – in fact served as a place to observe in order to reflect on what one had perceived, thereby reviving a particular meaning of the word *theatrum* from the seventeenth century. The stage, usually designed by Stein's regular collaborator Karl-Ernst Herrmann, and the costumes by Moidele Bickel, contributed to this effect. Such beauty along with that of the acting enabled, indeed encouraged, the spectators to consciously experience their own desire for a better life, and to reflect on the contradictions that had led to former failures. Despite Stein's painstaking philological engagement with the text and the joint historical research on the historical era concerned, the resulting productions can neither be labelled philological nor historical-archaeological or even historicist. Rather, I find only the term 'philosophical theatre' suitable here, as it describes a theatre that reflects on the preconditions for its coming into being through its genuinely own means and devices.

Just as Stein was obsessed with history as the subject of philosophical reflection on human action and failure, Ostermeier is concerned with contemporary times and their particular conditions for human behaviour. After studying directing at the renowned Ernst Busch Theatre Academy in former East Berlin, he began his career at the Baracke, a small experimental space at the Deutsches Theater Berlin, in 1996. He directed mostly contemporary British plays there, including Nicky Silver's *Fat Men in Skirts* (1996), David Harrower's *Knives in Hens* (1997), Mark Ravenhill's *Shopping and Fucking* (1998) and Enda Walsh's *Disco Pigs* (1998), but also Brecht's *Man Equals Man* (1997). The latter was his first production of many to tour abroad extensively. When Ostermeier was appointed artistic director of the Schaubühne at the age of thirty-one, he published a manifesto entitled *The Mission*, calling for a new realism in theatre, which he explained as 'a view of the world through an attitude that demands for change'.[11] The contemporary plays Ostermeier chose drew the spectators' attention to the miserable conditions under which the individual lives in today's Western capitalist societies; his preferred playwrights included Sarah Kane, Marius von Mayenburg, Lars Norén, Jon Fosse and Biljana Srbljanović.

When the director later turned to modern classics such as Ibsen, he treated the text as if it were a contemporary play. In *Nora* (2002) and *Hedda Gabler* (2005), his stage designer Jan Pappelbaum built a stylish interior of apartments reflecting a yuppie lifestyle as found, for example, in Berlin's hip, gentrified Prenzlauer Berg district. These classics were dealt with as ·contemporary plays addressing problems of Ostermeier's generation. The director therefore felt entitled to intervene in the plays where it seemed necessary for this purpose. The ending of *A Doll's House* has been notorious since Ibsen's times. It had caused an uproar amongst its late nineteenth-century audiences, to the extent that Ibsen felt compelled to change it for some productions to show Nora returning home. Ostermeier, too, changed it, but in order to maintain a taste of its original, outrageous impact: Nowadays, Nora simply leaving her husband would not enrage anyone; therefore, in Ostermeier's production, she shoots him. Moreover, Ostermeier continued to develop his new theatre aesthetics, which he had elaborated in his productions of contemporary British (and also Scandinavian) plays. He worked with uncanny special effects, horror projections of sorts, strong optic and acoustic signals, with quotations, figures and stereotypes derived from pop, comics, movies and soap operas, the finale turning out to be a veritable Western-style showdown. These devices had a rather affective strong effect on the senses of the spectators. *Nora* was directed according to the principle of 'montage of attractions', as developed by Soviet theatre and film director Sergei Eisenstein, to which Ostermeier frequently refers.[12] Yet, this by no means was Ostermeier's 'last word' on the topic. In *Hedda Gabler*, he avoided such 'loud' effects, instead concentrating on the characters and their story. In both cases, the bourgeois living room served as a kind of sociological laboratory.

This also holds true for the more recent *Enemy of the People* (2012). In the fourth act, Stockmann's speech before the assembled public was replaced by the French anti-globalization manifesto *The Coming Insurrection*. After that, the floor was opened for a discussion between the spectators and the characters – not the actors. The particular textual changes made in each of Ibsen's plays in order to emphasize their contemporariness all suggested a different way of staging that had repercussions on the aesthetics of the production. Even Shakespeare's texts were treated as if they were contemporary plays. In Ostermeier's 2008 *Hamlet*, Lars Eidinger played the lead role as a youth of today, as a 'spoiled brat':

> This intoxicated ego trip, this excessive self-infatuation, this utter indifference towards political processes, this shrugging cluelessness with which one moves and exhibits oneself in the social media – this does indeed characterize parts of this generation.[13]

Hamlet again toured all over the world, speaking to audiences all over Europe, the Near East, East Asia and Latin America – *not* as the performance of a classic but as a contemporary play.[14] In fact, in each place the strongest impact was felt at a different moment, as Eidinger adapted his improvisations in addressing the spectators to each city. He acted out a madness that knew no boundaries, taking the sentence 'His madness is poor Hamlet's enemy' (*Hamlet*, 5.2.250) very literally.

Just as Peter Stein had developed a new style for each production in order to investigate and expose the contradictions at work during a specific era, Ostermeier tries out different styles with each production in order to emphasize its contemporariness. This underlines the nature of his theatre as a sociological laboratory. Each production gives insight into different, psychic and/or social, political or cultural problems that haunt us and our contemporary society. Since many of these problems derive from the process of digitalization and globalization, Ostermeier's productions resonate with audiences all over the world – they address the problems people have to deal with everywhere. So it is not through 'universalism' or by evoking certain eternal values that Ostermeier's productions speak to global audiences, but because they relate to the questions and problems that contemporary conditions cause in our everyday lives – this is why I call Ostermeier's theatre sociological. This is not to say that Ostermeier believes that his theatre can solve any of these problems and change the world. Rather, he describes it as 'enlightening':

> An enlightening theatre [...] a kind of modern confession manual to examine one's own susceptibilities to corruption, lying, hypocrisy, or, inversely, to identify one's own positive traits, a micro-sociological enlightenment that investigates the lives of families and couples without realising it – I believe this kind of theatre to be absolutely necessary and important.[15]

While Stein's philosophical theatre during the years of his artistic directorship analysed and reflected on basic contradictions within a historical timespan that had an impact on the emotions, actions and behaviour of the people as well as on the formation and history of the bourgeoisie, in particular the German *Bildungsbürgertum*, Ostermeier's sociological theatre dissects different kinds of relationships on a micro-level, thus confronting spectators with very familiar phenomena and challenging them to contextualize themselves.

Both kinds of theatre bear the marks of their time without being determined by it – a fact that becomes obvious especially when we relate their work to that of other contemporaneous directors, in Stein's case, for instance, Peter Zadek, Claus Peymann and Klaus Michael Grüber, and in Ostermeier's case, Michael Thalheimer and Stefan Pucher. Such a comparison immediately makes us recognize the very particular responses Stein and Ostermeier had to their time. Stein's philosophical theatre was as unique in the 1970s and early 1980s as Ostermeier's sociological theatre has been in the first two decades of the twenty-first century. The particular aesthetics each of them developed for their own kind of *Regietheater* is intricately entwined with their respective theatre's overarching principles, guidelines and approaches. It is one of the great merits of the Schaubühne that its artistic directors, each with very strong personalities and being outstanding artists themselves, invited other acclaimed directors to also show their work there. Even if public opinion usually connects the Schaubühne with its artistic directors, it is an institution that from Stein's directorship until today has hosted the most distinctive and brilliant directors not only from the German-speaking countries but also from other parts of the world. It is the sum total of all the artistic work carried out at the Schaubühne – and not only that of their artistic directors – which has made it such an extraordinary theatre, a showcase for the most diverse kinds of *Regietheater* that have been developed over the last fifty years.

Notes

1 See Michael Patterson, *Peter Stein: Germany's Leading Theatre Director* (Cambridge: Cambridge University Press, 1981), 1–45.

2 Ibid., 11–13.

3 On the notion of *Regietheater*, see Marvin Carlson, *Theatre is More Beautiful Than War: German Stage Directing in the Late Twentieth Century* (Iowa City: University of Iowa Press, 2009), and Peter M. Boenisch, *Directing Scenes and Senses: The Thinking of Regie* (Manchester: Manchester University Press, 2015).

4 See Patterson, *Peter Stein*, 41–3.

5 See the interview with Ostermeier in the present volume, Chapter 4, esp. p. 43ff.

6 See Erika Fischer-Lichte, *The Transformative Power of Performance: A New Aesthetics* (Abingdon and New York: Routledge, 2008).

7 Quoted in Peter Iden, *Die Schaubühne am Halleschen Ufer 1970–1979* (Munich and Vienna: Hanser, 1979), 23–4. All translations from German sources are by the author.

8 See Patterson, *Peter Stein*, 168.

9 See Erika Fischer-Lichte, *Dionysus Resurrected: Performances of Euripides' The Bacchae in a Globalizing World* (Chichester: Wiley-Blackwell, 2014), 93–115.

10 See Erika Fischer-Lichte, *Tragedy's Endurance: Performances of Greek Tragedies and Cultural Identity in Germany since 1800* (Oxford: Oxford University Press, 2017), 294–312.

11 See the translation of this document in Chapter 1, p. 3.

12 See Peter M. Boenisch and Thomas Ostermeier (eds), *The Theatre of Thomas Ostermeier* (Abingdon and New York: Routledge, 2016), 174–6.

13 Ostermeier in Gerhard Jörder, *Ostermeier Backstage* (Berlin: Theater der Zeit, 2014), 110.

14 See also the contributions in Part Two of this volume, which deal more extensively with *Hamlet* and Ostermeier's other Shakespeare productions.

15 Jörder, *Ostermeier Backstage*, 129.

3

The Schaubühne's Civic Mission in the Age of Globalization: An Imaginary Island that Probes Society

Ramona Mosse

A close-up of a young woman's face. Then we move up with the eye of the camera through the head of the actor, up into the fly tower, breaking through the ceiling into the night skies, hovering at bird's eye view above the Schaubühne am Lehniner Platz on Kurfürstendamm in Berlin. Rain is pouring onto the building. We move out further beyond Berlin and into the world that is becoming an ever-widening map below until we are in outer space looking back at the globe at large. This video sequence is part of *Shakespeare's Last Play*, directed by Dead Centre, the Irish-English directors' duo of Bush Moukarzel and Ben Kidd, at the Schaubühne in 2018. A meta-theatrical game with Shakespeare's *The Tempest*, the production toys with the geography of theatre, mapping stages onto islands and islands onto stages, following a quest for what to do with the dramatic canon, and specifically Shakespeare, on the twenty-first-century stage. Borrowing from this imagery, this chapter will focus on the particular geography of the Schaubühne as a public theatre institution. It both maps the Schaubühne onto the contemporary German theatre landscape and locates it within an international and indeed globalized context. The idea of an island is key in a variety of contexts here. First of all, Ostermeier himself evokes the imagery discussing his decision to accept the offer of the Schaubühne's artistic leadership: 'The system offers you some freedom, I said to myself. You can build a small, habitable island here, a bit of real life within the fake. And that's what we have tried to do'.[1] Furthermore, the island speaks to an air of exceptionalism that has pervaded the Schaubühne throughout its institutional history. When it was founded in 1962 as a student-run theatre, it existed in a paradoxical borderland. West Berlin was an island of capitalist democracy behind the Iron Curtain, while the Schaubühne in its original location in West Berlin's Kreuzberg district was perched so close to the Berlin Wall that an engagement with the ideological contradictions of Cold War culture seemed self-evident.

It was a place set out to probe the political imagination. When it changed location in the 1980s to a newly renovated bespoke building in a different part of town, the sense of being set apart from its surroundings persisted. The Schaubühne has time and again been a space for reimagining the future of institutions rather than providing a vessel for preserving past tradition. It is therefore closely tied up with the island as the dominant political metaphor for the concept of utopia: an imaginary island that reinvents as well as critiques social existence.

From an international perspective, the Schaubühne has commonly been understood as synonymous with Ostermeier's directorial signature. He has translated the Western dramatic canon – notably Ibsen, Shakespeare and Schnitzler – into radically updated contemporary settings, be it the Sopranos noir situation of his *Hamlet* or the Berlin yuppie loft spaces that form the backdrop to his Ibsen productions. Yet from a German perspective, Ostermeier rose to fame when being handed the artistic direction of one of the most prestigious German theatres at the age of thirty, in return for having introduced new playwriting in English – the works of Sarah Kane, Mark Ravenhill and Enda Walsh – into the German repertoire. Ostermeier was first a director of contemporary playwrights rather than the classic canon. Beyond the sense of Ostermeier as a representative of the iconic German *Regietheater* engaging the classics, there are therefore several intertwining stories of his artistic direction at the Schaubühne, and of this theatre as a public institution shaped by its ensemble and associated artists, its audiences and its location in the former West Berlin. There is, for example, the story of the initial years of collective artistic direction at the Schaubühne, as much as the story of a process of internationalization of the German theatre landscape, with the Schaubühne as one of its prominent drivers. This chapter will explore these dimensions of the Schaubühne beyond the towering figure of Ostermeier – but still in dialogue with him – in a set of journeys from the local to the global.

Locating the Berliner Schaubühne

In order to gain a sense of the local geography of the Schaubühne, we shall return to Dead Centre's video sequence. Below lies the massive horseshoe-shaped modernist building with its large ventilation chimney and its rounded glass front driving a wedge into the pavement of the Kurfürstendamm, the former shopping artery of the old West Berlin. Designed by architect Erich Mendelssohn in the late 1920s, it originally housed a cinema and was part of an ensemble of buildings set to model progressive city life by combining culture, living, sport and shopping facilities. It is full of bare, clean lines provided by concrete and glass structures, entirely void of the stereotypes of stuccoed ceilings and plush red velvet seats that have come to be traditional for theatre auditoria. Architecturally as well as atmospherically, the Schaubühne am Lehniner Platz seems like a UFO that has landed in the far western end of the leafy upper-middle-class neighborhood of Charlottenburg-Wilmersdorf. Unlike the other big Berlin theatre institutions such as the Volksbühne, the Berliner Ensemble (BE) or the Deutsches Theater, which are all located in the cultural centre of the capital's Mitte area close to Friedrichstrasse, the Schaubühne am Lehniner Platz in the former West is neither central nor countercultural. Its proximity to the sedate atmosphere of old people's homes puts it in the cultural periphery of a twenty-first-century Berlin that has become famous for its buzzing club culture. Ostermeier's call of the 'small, habitable island' gains more specific relevance as always already set apart from its immediate Berlin context.

The original Mendelssohn building was renovated between 1978 and 1981 at a cost over 80 million Deutschmarks to be turned into a new versatile performance space for the Schaubühne, then under the artistic direction of Peter Stein. Its interior can be divided into up to three separate playing areas, while also allowing for the possibility to use the entire hall, spanning nearly 70 metres, as a single playing space:

> all the classical theatrical forms are fully realizable from a technical standpoint – using a proscenium stage, a transversal or thrust stage, an arena stage, an opera stage with orchestra pit, and even an amphitheatre or a kabuki stage – and the house is best prepared to accommodate any future requirements of stage experimentation.[2]

The creation of such a malleable performance space drew on the idea of a 'total theatre' that Walter Gropius and Erwin Piscator had envisaged in the 1920s, exploding the proscenium and substituting it with a flexible surround spatial experience. More immediately, the renovation responded to the experimental performance culture that Peter Stein, Klaus Michael Grüber and their ensemble had implemented with their multiple site-specific performances that had the Schaubühne rise to world fame during the 1970s. With productions such as *Shakespeare's Memory* in an old film studio, an *Oresteia* onsite in the Berlin exhibition halls or a *Winterreise* taking place in the massive round of the Olympic Stadium, the ensemble had intentionally moved outside the original facilities at the Hallesches Ufer in Kreuzberg.[3]

The new multi-purpose spaces at Lehniner Platz made such a refashioning of theatrical space the norm rather than an exception. The renovation

The Schaubühne's Civic Mission in the Age of Globalization   25

encapsulates the process of the Schaubühne's institutionalization, as critic Sybille Wirsing attested at the time:

> Already in 1975, Peter Stein suggested that the Schaubühne would have to develop from an experiment, as which it began, into an institution. It could only enter this new phase either properly established or not at all. That was an ultimatum. Now, the eighty-million [Deutschmark] theatre, which is being built on the upper Kurfürstendamm with the money of the senate [...] is supposed to provide such continuity.[4]

In an important sense, the new and flexible theatre space translated the idea of experimentation into the walls of the building, putting an invitation to think the future of theatre into stone. Yet, this passage into institutionalization proved to be decidedly difficult. In 1985, only four years after moving in at Lehniner Platz, Stein announced the end of his artistic direction. A number of renowned German theatre directors followed in his footsteps as artistic directors over the course of the next fourteen years, including Luc Bondy, Jürgen Gosch and Andrea Breth. While they were able to create individual productions that brought occasional successes, none of them managed to open a new institutional chapter for the Schaubühne. Only with the arrival of an entirely new generation of young theatre-makers as an artistic leadership team did a new era begin. In 1999, along with the then thirty-year-old Thomas Ostermeier, came his dramaturg Jens Hillje, choreographer Sasha Waltz and producer Jochen Sandig. From 2004, Ostermeier and Hillje continued until Hillje left in 2009. Since then, Ostermeier has been the theatre's sole artistic director.

The development of the Schaubühne as an institution under Ostermeier's direction marks a striking wrestling with the unique spatial possibilities inscribed into the building at Lehniner Platz.[5] Coming from the Baracke (literally: shack) of the Deutsches Theater (Ostermeier and Hillje) and the Sophiensäle (founded by Waltz and Sandig, together with fellow choreographer Jo Fabian, in a former craftsmen's house in Berlin Mitte) the new artistic team had moved from small, somewhat makeshift stages, to one of the city's largest. As set designer (and Bauhaus-trained architect) Jan Pappelbaum describes:

> From today's point of view, I would say that we fell into the trap of being too preoccupied with the question of giving form to the space. The actors had little chance to stand their ground within the spaces we created. They were literally lost in space. The spaces looked visually stunning, but one of the biggest problems was that you could barely see and hear the actors. [...] We therefore eventually decided to bring calmness into the Schaubühne space by building, within the big shell of the Schaubühne,

three permanent auditoria of various size, which all are, as far as their dimensions are concerned, more intimate chamber theatres [*Kammerbühnen*]. This basic set-up seemed to fit best the manner of playing and effect desired by Thomas's approach, and that of most other directors working at the Schaubühne.[6]

In addition to such aesthetic preferences, a pragmatic problem was also how to fill such a massive space on a daily basis. The collective artistic direction that combined dance and dramatic theatre was one way of broadening audiences, and, particularly in the early years, Sasha Waltz's performances drew large audiences, as did, soon after, Ostermeier's turn to canonical authors such as Ibsen.[7] These artistic and repertory choices went hand in hand with an increasing development of spatial downsizing and the decision for a more permanent division of the principally flexible theatre into three smaller, stable spaces.

The most recent transformation of the smallest of the three playing spaces occurred in 2014 with the building of a rounded auditorium around a thrust stage. This adaptation of a Shakespearean theatre does away with standing room for the groundlings but still privileges the Globe's immediacy between stage and auditorium by creating 'the atmosphere of a claustrophobic boiler-room – a stage enclosed by a wall of spectators', in which each visitor has the impression of being closest to the stage.[8] This permanent amendment of Hall C as an intimate, third playing space initially created the frame for Ostermeier's *Richard III*, yet beyond Shakespeare, the 'Schaubühne Globe' not only offers a new twist on the concept of the chamber play as mentioned by Pappelbaum, but it also enables an immediate encounter between actors and audiences, which was exploited also by Dead Centre's production referred to above, or by journalist Carolin Emcke's 2018 lecture performance *Ja heißt ja, und . . . (Yes means yes, and . . .)* that took on the #MeToo debate.

The material conditions and transformations of theatrical space thus also relate to the Schaubühne's continuous (re)negotiation of its place within the public sphere. In 2012, critic Rüdiger Schaper marked the theatre's fiftieth anniversary by stressing the necessity to create 'a biography of space', while connecting it with the Schaubühne's utopian legacy, and its challenge of 'always having to define itself anew as something extraordinary in response to just such expectations'.[9] Schaper here refers to the dual pressure of public expectation to fulfil an innovative civic mission and the necessity of responding to financial pressures that plagued particularly the early years of the new team's artistic direction. The Schaubühne, unlike state theatres such as Deutsches Theater and the Volksbühne, is a private cooperative that receives public funding in the form of the building lease and to provide for the salaries of its artistic and technical staff; production costs need to be raised by the theatre itself. This increases the implicit tension between a civic mission of political criticality and the pragmatism necessary to run such a large theatre with multiple stages. This tension also defines the difference in the critical against the public reception of Ostermeier's Schaubühne. In 2017, it played at 92 per cent capacity, making it the most popular theatre in Berlin.[10] And yet, 'in his native country, Ostermeier's work seems largely to slip through the net of mainstream critical reception'.[11] It ultimately points to the particular ideological bent of the German theatre criticism that echoes the Adornoan critique of the culture industry with its fundamental suspiciousness of commercial success that arguably forecloses compatibility with a critical, political bent.

The institution as a place of freedom

If an institution is a place, whose organization of space is fundamentally political, it is also a set of relations. In their programmatic 1999 manifesto, the new artistic leadership collective identified the loss of a 'mission' amongst German theatre makers as a fundamentally civic one that came with the privatization of social relations and a concurrent depoliticization of public life. They tasked theatre, instead, with modelling alternatives of social existence in order to create a new political consciousness in the public sphere, as 'the place of realization, and thus of repoliticization'.[12] In many ways, their wholesale attack on the established theatrical structures linked up to the 1970s Schaubühne, as Erika Fischer-Lichte noted in her chapter (Chapter 2). In addition to an innovative schedule of contemporary work, they also implemented a new participatory management structure, which, however, was voted out by the ensemble after two years.[13]

Another sentence in the manifesto proved equally provocative: 'Theatre is connected to the world through the authors'.[14] While this would imply a commitment to dramatic representation in the English-speaking theatre world, in the German context dramatic form itself had turned into a site of contestation. Hans-Thies Lehmann's *Postdramatic Theatre* had just been published (in 1999), foregrounding the progressive potential of contemporary performance based in deconstruction. The postdramatic turn classed dramatic representation *per se* as an affirmation of capitalist structures and established authority, and the directorial and performative ability to deconstruct or deprioritize the text was seen as an indicator of political commitment. All in all, this amounted to a rejection of textual as well as institutional authority in favour of conceptualizing performance as a fundamental act of resistance.

Putting the author at the centre of one's mission therefore suggested a different understanding of the political dimension of theatre. Ostermeier, in particular, saw the postmodern perpetuation of critique ultimately as self-serving and thus reinforcing rather than resisting capitalist structures, as it championed increasing social complexity without retaining space for political agency.[15] For Ostermeier, dramatic representation was precisely the tool for understanding the contradictions and shortfalls of contemporary capitalist society. He envisaged the Schaubühne as continuing a Brechtian legacy of acute analysis of social structures through story-telling, yet in order to activate this 'contemporary' potential fully, authors would need to overcome what dramaturg Jens Hillje describes as their 'Heiner Müller impasse':[16] in short, the dominant approach of the deconstructive appropriation of the theatrical canon as the only path for creating a politically engaged theatre.

From the outset, then, Ostermeier positioned himself against what he identified as a binary between 'the affirmative institutional world, and [...] the world of resistance outside the institutions'.[17] His embrace of the creative potential of institutions as a place that may foster political consciousness and offer an alternative social imaginary would continue to inform his work at the Schaubühne, both as director and as intendant. His commitment to theatre as a crucial part of the public sphere echoes Christopher Balme's notion of the theatrical public sphere as 'integral to our notions of the future and futurity, because it provides a discursive prerequisite for shaping things to come'.[18] Ostermeier iconically realized his vision of theatre as a discursive civic space in his production of Ibsen's *Enemy of the People* (2012), which in the fourth act erased the distinction between stage and auditorium, as house lights were raised and characters and audience met for a joint debate about the political decision-making processes laid out by Ibsen's play (see Figure 2). As Hana Worthen argued, in 'arranging the audiences into both a demos, a voting voice, and voicing agents within the frame of each performance', the production aimed at 'stag[ing] the becoming of an active and pluralistic spectatorship, an audience whose performance produces the event and its significance'.[19] The theatre as a place for, in her terms, 'skeptical' public debate is what has shaped the Schaubühne's civic mission far beyond its theatre productions. It offers regular events, such as the monthly roundtable discussions *Streitraum* ('room for debate') that date back already to the Baracke. The 'voicing agents' of the production return here as the theatre extends into a public debating forum.

The idea of the theatre as a probing platform for democratic processes became even more pronounced in the Schaubühne's cooperation with Swiss theatre-maker Milo Rau, whose re-enactment approach shares Ostermeier's concern with the scope and status of realism as an alternative to deconstruction.

Figure 2 In Thomas Ostermeier's production of Ibsen's *Ein Volksfeind* (*An Enemy of the People*, 2012), characters and audience met for a joint debate that reflects the Schaubühne's civic mission far beyond its theatre productions: David Ruland as newspaper editor Aslaksen (left on stage), and Stefan Stern as Ibsen's Doctor Stockmann (behind the lectern), during the discussion scene in the performance on 8 September 2012. © Arno Declair/Schaubühne.

More drastically than Ostermeier, Rau explodes the notion of a distinct theatrical reality and instead understands the theatre as directly intervening into the public sphere to propose political alternatives. In 2017, his *General Assembly* opened at the Schaubühne as a three-day political event that modelled a global parliament, offering a speaking platform to activists from around the globe and forming what Rau called 'the global third estate'[20] to discuss the possibility of a global democracy. Both Ostermeier and Rau envision a civic 'mission' that places the remodelling of existing hierarchies and institutions centre-stage. Importantly, the example of Rau shows how much such commitment to a civically engaged theatre has shifted from a local to a global level over the past decades.

The global Schaubühne

Let me start this next journey with a personal anecdote: I watched my first Schaubühne production not in Germany but in Brooklyn, at the 2004 BAM

Next Wave Festival. *Nora*, Ostermeier's version of Ibsen's *A Doll's House*, was set in the minimalist style of Berlin yuppie-dom and allowed Nora to evoke Lara Croft both in costumes and in behaviour in the closing sequence of the play: she exits no longer with the bang of a door but with that of a machine gun with which she takes out her husband. And yet, this curious encounter abroad may not have so much to do with my own nomadic existence at the time but rather with the strong impetus for internationalization that the Schaubühne has fostered on multiple fronts. The Schaubühne has, indeed, grown into a global theatre company in as much as Berlin simultaneously has developed into a global city. As the city opened up to an influx of a new multicultural population and experienced greater international visibility after the fall of the Berlin Wall, the cultural sector began to formulate responses to these changing demographics.

Two Berlin theatre institutions stood out for spearheading the movement towards internationalization in the German theatre scene, which for language as well as structural reasons bound up with the repertory system had existed in a largely inward-looking celebration of its own privilege. The first is the HAU ('Hebbel am Ufer'), a three-stage production house in Kreuzberg that was founded in 2003 under the artistic direction of Matthias Lilienthal right in the Schaubühne's old home at Hallesches Ufer. Without its own ensemble, it exclusively provides a stage for international guest performances, which it also co-produces. It continues the ground-breaking work of theatre producer Nele Hertling (b. 1934), who in 1989 had created an innovative institution at the Hebbel Theater (now part of the HAU) that was able to 'add something to the city that is indeed different and truly international, and does not have a problem with foreign languages and that is mixing up forms'.[21] While these activities have transformed Berlin and German theatre more widely by creating institutional infrastructures for bringing international performers and ensembles to the capital, Ostermeier's achievement lies in embedding this level of internationalization into the existing repertory structure of the German theatre. Eventually, where Hertling and Lilienthal imported, Ostermeier exported at an exceptional rate.

At the centre of the Schaubühne's internationalization stands its expansive touring schedule, running at around 100 guest performances annually, a number that has been relatively consistent over the two decades of Ostermeier's artistic direction.[22] The most toured productions in the last five years (2014–19) were Milo Rau's *Compassion – History of a Machine Gun* (2016), in addition to Ostermeier's own productions of *Enemy of the People* (2012)[23] and *Richard III* (2015). In addition, the Schaubühne is a founding member of the European theatre network Prospero that, since 2008, has sought to further production exchanges and joint actor training across the continent; it enabled co-productions such as Milo Rau's *Compassion – History of a Machine Gun* (2016) and, more recently, Katie Mitchell's *Orlando* (2019).[24] Wide-ranging efforts to surtitle performances in several languages, which initially served to facilitate the touring schedule, have now gained equal importance as an offering for the international audiences frequenting the Berlin theatre. The intense touring both responds to a globalizing *Zeitgeist* and is tied up with the more pragmatic necessity of generating income to finance the theatre's production work that is not covered by state support. Commenting in 2019, Ostermeier suggested that when taking on the co-artistic direction twenty years earlier, the biggest pressure was not to run the company into debt: 'in these economically dominated times, you can think and say anything, but you are not allowed to go bankrupt, that is the last cardinal sin'.[25] The international success initiated with the Ibsen plays *Nora* (2003) and *Hedda Gabler* (2005) and then manifested through *Hamlet* (2008) proved a crucial turning point in the volatile financial situation of the company.

Parallel to its touring, with which the Schaubühne taps into international festival circuits and builds institutional co-operations, its own festival, FIND (Festival of International New Drama) has provided an important platform for inviting international productions and artists to Berlin. While the chapters by Jens Hillje (Chapter 10) and Marina Ceppi (Chapter 12) focus in greater detail on the history and scope of the festival, I would like to use FIND as a starting point for thinking about the Schaubühne as a global institution, both literally engaging in transnational collaborations and conceptually taking on global political debates. Three interconnected examples illustrate in the following section what a 'global Schaubühne' might imply: first, the Schaubühne's engagement with its guest artists Bush Moukarzel and Ben Kidd of Dead Centre, mentioned at the outset of this chapter; second, *Pearson's Preview*, a blog on the Schaubühne website; and third, the playwriting work of dramaturg Maja Zade as an example of how the question of the local and the global is negotiated on a more conceptual level.

Most imminently, FIND functions as more than an add-on seasonal event but provides a rich sourcing ground for new artistic collaborations, such as the one with Dead Centre. The company's six productions to date offer part absurd, part philosophical running commentaries on the modern dramatic canon: Chekhov, Shakespeare and more recently Beckett. They were repeatedly invited to FIND (with *Lippy* and *Chekhov's First Play* in 2016, and *Hamnet* in 2017) to then collaborate on the in-house season schedule with a co-production. Other examples of this producing model include Álex Rigola, Rodrigo García, and more recently Milo Rau and Anne Cécile Vandalem. In Dead Centre's case, the collaboration led to further exchange, since Moukarzel himself was included, as an actor, in the English-language cast for Ostermeier's *Returning to Reims* (2018), while two Schaubühne actors (Moritz Gottwald and Christoph Gawenda) participated as recorded voices in Dead Centre's production *Beckett's Room* (Dublin Theatre Festival, 2019). In 2018, Dead Centre and the Schaubühne created the already mentioned *Shakespeare's Last Play* for the Schaubühne's Globe stage. Their case exemplifies a lively back-and-forth of exchange and allows another shift in perspective on the Schaubühne, reflecting on the peculiarities of the theatrical structures within which it exists. Moukarzel, in a personal interview about his collaboration with the Schaubühne, stressed two aspects about this theatre institution: the power of the ensemble and the power of the directorial figure:

> [A] place so well resourced, and so well structured, and also with such a clear leadership. [...] They can react very quickly, and that is quite an important thing because theatres are usually quite slow: they make a decision, and it can only be implemented three years later. [The Schaubühne] obviously has a structure that can be very reactive to the world.[26]

Moukarzel sees the power of the director as paired with the strong position of the ensemble actors, who take an equal share in shaping the institution of the theatre. Most striking to him was both the energy and virtuosity the performers drew from knowing each others' acting strengths, together with their approach to the production: 'they really want to feel they have ownership of it.'[27] The ensemble thus became an important counterpoint to directorial power, which echoes Ostermeier's own emphasis on an actor-based theatre in his theoretical writings on his approach to directing.[28]

Moukarzel's observations foreground the fundamental combination of autonomy and collaboration that form the institutional backbone of the Schaubühne. Ostermeier's autonomy in leading this institution, implicit in the fast reactiveness that Moukarzel highlights, has enabled a unique engagement with the changing social and political climate, promoting the theatre as an important extension of the public sphere. His two recent productions of *Italian Night* (2018) and *Youth Without God* (2019) by the Austrian Ödön von Horvath, plays from the 1930s, take on the rising right-wing populism in Germany, and engage in close dialogue with a co-production such as *Danke Deutschland – Cảm ơn nước Đức* (2019), which explores the status of a multicultural society and the latent racism through the fate of Vietnamese immigrants in Germany today. It was directed by another regular FIND artist, Sanja Mitrović. These examples illustrate how FIND and the collaborations that have emerged from it have functioned

The Schaubühne's Civic Mission in the Age of Globalization   33

as a tool through which the Schaubühne reflects on its own methods of working in order to generate new artistic voices and new approaches to theatre-making. The international collaborations also offer an urgently necessary valve for challenging the institutionally stratified and homogenous training and career paths in the repertory theatre system in Germany, which continues to lack diverse ethnic representation among its actors and artistic staff.

A different instance of critical self-distancing is provided, within the digital sphere, by the blog *Pearson's Preview*.[29] It began as a live blog during the 2014 FIND, and has since continued to cover both the annual festival and all premieres in the theatre. The blog is written in English (alongside a German translation) by the Berlin-based Canadian writer and historian Joseph Pearson. It consists of a mixture of essays and interviews that are the product of Pearson's rehearsal visits:

> The interest was to have someone come in who is not going to judge whether a production is good or bad [. . .] but rather come in at an earlier stage to reflect on creation: the ideas behind a production, where things might go or how rehearsal works. What does it feel like to go behind the curtain and look at the process?[30]

Once more, the outsider perspective – here one that Pearson as an immigrant to Germany and a non-specialist in theatre provides – takes a central role in diversifying the voices that make up the Schaubühne intervention in the public sphere. The blog functions both as an outreach and as documentation tool, also charting the intensity of international collaboration at the Schaubühne: Pearson so far has interviewed more than sixty international guest artists and ensembles that have been hosted at the theatre, such as British director and actor Simon McBurney in 2015, Egyptian theatre-maker Ahmed El Attar in 2016 and Chinese director Li Jianjun in 2019. In addition, it acknowledges with its insights into the rehearsal process a part of the theatrical apparatus usually left out of sight. *Pearson's Preview* is a prominent example of the institution's openness to look critically at its own workings, as well as evidencing an avid sense for the use of digital media to expand the reach of its own institutional frame, alongside the theatre's expanding online media library that includes videos from touring, of Streitraum debates, production trailers and interviews, and 'behind the scenes' portraits of ensemble actors in specific roles.

Pearson's blog builds the bridge to a wider conceptual level through which global political debates enter the Schaubühne's theatre work, as can be shown through the example of the *#MeToo* debate. In a text on the 2019 FIND,

Pearson highlighted how several festival productions picked up the question of sexual politics, a 'Zeitgeist [that] is also very much present in the house productions, such as the direction of Patrick Wengenroth and Maja Zade's plays'.[31] This focus on sexual politics, however, also responded to intense criticism of Ostermeier the previous year for presenting a season schedule that consisted entirely of male playwrights.[32] The debate threw a spotlight on a systemic power imbalance not exclusive to the Schaubühne but endemic across the German theatre system with its dearth of female artists in comparison to, for instance, the UK or US. Hence Maja Zade, long-time principal dramaturg in the Schaubühne's artistic team, may serve as a final example, with her debut work as a playwright, in which she tackled the topic of sexual politics head on. Her *Status Quo* (2019), directed by Marius von

Figure 3 Maja Zade's *Status Quo* (dir. Marius von Mayenburg, 2019) lambasted misogynistic power dynamics in the contemporary work place, including the theatre, by flipping the gender hierarchies: Jenny König, Jule Böwe and Carolin Haupt gave a juicy parody of rehearsal room practices. © Arno Declair/Schaubühne.

The *Schaubühne's* satire that inverted the power dynamics between the genders, as men were shown being exposed to the every-day sexism in work and social life, while women hold the positions of power and authority. In this inverted world, Zade's play offered a meta-theatrical lens on the power dynamics implicit in theatre-making itself, with a whole strand of the play set in a theatre rehearsal room (see Figure 3). Pearson described the scene as 'a brilliant take-down of the theatre director's perceived omnipotence' and also an occasion for an extended debate among the ensemble members about their experiences with theatrical power structures.[33]

Zade's satirical glance at her own existence in the theatre offered a necessary critique of the intensely hierarchical structures of the German theatre system more generally, which centralizes institutional authority around the figure of an *auteur*-director, such as, in this case, Ostermeier himself. Overall, the structural division of a publicly highly visible male director paired with a female dramaturg in the background is far from atypical in the German context. At the same time, her own move into the front row of playwriting showed an awareness of and willingness to address the existing power stratifications on the part of the Schaubühne team. Ostermeier himself directed Zade's next play, *Abgrund* (*Abyss*, 2019). Furthermore, the situation of sexual politics at the Schaubühne presents itself as more complex than the issue of an all-male season schedule might suggest. While it is true that the public face of the Schaubühne boasts a range of male figureheads, such as Ostermeier himself but also Lars Eidinger, the theatre also has built several long-standing relationships with female theatre makers such as Katie Mitchell and the Argentinian choreographer Constanza Macras. Likewise, Carolin Emcke's curation of the *Streitraum* debate can also be classed as an important outward-facing feature of the Schaubühne programming. The case thus also points at the institutional flexibility and awareness with which the Schaubühne since 2000 has worked to subvert the stratifications implicit in existing institutional structures.

The Schaubühne's achievement as an institution lies not least in such willingness to think beyond and to rework the existing structures, and also unique privileges, of the German subsidized theatre system, from the participatory management models of the early days to the establishment of a broad and diverse global network of cooperating artists, whose alternative perspectives, aesthetic visions and practices have provided a continuous resource of new impulses and encounters for its artistic team and ensemble. As Pearson described it in our conversation:

> The Schaubühne is a surprising hybrid of traditional and alternative elements. On the face of it, it is a bourgeois institution on one of Berlin's

most expensive streets, which has a desire to engage with its neighborhood. On the other hand, it breaks out of that shell, engages with more radical politics, finds different publics internationally. This makes it a theatre that is a little out-of-place in, but also part of both worlds.[34]

This sense of being perpetually out of place is also what has allowed for the continuous transformation of the Schaubühne as an institution and its ability to stay 'contemporary', even twenty years on from its original mission statement. It is this 'out-of-placeness' that defines the civic mission of the Schaubühne. Such utopian 'out-of-placeness' might then create also spaces of dissent, not least through a perceptual alterity as an aesthetic basis of its version of a directorial *Regietheater*.[35] More than a particular aesthetic style or focus on a particular body of dramatic work, Ostermeier's artistic leadership at the Schaubühne gains its cohesive arc through this search for engendering sites of discursive dissent, not only within the prolifically diverse range of productions but also in negotiating its institutional place in the cultural landscape. 'Being out of place' may also be another way of describing the island with which we began. If there is a utopian impulse in building an institution, it lies not so much in having made the perfect place, but in continuously embracing the labour of readjusting the infrastructures that this institution affords. What the journeys of the Schaubühne as an institution illustrate is that this island has never been a retreat but rather a launching pad for diverse forms of mobility (mental as well as actual) and commitment.

Notes

1   Gerhard Jörder, *Ostermeier Backstage* (Berlin: Theater der Zeit, 2014), 49.
2   Schaubühne Berlin, 'Architecture', www.schaubuehne.de/en/pages/ architecture.html (accessed 15 October 2019).
3   See David Bradby and David Williams, 'Peter Stein', in *Director's Theatre*, 2nd edn, ed. Peter M. Boenisch (London: Red Globe Press, 2020), 131–54.
4   Cited in Karl Ernst Herrmann, ed., *Schaubühne am Halleschen Ufer & Lehniner Platz, 1962–1987* (Frankfurt am Main: Propyläen, 1987), 302.
5   See also the chapters by Jens Hillje (Chapter 10) and Sabine Huschka (Chapter 13).
6   Jan Pappelbaum, 'Creating Stage Spaces Like it is not Possible Anywhere Else', in *The Theatre of Thomas Ostermeier*, eds Peter M. Boenisch and Thomas Ostermeier (Abingdon and New York: Routledge, 2016), 33. (Thomas and I, on the cover, are listed as co-authors rather than editors of the book, even though there are contributions by others in there as well.)
7   See Jens Hillje's comments in his essay in Chapter 10.

The Schaubühne's Civic Mission in the Age of Globalization   37

8   Pappelbaum, 'Creating Stage Spaces', 39.
9   Rüdiger Schaper, 'Zu Luft wird hier der Raum', *Der Tagesspiegel*, 16 September 2012, www.tagesspiegel.de/kultur/50-jahre-schaubuehne-zu-luft-wird-hier-der-raum/7138916.html. See also Jack Zipes, '"Utopia as the Past Conserved"; An Interview with Peter Stein and Dieter Sturm of the Schaubühne am Halleschen Ufer', *Theater* 9, no. 1 (1977): 53.
10 Hildburg Bruns, 'Lars Eidinger lässt die Schaubühnen-Kassen klingeln', *Berliner Zeitung*, 12 March 2018, www.bz-berlin.de/kultur/lars-eidinger-laesst-die-schaubuehnen-kasse-klingeln (accessed 25 February 2020).
11 Boenisch and Ostermeier, *The Theatre of Thomas Ostermeier*, 2.
12 Chapter 1, p. 3.
13 See Ostermeier's account of this episode in Chapter 4, p. 43–4.
14 Chapter 1, p. 4.
15 See his exemplary essays 'Theatre in the Age of its Acceleration' and 'A Defence of Realism in Theatre', in Boenisch and Ostermeier, *The Theatre of Thomas Ostermeier*, 13–25.
16 See Chapter 10, p. 125.
17 Boenisch and Ostermeier, *The Theatre of Thomas Ostermeier*, 230.
18 Christopher B. Balme, *The Theatrical Public Sphere* (Cambridge: Cambridge University Press, 2014), 18.
19 Hana Worthen, 'For a Skeptical Dramaturgy', *Theatre Topics* 24, no. 3 (2014): 180.
20 Milo Rau, 'General Assembly', www.general-assembly.net/en (accessed 4 February 2020). In 2018, Rau became artistic director of NT Ghent in Belgium, publishing a much debated manifesto that outlined the path towards 'a city theatre of the future', echoing the call for a new 'mission' in the Schaubühne's manifesto from two decades earlier. Rau's manifesto from 2018 echoes the call for a new mission for the theatre that the Schaubühne had formulated at the beginning of Ostermeier's tenure in 2000 (see NT Ghent, 'The Ghent Manifesto', www.ntgent,be/en/manifest, accessed 4 February 2020).
21 Cited in Bonnie Marranca et. al., 'Berlin Conversations', *PAJ: A Journal of Performance and Art* 22, no. 2 (2000): 57.
22 Boenisch and Ostermeier, *The Theatre of Thomas Ostermeier*, 1.
23 The Schaubühne has published an extensive online archive documenting the international touring specifically of *An Enemy of the People*, www.schaubuehne.de/de/video/index.html (accessed 25 February 2020).
24 See www.prospero-theatre.eu/en/ (accessed 5 November 2019).
25 Ulrich Seidler, '20 Jahre an der Schaubühne: Thomas Ostermeier über Wunder und Verantwortung', *Berliner Zeitung*, 29 June 2019, https://archiv.berliner-zeitung.de/kultur/theater/20-jahre-an-der-schaubuehne-thomas-ostermeier-ueber-wunder-und-verantwortung-32772114 (accessed 25 February 2020).
26 Bush Moukarzel, personal interview with author, 24 October 2019.
27 Ibid.
28 See Boenisch and Ostermeier, *The Theatre of Thomas Ostermeier*, 132–84.

29 Joseph Pearson, 'Pearson's Preview', www.schaubuehne.de/de/blog/index. html (accessed 25 February 2020).

30 Joseph Pearson, personal interview with the author, 21 October 2019.

31 Joseph Pearson, 'Staring the Accused in the Eye: Talking Gender at FIND 2019' (14 March 2019), www.schaubuehne.de/en/blog/find-preview-1.html (accessed 25 February 2020).

32 Barbara Bogen, 'Warum an Theatern die Männer dominieren', *Bayern Radio*, 14 May 2018, www.br.de/nachrichten/kultur/warum-an-unseren-theatern-die-maenner-dominieren,Qs1fMFy (accessed 4 February 2020).

33 Joseph Pearson, '*Status quo*'s Mirror on Injustice (and Patriarchy in the Theatre)', *Pearson's Preview*, 8 January 2019, www.schaubuehne.de/en/blog/statusquo.html (accessed 4 February 2020).

34 Pearson, interview.

35 Peter M. Boenisch, *Directing Scenes and Senses: The Thinking of Regie* (Manchester: Manchester University Press, 2015), 22–3.

4

'Audiences Know Their Cause will be Treated': Making Political Theatre at the Schaubühne

Thomas Ostermeier in conversation with Clare Finburgh Delijani

Clare Finburgh Delijani (CFD): *Can you describe the institutional identity of the Schaubühne?*

Thomas Ostermeier (TO): There is a tendency to think that the Schaubühne was founded in 1970 by the great German director Peter Stein, whereas in fact it began nearly a decade earlier. The history of the Schaubühne, notably its first eight years, is crucial for understanding the spirit of the Schaubühne today. It was started in 1962 by a group of students who decided to discontinue their theatre studies and make theatre instead.[1] One of the five, Jürgen Schitthelm, was managing director until 2012, and he is still a shareholder in the company today. At the time, he was twenty-two. Together with four other theatre fanatics – Leni Langenscheidt, Waltraud Mau, Dieter Sturm and Klaus Weiffenbach – he launched this project in order to make practical theatre independently. The fact that the first company was independent is still very significant with regard to the identity of the Schaubühne today: it was a theatre initiated by students, with no public money involved. The five students all came from different backgrounds. Significantly, Schitthelm was from East Berlin and had moved to the West just before the Wall was built in August 1961. When he was a teenager in East Berlin, after school he used to attend rehearsals at the Berliner Ensemble (BE), the theatre established by Bertolt Brecht and Helene Weigel in 1949. The company thus started, in 1962, with a very politically engaged programme, not dissimilar to the programme with which we started the Baracke, the small experimental space at the Deutsches Theater Berlin, in 1996. For example, they staged Sean O'Casey's *Shadow of a Gunman* and Arnold Wesker's *Roots* in their first season. Formally, these were all very realist plays, what you might call 'kitchen sink' dramas, but in essence they were politically provocative agit-prop.

40 *The Schaubühne Berlin under Thomas Ostermeier*

Politics have also been embedded in the very name of the theatre. There are two reasons why they called their project 'Schaubühne'. One is the political German playwright Friedrich von Schiller's famous text *Die Schaubühne als eine moralische Anstalt betrachtet* (*The Theatre Stage Considered as a Moral Institution*, 1784), which asks what good theatre can do for the moral principles or ethics of a society. The other is the magazine called *Die Schaubühne*, published in the Weimar Republic of the 1920s by the progressive intellectuals Siegfried Jacobsohn, Kurt Tucholsky and Carl von Ossietzky. From the start, the theatre enjoyed support from West Berlin critics, most notably the most influential West Berlin theatre critic, Friedrich Luft (1911–90). He followed the young theatre company closely, and identified that they were seeking to create the identity of an ensemble, even if they did not have the financial means to establish a permanent company. They would engage actors according to each production, as in the British or French systems, yet in fact these soon ended up mostly being the same actors all the time. The consequence was that their very politically conscious, social realist programme of plays was performed by a politically militant group of actors on stage.

Then came Peter Stein. In 1968, he had been kicked out of the Munich Kammerspiele, because he collected money for the Việt Cộng after his production of Peter Weiss's *Vietnam Discourse*. The Schaubühne took over this controversial production after it had been closed in Munich. At the Kammerspiele, Stein had been assistant director to Fritz Kortner, one of the most important post-war German directors. Before the Second World War, he had been one of the greatest actors in the German-speaking world, but being Jewish, he had to flee from the Nazi regime, yet later returned from exile. Kortner's work inspired a whole generation of young German theatre-makers of Stein's generation. Stein's first own production as director, at Kammerspiele, is considered to be a landmark production of Edward Bond's *Saved*. After his dismissal from Munich, he worked in Zurich and in particular in Bremen, where in 1969 he directed Goethe's *Torquato Tasso*, with the now legendary actors Bruno Ganz, Edith Clever and Jutta Lampe. He was then invited to become artistic director of the Schaubühne. The city of Berlin was clever enough to invite not only Stein, but along with him his very promising group of performers, and also other directors who had worked with them at Bremen, such as Klaus-Michael Grüber, Frank-Patrick Steckel and Claus Peymann, who all took up residence at the Schaubühne.

It is the following episode in the history of the Schaubühne that remains famous today, an era marked by a commitment to democracy and participation. Stein introduced an egalitarian wage system, just like we had at the start of my mandate, as well as a politically engaged *Spielplan*, or season

Making Political Theatre at the Schaubühne 41

programme, which he started off by directing Brecht's adaptation of Gorky's *The Mother*. Importantly, Stein cast the actor Therese Giehse in the lead role. She was a leftist Jewish Bavarian actor who had performed with Brecht at the BE. She had two clear and different artistic identities: she was a highly politically engaged actor, and at the same time she was a Bavarian *Volksschauspieler*, a popular actress, coming from a working-class background, who throughout her life performed in her Bavarian dialect and not in 'stage German'. It was therefore highly symbolic that Stein placed his young emerging actors in a constellation around this icon of Brechtian political theatre. Just like Jürgen Schitthelm, who had been influenced watching Brecht rehearse *The Caucasian Chalk Circle* at the Berliner Ensemble, Stein also brought Brecht's legacy into the Schaubühne. As a result, Brecht and an admiration for Brecht are engrained in the Schaubühne's identity.

Stein then introduced weekly lessons on Marxism and Leninism for the entire ensemble of actors, which led, in 1972, to the Conservative Party of Berlin declining to give subsidies to the theatre, arguing that they refused to support a theatre that promoted communism. For an entire year, the theatre received no subsidies from the city, which resulted in their going into debt. Stein and his ensemble continued to stage highly political plays, like Vsevolod Vishnevsky's *An Optimistic Tragedy* (1972), a play about the Russian Revolution, and Marieluise Fleisser's *Purgatory in Ingolstadt* later the same year. His production of Ibsen's *Peer Gynt* (1971) had meanwhile further demonstrated the Schaubühne's emphasis on ensemble work, with several actors sharing the lead role. However, it is also important to point out that, within the ensemble, there were different factions. Claus Peymann, an associate director at the theatre for the first year, decided to stage Peter Handke's *Der Ritt über den Bodensee* (*The Ride Across Lake Constance*, 1971) which provoked tensions between the moderate members of the ensemble and the radical leftists, represented mainly by the actor Michael König, who was a Maoist and believed that Handke's theatre was not sufficiently political to be staged at the Schaubühne, even that Handke was a reactionary. Two years after Stein arrived, he and his actors abandoned egalitarian wages, meaning that the actors who had by then become stars, notably Bruno Ganz, Corinna Kirchhoff, Edith Clever, Jutta Lampe and Otto Sander (with the exception of Ganz, they all became stars thanks to the fact that they had been actors at the Schaubühne, not from their cinema or television careers) received more than the rest.

It is important to remember that these were very different times. One must consider the Schaubühne in its material circumstances. It was not only the talent and brilliance of the Schaubühne's artistic director and his actors that shaped the institution, but also the geography and the history in which

42 *The Schaubühne Berlin under Thomas Ostermeier*

it found itself. Initially, when it was based at Hallesches Ufer, the Schaubühne was striving to find its identity right next to the Berlin Wall that stood just behind the theatre. West Berlin at the time was a Western shop window right in the heart of communist East Germany. It felt obliged to promote the idea of freedom and democracy, and was supported in this by the Allied Forces who still governed the city and its British, American and French sectors, until 1989. At the same time, the isolated city suffered a dramatic brain drain, as it was geographically cut off from the rest of West Germany, and its citizens were, in fact, not even fully West German; they did not get the German *Personalausweis* identity card. This is also the reason why the famous Theatertreffen theatre festival was founded in the city: in order to bring the most beautiful examples of West German culture to Berlin each year, and to show them off as achievements of democratic free culture, signalling to the East, but also to the West Berlin citizen who could not easily travel out of the isolated city.

Because of this isolation, the young and talented sought their careers elsewhere. This was a problem for the few large companies and industries in the city, for example Siemens and Bayer, yet also for culture. This, in fact, was the reason why the city had asked Peter Stein, one of the most talented and politically edgy directors of a new generation, to come to Berlin. The Schaubühne – remember it was a student company – had become so important because after the Wall was built, almost all theatres lay in the eastern part of the city. The Schaubühne was, with the Schillertheater, one of only two stages remaining in West Berlin, later joined by Piscator's Freie Volksbühne, which was founded just before Stein was brought to the Schaubühne. The city took a gamble that paid off, since the Schaubühne became world famous. In fact, it became a model for other German theatres, as it represented and promoted the idea that actors should not only learn their lines and excel on stage, but that they should also be familiar with the history of the play, with academic research on the play and with the play's dramaturgy. At the Schaubühne, rehearsal periods were extremely long – six months, even a year – and a great amount of time was spent around the table, as experts and specialists were invited to explain the main issues in a play. In preparation for *As You Like It*, his first Shakespeare production, Stein conducted research over a two-year period, resulting in his own adaptation entitled *Shakespeare's Memory*, which presented the ensemble's research into Elizabethan history, Elizabethan science, the Globe Theatre and other aspects of early modern life. In this way, he applied a thorough research process to the theatrical event. Such intense preparation gave rise to a nuanced realism in which Stein and his actors paid particular attention to the historical background. The productions performed during the first ten years of Stein's

Making Political Theatre at the Schaubühne   43

directorship were ground-breaking, admired and respected, eventually far beyond West Germany, specifically for the meticulous intellectual preparation that took place during rehearsals.

At the end of the 1970s, the company moved from the former Union Hall at Hallesches Ufer into the building where we are now, an old cinema built in 1927, which was converted specifically for Stein. Once again, he benefited from the generous support of the city, as it wanted to show off its superiority to the communist East, and invested some 80 million Deutschmarks into a high-tech refurbishment. The inaugural production at Lehniner Platz was Stein's celebrated eight-hour *Oresteia* (1980), followed by his series of famous Chekhov interpretations, including *Three Sisters* (1984) and *The Cherry Orchard* (1991). By the end of the 1980s, when I first started seeing Schaubühne productions, they had changed considerably from the productions of the 1970s, when the storytelling was extremely nuanced and detailed. The Schaubühne had become a temple of West-German theatre, staging the biggest stars, and adopting what one could describe as a mannered, somewhat pretentious style of acting. The vowels appeared much longer, the way of acting was no longer naturalistic, even if the scenography was highly detailed and realist. We now tend to look back at this time as the golden age of the Schaubühne, but reading the reviews, it is clear that early on, they were criticized. Reviews suggested that the actors were stifled by their own aesthetic experimentation; that the sets, while beautiful, were overblown; and that Stein was simply repeating a successful formula with less and less political relevance, becoming his own museum.

CFD: *What was the legacy of this history of the Schaubühne that you inherited as you took over the theatre in 1999?*

TO: When I took over, Stein had been gone for fifteen years. So I am not his successor. He stepped down as artistic director in 1985, but continued to stage a number of productions at the Schaubühne until 1989. He was succeeded by Jürgen Gosch, Luc Bondy and eventually Andrea Breth who took up the legacy of Stein's later productions by working in a very naturalistic way with her actors, paying acute attention to historical detail and staging plays in period costumes and set.

When I started as artistic director, I reinstated the model of *Mitbestimmung*, of co-determination and participation by all members of the creative team. Every week, all actors had to attend a general assembly. They were all obliged to read all the plays that we considered, and were involved in discussing whether or not to stage them. Actors were also present at all administrative meetings. For example, two actors would come as delegated representatives

44 *The Schaubühne Berlin under Thomas Ostermeier*

to our weekly finance meetings, and to our dramaturgy meetings, where we discussed new plays and productions. They were then responsible for reporting back to the other actors. When we had our next general assembly, every actor would therefore be informed and ready to discuss the theatre's prospective programme of plays, and who would direct them. The actors all had contracts which specified that they were not permitted to work outside, in cinema, television or radio; they had to commit themselves entirely to the Schaubühne project.

But after two years, a two-thirds majority voted to abandon this policy. I still do not think this was a wise idea, as only maybe 10 per cent of them ever made a career in these other industries; but they voted to abandon our original contracts, which had stipulated equal pay for all the actors (and it is important to note that, like under Stein, this only concerned the actors – having an equal pay policy for all staff would have been the right thing to do, but it would have exploded the budget). Each actor, during these early years, received a monthly salary of 6,000 Deutschmarks. But this equal pay was abandoned, as were the regular weekly assemblies. The actors already had increasingly pulled out of the weekly meetings, there was less and less interest; soon we only held them once every month, and after a while only when a need for them was felt. The participation system meant a lot of off-stage work for the actors, and I realized that it completely destroyed the spirit of the company. But one cannot have only the advantages of such a democratic system, without putting in the work; this is all part of the political reality. One of the biggest problems was that I had introduced these ideas, and they were felt as an enforced democracy.

I had to accept that we had tried to instil this system of democracy at a time that was entirely different from when Stein had tried. Yet at this time, in the early 2000s, the *Zeitgeist* was a triumph of consumerism, of individualism, of fashion; it was a time of start-ups. So this system was experienced like the rules of some ancient monastery in a world whose principles had completely changed. It was a democratic decision to abandon egalitarian pay, but personally I consider this to be the biggest failure of my life. Actually, I cannot even say it was a democratic vote, as not even enough people showed up to make it a fully quorate, representative vote. Even today, I think few of the actors in my ensemble understand why this idea of a general assembly was so fundamental for me. But in 2016, a group of actors started up a new general assembly themselves, in response to the rapidly changing times. So there is a new spirit of democracy now at the Schaubühne.

CFD: *I assume that Peter Stein's legacy of political theatre, which you have described, was important for you when you first arrived at the Schaubühne.*

Perhaps it had influenced you earlier, if we also consider the work you had staged at the Baracke, mainly by the British 'in-yer-face'-generation of writers?

TO: As a private person and as a citizen, I would consider myself to be politically engaged. However, as a theatre-maker and an artistic director, I do not have a political agenda for the Schaubühne. If you have a certain ideology or programme, you narrow your view on the world. But of course my politics do come across in the themes and works I select. You can see my observation of social reality in Germany, of the world we live in, of what we are dealing with. That is what I try to reflect in theatre. As both a theatre-maker and a theatre programmer, I see myself as a membrane: a very thin skin to the outside world, a skin that is highly sensitive to what is happening.

But my priority when I took over the Schaubühne was to make it an international theatre, in contrast to the idea of a national theatre that is so important in Germany. The internationalism I envisaged for the Schaubühne was 'internationalist' in the communist sense of the International. Internationalism was first conceptualized by the communists long before globalization ever had a name. We are very lucky at the Schaubühne with respect to the fact that we tour internationally, that we are internationally connected and that we have an internationalist outlook. We have a lot of international people coming to the theatre because they have seen our shows abroad and they want to see the 'cradle' of the theatre, so to speak, when they visit Berlin. In addition, Berlin today has large communities of people from Greece, Italy and Spain who have been forced by the financial crisis to leave their countries, not to mention the migrants from conflict zones such as the Middle East. There are even people from France, the UK and the USA who come to Berlin because it still has lower rents than other major cities in the world, and people can still just about afford to have a career in the arts. These people provide the Schaubühne with a very international audience. We make sure that a number of shows per month are surtitled, mainly in English and French. We were the first and for a long time only theatre to do this in Berlin; now all the big Berlin theatres, and actually many theatres across the entire country, do it. We ensure that in our theatre we do it highly professionally, because our surtitles appear integrated into the set, and not somewhere to the side where you need to look away from the stage to read them. So without necessarily putting on a specially dedicated programme, we have cultivated a very diverse, global audience.

CFD: *Globalization, however, means above all the ever increasing move towards models of individualism rather than the spirit of communitarianism*

46 *The Schaubühne Berlin under Thomas Ostermeier*

that you have mentioned in the context of the failure of your ideal of a Schaubühne general assembly. Against this spirit, you have been very successful in your commitment to the Schaubühne's ethos of the ensemble.

TO: I will always defend the idea of an ensemble, especially considering the situation in theatres in the UK and France. For me, having the opportunity continuously to conduct research into theatre and acting methods is fundamental, and this is only possible with a permanent ensemble. To take just one example, my production of Schnitzler's *Professor Bernhardi* (2016) would never have been possible with any random sixteen actors. To have such a large group of actors working so well together on stage requires the experience of continuously working together. There were, in fact, a lot of newcomers in the show, who had just joined the ensemble at the time. But they worked with the core of actors who know each other very well, who are aware of how everyone functions, who support each other on stage, who know that they can do anything at any moment and will be carried by the others – who thus trust each other completely. One might even say that some of these actors had been rehearsing together for this production for the past fifteen years. I strongly believe that the most important periods in theatre history, and the most famous directors, have always been linked to an ensemble. Stein, and also the Volksbühne under Frank Castorf, are examples in recent German theatre history, but also think of Stanislavsky and the Moscow Art Theatre, and of Brecht and the Berliner Ensemble. In order to develop, theatre directors need this continuous work with an ensemble of actors.

I feel that with the ensemble at the Schaubühne we have made great progress over the past years. The ensemble has really gained in quality. We have a group of incredibly gifted actors, a mixture of some who have grown and developed with us over the years and have reached middle age, and young new actors who, I can safely say, are the most talented of their generation. We can attract the very best young actors because they are aware that if they join our company, they will be able to grow and develop their skills and fulfil their potential to a maximum. The project, going into the future, is to develop further the ensemble in order to make it grow even stronger, and to deepen the way we work and play together. Marius von Mayenburg recently pointed out that what he thinks we have achieved at the Schaubühne is not only to make successful theatre, but also to create a certain way of acting. So the success of the theatre has gone hand-in-hand with developing the ensemble, which is absolutely central to my ethos both as an artistic director and as a theatre director.

CFD: *Let me return once more to the move towards individualism, and to today's neoliberal economic landscape, also thinking of today's populism and* *the far right, with which your recent productions engage. What are the battles you have to fight in your theatre in this respect?*

TO: Today, our biggest challenge, indeed, comes from outside the theatre. We face an attack by neoliberal economics on culture more broadly. Theories coming out of the Chicago School of Economics, first implemented by Ronald Reagan in the USA and Margaret Thatcher in the UK, are continuing apace, as my recent shows, like *Returning to Reims*, highlight. Even if we have a social democratic government, as we have in the city-state of Berlin, centre-left politics have become infiltrated by neoliberal economics. If this is taken to its conclusion, the brutal truth we will have to face is that theatre and the arts will no longer be subsidized at all, but will be driven by a model of cultural policy that involves having dinners and attracting as many corporate sponsors as possible. Everyone thinks Germany is awash with subsidies for the arts, and that it is just great to work in German theatre. The truth is that a mere 0.7 per cent of Berlin's budget is spent on theatre. If it were 2, 5, 7 or 10 per cent, one might think that Germany really promotes culture. But, of course, even 0.7 per cent is much more than in the UK, the US, and other countries.

Yet in considerable contrast with when I took over the Schaubühne twenty years ago, nowadays, the politicians in the Berlin parliament make considerations about how much money they give us based on the number of spectators we have. They apply a formula to calculate how much they will subsidize each theatre seat, and then compare it with previous years, and with other theatres. So it has clearly become only about money. It is no longer about quality, about developing new audiences, or creating audiences for the future, about working with students or school children, about educating people to think about ideals and human conflict, and being human and living in the world. It is just about money. I was shocked when I had a conversation with the former French prime minister Jean-Marc Ayrault, just after the 2015 Paris attacks, and he said, 'Thomas, we have to do something for the young people in the *banlieues*. We have to bring culture to them. We want to talk to them. Do you know how we can solve the problem? Do you know how theatre can help?' Other than money, there seems to be no idea of how to keep the fabric of society together; everything else has been abandoned – and the real humanist value of culture, of art and of theatre, is only recognized when it is too late, and something drastic has happened.

CFD: *You are the Schaubühne's artistic director and also a theatre director. Do you see these two responsibilities as a logical extension of one another, or do you sometimes perceive them as in conflict with each other?*

TO: I do not see a conflict between the two jobs, I see them as existing in parallel. This is because I have a really excellent team round me. We have 220 permanent employees at the Schaubühne, so I always know the theatre is in capable hands while I am in rehearsals. Every now and then, when things get too political, I have to step in for them, since with my reputation and recognition I can fight on behalf of the theatre, and I am prepared to fight hard for my art, for my ensemble and for the entire building. But recently, we received a lot of money for our technicians and administrative staff, as a direct result of the success of the art we are making.

Other theatres in German-speaking countries have a managing artistic director, who does not direct shows himself. But I feel that in most cases, this is detrimental to the spirit of the company. Being a stage director as well as the theatre's artistic director, I have been able to develop an ensemble of actors that attracts directors of the calibre of Simon McBurney, Romeo Castellucci, Milo Rau and Katie Mitchell, who want to work with them. Ivo van Hove came several times, and Falk Richter worked with us for many years. Only an artistic director who is also a theatre director, and who can train actors not only in the art of acting, but also in the ethics of rehearsal, of working together – instead of only thinking about promoting themselves and getting famous – is able to develop a quality ensemble like ours, who so many directors want to work with.

CFD: *But what about diversity and inclusion? In the UK, funding from the Arts Council has shifted away from theatres that predominantly programme white, male playwrights staged by white male directors. Are ideas of 'diversifying' your ensemble a concern? One might argue that an ensemble impedes diversification.*

TO: This is a major question. But I do not agree that ensembles are an obstacle to diversity. It is true that our ensemble is not as ethnically diverse as the German society around us. But I have also been a teacher of *Regie*, or directing, at the Ernst Busch Academy of Dramatic Arts since 2005, and I am very passionate about finding talent among students from immigrant backgrounds, and from immigrant and working-class backgrounds. For me, diversity is not only a question of including people from different ethnic backgrounds, but it also has to do with class. Today it is simply not financially possible for students from more modest backgrounds to go to theatre school any more, especially in the USA and in the UK. The only way to diversify the theatre is to start diversifying the students we let into drama schools. Social background is extremely important to me. It has always played a major role in decision-making when it comes to actors I engage in my company. Since many of the actors in our ensemble have worked here for many years, they come from a time when it was still possible for young people from working-class or petit-bourgeois backgrounds to join theatre schools. A lot of them are also from the former East Germany, which has a completely different social make-up and cultural history.

You can also tell from the subject matter of my productions, from *Shopping and Fucking* at the Baracke to *Returning to Reims* and *The History of Violence* today, that I am very engaged in questions of the marginalized. I am also very interested in questions of high and supposedly low culture, and how snobbish and elitist high culture is. I think audiences know their cause will be treated at the Schaubühne. They know that many subjects that they are dealing with, for instance globalization, marginalization, the New Right, LGBTQ rights etc., will be treated. I am not a big promoter of the idea that you have to organize a special campaign or design a specific programme in order to attract a diverse audience, because I always say that the plays and the productions should speak for themselves. We have never had an agenda to get younger audiences or more diverse audiences. It just happened because as an artistic team we are socially engaged. We are interested in social questions, and aspects of injustice, so audiences can recognize themselves in the work we do.

Socially engaged theatre is directly related to the idea of making theatre that is popular, but that does not become a consumer product. I feel passionately about breaking down the binary between what is perceived as 'low' and 'high' culture. I have no problem with incorporating popular music, and having a rap in the middle of the show, or fight scenes, martial arts and fencing or video. For me, theatre is the art of entertainment, and all my senses need to be stimulated. That does not mean making a musical, where it is only about entertainment. I fully support Brecht's idea that thinking can be entertainment. It can be very entertaining to follow a philosophical or socio-political argument. And this argument can be juxtaposed with music or comic scenes, or physical theatre. This is the same tradition as Elizabethan theatre, where stupid clowning and highly developed philosophical thinking sit side-by-side on the stage. So my theatre situates itself where popular theatre meets high art. I dream of a true mash-up, a flux where all different art forms come together to create something entirely new. Every perspective on the world is relevant. None should be excluded.

Note

1   See also Erika Fischer-Lichte's chapter (Chapter 2), and the chronology of all productions offered by Jürgen Schitthelm (ed.), *50 Jahre Schaubühne* (Berlin: Theater der Zeit, 2012).

Part Two

Thomas Ostermeier at the Schaubühne: Reinventing 'Directors' Theatre'

5

Socialist Realism, Capitalist Realism, Ostermeier Realism

Marvin Carlson

Capitalist realism has gained new prominence in the English-speaking world with the appearance of the late Mark Fisher's 2009 book, *Capitalist Realism: Is there no Alternative*. The term, however, has been circulating in the German art world since the early 1960s, when it was given prominence by a group of German painters who launched, in 1963, a movement calling itself 'Kapitalistischer Realismus'. It shared some features with the contemporary American Pop Art Movement. Its name, alluding to the Soviet-imposed artistic doctrine of 'Socialist Realism' in Eastern Europe, suggested an ironic and political turn to the Western consumer 'doctrine' of capitalist products, publicity and advertising. Within the world of German theatre, this idea, however, had barely any circulation before Thomas Ostermeier used it to put his own work into a contemporary perspective. In the German theatre journal *Theater Heute*, he expressly distanced his work from that of Western Capitalist Realism, as well as from the long-time dominant East German and Soviet approach of Socialist Realism. The latter, Ostermeier asserted, was dedicated to 'the affirmation of a particular existing social organization', while the former was based upon the aesthetic of 'Anything Goes':

> where every reading and interpretation is allowed and where it is continuously made clear that the core of a self-determined, subjective individual no longer exists, and therefore everything is up for deconstruction.[1]

It may warrant a brief discussion for an English or American audience just what is being argued here. Even a serious theatre-goer, especially in New York, has little exposure to the sort of work Ostermeier is referring to as 'capitalist realism', and may think that the reference is to politically engaged works dealing in a realistic manner with contemporary society, such as Broadway productions of David Mamet for example. Terms such as 'deconstruction' and phrases like 'every interpretation is allowed' should make it clear, however, that this is not at all what Ostermeier has in mind. His reference is to a kind of theatre that forms an important part of the offerings in German theatre centres such as Berlin or Munich, but is almost unknown in London and New York. Indeed the term 'deconstructionist' was often applied to many examples of such work in Germany during the 1990s.

Many leading German theatre directors of that decade (and since) have been associated with such work. One of the first and most prominent was Frank Castorf at the Berlin Volksbühne, the most talked-about director in Germany in the mid-1990s, when Ostermeier began his professional career. Ostermeier, like most of the leading theatre figures of the 1990s, admired Castorf. In an interview in May 1997, he described Castorf's theatre as the most important in Berlin. Nevertheless, he also insisted that he himself had little interest in the sort of 'destruction of plot and character' found in Castorf's work. He instead preferred finding examples of 'well done writing' and representing them respectfully. To a German reader at that time, Ostermeier's pronouncement might have suggested an approach similar to that of Peter Stein, especially in the direction Stein was moving at this later period of his work. Long considered one of the most radical and innovative theatre directors in Germany, he had moved more and more towards a classic and traditional style, of which his monumental 1989 *Cherry Orchard* was considered as an outstanding example. Unlike his earlier striking and unconventional reinterpretations of works such as Ibsen's *Peer Gynt* or Kleist's *The Prince of Homburg*, dating from 1971 and 1972, Stein sought to capture in complete detail every element of the original Moscow Art Theatre production, with perhaps even greater attention to physical details of the setting and acting. The beauty of the production became almost a cliché along with its scrupulous respect for both the text and the theatrical tradition, qualities that would mark Stein's projects from this time onward.

When Ostermeier spoke of presenting works 'respectfully', however, he was clearly not thinking of this kind of scrupulously researched projects with which Stein was engaged. Indeed he specifically rejected, along with the deconstruction of Castorf, precisely such an approach based on the cult of beauty and reverence for the past, which he characterized as the 'museum style' of contemporary German theatre. What he proposed to develop instead was something he considered distinctly different from either of these approaches. This would be a vital and critical engagement with 'contemporary authors dealing with material of the here and now'. Lacking a current German theatre model for work of this sort, he turned to England, where he found inspiration in London's Royal Court Theatre, its director Stephen Daldry, and Daldry's recent productions of such dramatists as Mark Ravenhill and Sarah Kane.[2]

Socialist Realism, Capitalist Realism, Ostermeier Realism   55

Ostermeier's association with the Royal Court of the 1990s and the dark and gritty realism of its authors and production style at this time was essential to the development of his reputation and his style. In 1997, he was then invited by Thomas Langhoff, then director of the venerable Deutsches Theater, to lead a new small experimental theatre in a former workshop space next to the theatre, called the Baracke (shed). In response to the enormous popularity of Castorf's productions at this time, especially among younger theatre-goers in Berlin, Langhoff hoped to create a new theatre that would be able to compete for these audiences without going in as radical a direction as Castorf. Ostermeier's first Baracke production was a dark grotesque contemporary comedy, *Fat Men in Skirts*, by US playwright Nicky Silver, which included cannibalism, incest and murder. Ostermeier's gritty realistic interpretation was a revelation to Berlin audiences, and, buoyed by this success, Ostermeier announced a programme of five plays a year at the Baracke, which he announced would deal 'in the most unadorned way with such subjects as drugs, criminality, sex and power, to once again reflect reality'.[3] The first play to follow was a new work from Britain, David Harrower's innovative *Knives in Hens*, which attracted only modest attention. An attempt at utilizing a biomechanical approach in the style of Meyerhold for Brecht's *Man Equals Man* was even less successful, probably most noteworthy for being the first production in which Ostermeier worked with designer Jan Pappelbaum, who would become the designer closely associated with the director's work until the present day.

It was not until Ostermeier returned again to the experimental London stage that he came upon a powerful group of new dramatists and new works that proved precisely suited to his developing aesthetic. At the Royal Court Theatre, its then new director, Stephen Daldry, sought to revive the excitement that this theatre had last experienced in the 1950s with the appearance of the 'angry young men'. A new, shocking and confrontational style of theatre was emerging that would be given the term 'in-yer-face' theatre by British theatre critic Aleks Sierz. The leaders of this movement were Royal Court dramatists Sarah Kane and Mark Ravenhill, whose *Blasted* (1995) and *Shopping and Fucking* (1996) had made them the central figures in this new school. The international department of the Royal Court arranged for these two young dramatists to visit Berlin in the spring of 1997 and present readings of their work at the recently opened Baracke. Their approach precisely suited the vision of Ostermeier, and he essentially made his and their reputation in Germany by premiering their works.

The production that more than any other established this new gritty realist approach was his staging of Ravenhill's *Shopping and Fucking* in February 1998, two years after its London premiere. The powerful naturalistic production was an enormous success, and the ninety-nine seats in the Baracke became the most sought-after theatre tickets in Berlin. That year *Theater Heute* selected Ravenhill as 'author of the year', the Baracke as 'theatre of the year' and Ostermeier as 'emerging director of the year'. The journal reported that the Baracke had created a 'boom' of interest in the new English drama and continued, 'the pioneer of the English mode on German stages has been primarily the Berlin Baracke, working closely with the London Royal Court, the breeding ground of the English playwriting miracle'.[4] It was this success, especially with *Shopping and Fucking*, that led to Ostermeier's appointment to assume direction of the Schaubühne, one of the leading theatres in Berlin, associated mostly with the name of the now legendary Peter Stein.[5] While a series of well-established artistic directors had followed him – Luc Bondy, Jürgen Gosch, Andrea Breth – and although all enjoyed some success, none seriously challenged the memory of the Stein era. Yet Ostermeier faced an even greater challenge than any of his predecessors at the Schaubühne. Unlike any of them, when he received this invitation in 1999, he still had only a few productions under his belt, and actually had never yet directed a production in a large theatre.

Moving from the tiny Baracke to this huge three-stage complex was a staggering undertaking for a young director, and an almost unprecedented vote of confidence in a relative newcomer to the theatre scene. Much attention therefore was given to his first large-stage production, which took place during his final Baracke-season on the main stage of the Deutsches Theater, to which the Baracke had served as an auxiliary stage. His choice was somewhat surprising: Maeterlinck's *The Blue Bird*, a 1908 symbolist fairy-tale whose tonality could not have been further from the gritty realism of the Royal Court dramatists. Very likely Ostermeier wished to demonstrate that he could significantly expand his directorial range to adjust to his new situation, but also that he could undertake a work from the classic European repertoire, which he had not yet demonstrated. In fact, he made Maeterlinck's rather sentimental and whimsical fairy tale into something much closer to the nightmare world of Sarah Kane, with almost catatonic protagonists wandering through a grotesque world of maimed figures, some in orthopaedic gear, seemingly intent upon damaging themselves and others. Significantly, Ostermeier's partner in creating this grim dystopian vision was scenographer Jan Pappelbaum. Reviews were mixed, but this production made it clear that although Ostermeier was not opposed to presenting classic works, they were going to be filtered through his particular dark view of the contemporary world.

For the actual opening of his direction at the Schaubühne in January 2000, Ostermeier did not choose a work so far from his established repertoire. Once again with Pappelbaum providing the design, he opted for a

Socialist Realism, Capitalist Realism, Ostermeier Realism   57

contemporary realist whose work had much in common with the new British realists: Swedish playwright Lars Norén. Unlike the Royal Court dramatists, however, he was already a well-known writer on German stages at the time, having been introduced by Claus Peymann almost twenty years before. During the 1980s, Norén had created a series of dark, intimate family dramas, recalling for many the naturalistic dramas of his countryman Strindberg. The work Ostermeier presented, however, Norén's 1998 *Human Circle 3.1*, was much larger in scope, portraying the breakdown of civil society in a modern metropolis, prey to drugs, violence and marauding street gangs. Even the theatre did not escape Norén's condemnation. Dramaten, the Swedish national theatre, was characterized as a 'Capitalistic whore-house' in the play, and its most famous director, the internationally admired Ingmar Bergman, as a 'brutal despot', whose company were merely 'fawning ass-lickers'.[6] Such extreme rhetoric did not disturb Ostermeier, who found Norén a 'logical choice' to open his administration of the Schaubühne, seeing in the work of the Swedish dramatist a close parallel to his own concerns. He elaborated on this convergence in a newspaper interview that appeared on the day of the premiere:

> During the eighties Norén was concentrating on family situations, dealing with themes of killing the father, incestuous relationships, jealousy, and psychological terror within one's own four walls. Then, after the fall of the Wall, he said he must now widen his horizon and look elsewhere. There is a remarkable similarity to our own trajectory; emerging from the Baracke we put aside family dramas and the microcosm that had up to then occupied us. And we came upon this author who had followed a similar path and announced that he, like us, was now seeking a sociological theatre which would be closer to the thoughts of Pierre Bourdieu on society. Theatre would deal with the loss of utopia, not only in general but in the case of each individual. This relates directly to the history of the twentieth century and to the history of a Western European society with strong social democratic features at the moment when it must say farewell to all that was once certain.[7]

In another interview at the time, Ostermeier returned to his ongoing interest in his own approach to contemporary realism:

> Realism is not the simple depiction of the world as it appears. [...] It is a view of the world with an attitude that involves an alienation born out of suffering and injury. This inspires writing which seeks revenge on the blindness and stupidity of the world. The individual suffers, even if the

58   *The Schaubühne Berlin under Thomas Ostermeier*

> subject is only constructed and without a core. Man realizes himself in
> pain, if he does not lose himself in dreams or lies. The basis of realism is
> the tragedy of everyday life.[8]

In this clear statement on the subject of realism, Ostermeier's distance from
both socialist realism and capitalist realism is clear. The former subsumes
pain in the larger social goal, the latter ignores it as an irrelevant side-product
of a no longer existing subject. Pain and suffering, Ostermeier insists, are
central even to the constructed subjects of capitalist realism, and certainly to
the misled dreamers of socialist realism.

The Schaubühne opening with Norén was then followed by Ostermeier's
production of the Royal Court dramatist most associated with his directorial
work, Sarah Kane, who had died the previous year. Kane could hardly be
called a realist, and *Crave*, Ostermeier's first own production of her work, was
one of the most abstract and stylized of her works. Its central concern with
contemporary human suffering, as manifested in such phenomena as rape,
drug addition, mental instability, suicide, and murder, made it, despite its
rejection of conventional realism, an excellent example of the new mode of
psychological and social realism that Ostermeier was pursuing.[9] Kane's work
became so central to the new Schaubühne realism that all her other plays
were gradually added to the repertoire, until by 2005 the theatre had become
the only theatre in the world to have every one of her plays in its active
repertoire.

Alongside them appeared other new works, both German and foreign, that
followed even more clearly in the spirit of the Baracke realism. Marius von
Mayenburg, also the German translator of *Crave*, was one of Ostermeier's
most important discoveries. His radio play *Haarmann* was presented, directed
by Wulf Twiehaus, in a reading at Ostermeier's Baracke in 1999. It was a dark
study of the modern psyche, an in-depth, essentially non-judgmental study of
mass murderer Fritz Haarmann, the so called 'Butcher of Hannover', who was
in 1925 convicted of the sexual assault on and murder of twenty-four boys and
young men. Mayenburg's first proper stage play, *Feuergesicht* (Fireface),
directed (though not premiered) by Ostermeier at Schauspielhaus Hamburg
later the same year, established the playwright as a significant new voice in
German drama. The play was a sensationalistic story involving incest, parricide
and pyromania, very much in the extreme style of the Royal Court dramatists,
but taking place within a seemingly normal middle-class German family. It
was presented in the theatre's small Malersaal, a studio space very similar to
the Baracke. On a long, shallow stage, Pappelbaum created three rooms in the
family house – dining room, bedroom and bath – in detailed reproduction of
a typical middle-class interior. Thanks in large part to Ostermeier's growing

Socialist Realism, Capitalist Realism, Ostermeier Realism 59

reputation, the production toured to Warsaw, Budapest and in the autumn to the Edinburgh Festival. Audience and critical response clearly was influenced by whether the public was familiar or not with the 'in yer face'-realism that had come out of London. In Warsaw, the scenes of nudity and incest created a minor scandal, while in Edinburgh it was dismissed as a rather 'weak dilution of the work of the likes of Mark Ravenhill and the late Sarah Kane'.[10] When Ostermeier came to the Schaubühne, Mayenburg joined him as dramaturg and writer-in-residence, positions he has retained ever since – still significantly contributing after two decades to the style and tone of Ostermeier's enterprise. English critics particularly continued to cite his close relationship to the Royal Court dramatists of the 1990s. When his 2004 drama *Eldorado* was offered by London's Arcola Theatre in 2014, reviewers almost unanimously discussed its similarity in tone, style and subject matter to Sarah Kane's dystopian apocalypse in her *Blasted*. Mayenburg's interest in social tensions never diminished, yet his range of approach has much broadened. His more recent Schaubühne works, such as *Plastic* (2015) and *Peng* (2017), are black comedies on class, art and political populism, more reminiscent of the boulevard comedies of Yasmina Reza than the British 'in-yer-face' writers.[11]

Ostermeier also introduced to the German stage in the summer of 2000 another Scandinavian dramatist whose realism bore a close resemblance to that of Norén and Mayenburg: Jon Fosse. Ostermeier presented Fosse's recent *Der Name* (*The Name*), showing a troubled, self-destructive family who barely speak to each other, but are forced to live under the same roof. Ostermeier himself commented jokingly on the proclivity of his theatre for works with a similar dark view of contemporary society. 'If I do another play this depressing,' he wryly remarked in an interview, 'I will need psychiatric care'.[12] In his already cited interview from the previous year, the German director had commented on the recent dilemma that was faced by a crushing world unredeemable by either of the two post-war alternatives of the twentieth century, capitalist humanism or the socialist vision. In his work to come, he would find a similar scepticism, frustration and lack of viable paths forward in other periods of history. Already in the 1999 interview, he suggested Georg Büchner's *Danton's Death* as an important example of a premodern work whose world-view was compatible with his own, and he would then select this play as the first classic he directed at the Schaubühne, in 2001.[13] Büchner's bleak and soul-consuming post-Revolutionary world was rendered with strong contemporary touches, such as handheld microphones, preparing the way for Ostermeier's subsequent resettings of Ibsen in recognizable contemporary surroundings.

It was in fact Ostermeier's 2002 production of Ibsen's *A Doll's House* (called *Nora* in German) that clearly demonstrated how the director's contemporary

60   *The Schaubühne Berlin under Thomas Ostermeier*

realism could be applied not only to modern European dramatists, but even to a classic of the modern version of so-called realistic drama. Ostermeier converted Ibsen's nineteenth century bourgeois couple into Berlin yuppies of the present, with Nora as a trophy wife and Torvald as a rising young entrepreneur, constantly utilizing his cell phone and digital camera. Their elegant contemporary multi-level apartment featured contemporary art, designer furniture, an aquarium and a huge hi-fi. In order to restore the shock of the original, Ostermeier had Nora shoot Torvald, leaving him to drown in the huge aquarium. A Berlin reviewer, recalling the shock and edginess of Ostermeier's Baracke work, and perhaps even recognizing an important similarity beneath the glittering surface of the new work and the grime and squalor of the old ones, hence entitled his review, 'Shopping and Fishing'.[14] Designer Jan Pappelbaum, in the first of what would become a series of striking uses of a full-stage turntable, rotated the entire set for the ending, showing Nora outside the famous front door, but not in triumph, rather collapsed against it, stunned by the enormity of what would now await her.

Although Ostermeier would soon continue his studies of the alienation of the privileged upper-middle class under capitalism with Ibsen, his two productions that followed in 2003 first returned to the depiction of the socially underprivileged. So close in fact was the spirit of Ostermeier's next production that it was widely seen, despite its shift back to the working class, as a sequel to *Nora*: this was Franz Xaver Kroetz's powerful 1970s monodrama *Wunschkonzert* (*Request Concert*) about a woman, crushed by a monotonous and repetitive existence, who commits suicide.[15] The emotional parallels between the two works were doubtless strengthened by the fact that the same actress, the much-admired Anne Tismer, played the central role in both. For his other 2003 production, the director returned to Büchner and to one of the most familiar representatives of the dehumanized victim of the modern social order, Woyzeck. For this production Pappelbaum created one of his most ambitious settings, a cinemascope-panorama set evoking a large deserted area of East Berlin, a ghastly no-man's land, which served as physical equivalent to the empty psyche of Büchner's protagonist. At the rear of the gigantic performance space was a concrete wall, out of which a drainage pipe continually poured raw sewage into a cesspool full of trash and garbage. Beyond the wall, one could see icons of modern capitalism, such as giant billboards, electric pylons, tenements, and, in the distance, even the distinctive TV tower on Berlin's Alexanderplatz. A modest reflection of this entrepreneurial display was offered by a seedy Currywurst kiosk near the cesspool, providing what sustenance the denizens of this district could afford. At the climax of the production, Woyzeck murdered Maria, raped her lifeless body, and then threw it into the raw sewage – as crass and revolting a sequence as almost anything offered by England's 'in-yer-face'

Socialist Realism, Capitalist Realism, Ostermeier Realism 61

drama. The production was invited to open the Avignon Festival that summer, where Ostermeier was the year's 'artistic associate', the first German director ever to be invited, an important tribute to Ostermeier's growing international reputation. His work was thus particularly prominent at the year's festival, with *Nora, Wunschkonzert* and *Disco Pigs* all presented in addition to his *Woyzeck*.

Ostermeier's next major offering at the Schaubühne, meanwhile, was even more in keeping with his earlier work: his 2004 staging of Wedekind's *Lulu*. As with *Nora*, Ostermeier updated the play to a contemporary setting, making Wedekind's protagonist (again played by Tismer) a victim of contemporary social and economic forces. The performance opened with an act curtain that was a giant 'Victoria's Secret' ad, whose sleek depiction contrasted sharply with the protagonist, seen near the end of her career, battered, skimpily dressed, her lipstick smeared, barely able to walk. Pappelbaum extended his scenic device from *Nora* to utilize a continually rotating set, with a dizzying and nightmarish panorama of objects, properties and puppet-like figures: a kind of postmodern dance of death through which the dazed Lulu staggered.

Later in 2004 Ostermeier returned to Ibsen, creating *The Master Builder* for the Vienna Burgtheater. Many of the characteristics found in *Nora* reappeared; the play was reconceived in a stylish modern upper-bourgeois setting, with elegant transparent sliding panels for walls. Once again Ostermeier radically altered the ending. The production began with a dream sequence showing Solness, played by the late Burgtheater star Gert Voss, as a kind of dominating colossus. The production did not end with his fall, but with him awakening with a nosebleed from what was apparently a recurrent nightmare that encapsulated his ongoing fear of being displaced from his position of power. The evening then ended with the repetition of an earlier dialogue, now not with Hilde but with his wife Aline. Thus the strange non-realistic elements of the play, always something of a problem for realistic directors, were safely relegated to a dream world.[16] The production as a whole still served the purpose of making Ostermeier's point about the destructive forces of modern competitive capitalism, but the experience of working within the conservative Burgtheater with its excellent but traditional actors seems to have muted Ostermeier's usually direct style.

In February 2005, Ostermeier then attempted to update, at Kammerspiele Munich, a classic of the naturalist German theatre: *Vor Sonnenaufgang* (*Before Sunrise*) by Ibsen's contemporary Gerhart Hauptmann. The director relocated the play to an Asian jungle in the modern globalized world, with imperialist German capitalists as the agents of oppression and ecological destruction. Despite its clear contemporary political relevance, the project did not succeed. The characterizations were considered too abstract,

62   *The Schaubühne Berlin under Thomas Ostermeier*

suggesting to many not realism but a kind of Brechtian parable play, yet lacking Brecht's sharp edge or effective stage language. Ostermeier's other 2005 productions, created in his own theatre and working with two dramatists who inspired some of his best work, Sarah Kane and Ibsen, were meanwhile both far more successful. Kane's *Zerbombt* (*Blasted*), her first play, completed the five-year project to produce her complete canon for the Schaubühne repertoire, following the play's earlier production at the Baracke, in 1998, by the now forgotten Rüdiger Burbach. Now, under Ostermeier's own direction, Pappelbaum's bright, modern hotel room with its apocalyptic destruction and Thomas Thieme's horrific portrait of the soldier murderer, rapist and cannibal, made this one of the most extreme, but also one of the most popular of the Schaubühne's Kane cycle.

It was followed by an even greater success, Ibsen's *Hedda Gabler*, which became one of Ostermeier's best known and most widely produced stagings of his first decade at the Schaubühne. Like *Nora*, *Hedda* was set among the bored and directionless yuppies in contemporary Germany, its main performance area a sleek, glass-walled minimalist living room. The modern digitalized world was again evoked, most notably when Hedda, instead of burning Lövborg's manuscript, gleefully trashes his laptop with a hammer. The surprising and highly effective ending again, as in *Nora*, made powerful use of the turntable. As in the playtext, Hedda shoots herself offstage, but instead of rushing off to discover her, the other characters remain onstage, carrying on their banal conversations unaware of her tragedy. Meanwhile, the revolving turntable alternates our own vision between their ignorant banality, and the horror of the dead Hedda with her blood and brains scattered on the glass wall behind her slumped body.

The strong tradition of American family drama, owing much to Ibsen, not surprisingly attracted Ostermeier's attention in the following years, beginning with one of the first major classics in that tradition, O'Neill's *Mourning Becomes Electra*. Ostermeier announced he was approaching O'Neill, as he had the Ibsen works, as a study of the breakdown of bourgeois family relationships and the bourgeois faith in a secure future.[17] Once more, the director and his set designer Jan Pappelbaum moved the scene into a contemporary German setting. O'Neill's Mammons became the Papenbeers, ex-Nazi industrialists living in an ostentatious home of glass and sliding panels, sleeping on futons, drinking whisky and playing golf. O'Neill's heavy Freudianism was replaced by conflicted emotions about the father's Nazi past and the spiritually empty present. A more contemporary American work, Tennessee Williams' *Cat on a Hot Tin Roof*, followed in early 2007. The production had very few surprising shifts in the plot and little physical violence, although in one of the memorable moments of the evening Maggie

Socialist Realism, Capitalist Realism, Ostermeier Realism   63

pushed the irritating Meg face first into the mountainous whipped-cream topping on Big Daddy's birthday cake. The setting was another one of Pappelbaum's modernistic glass boxes, but supplemented by overhead video projections of modernity (racing cars) and corruption (swarming maggots). Over the entire setting was another glass box, this one containing a large live bird of prey. Clearly Ostermeier wanted the sexual tensions in Williams to be tied to his familiar themes of contemporary social disorder and degeneration.

Into the second decade of his tenure at the Schaubühne, Ostermeier then mounted three further productions of Ibsen. Ostermeier has now staged eight out of the ten plays in Ibsen's so-called 'realistic' period. All have been re-imaged scenically and structurally and all updated to call attention to what they reveal about the soul-destroying materialism of the modern capitalist world. The venues of these three productions clearly testify to Ostermeier's current international reputation. *John Gabriel Borkman* premiered in 2009 in Rennes, at the National Theatre of Britanny; *The Enemy of the People* was first presented at the Avignon Festival of 2012, though both of them in German and with the Schaubühne ensemble and guest actors, while *Ghosts*, which Ostermeier had directed in 2011 in Dutch for Toneelgroep Amsterdam, was restaged, in 2013, in a French version with Théâtre Vidy Lausanne. By far the most innovative and successful of these was *Enemy of the People*. *Borkman*, although featuring three of the leading stars of a senior generation of actors in German theatre, Josef Bierbichler, Angela Winkler and Kirsten Dene (the latter both actors at Stein's Schaubühne), was generally considered too cold and abstract, with its minimalist setting by Pappelbaum suggesting the interior of an ice cube with cracks through which a chilling fog constantly seeped. The major scenic challenge of the play's conclusion, which takes its characters out of the mansion and up a mountainside, the production solved by a change as radical as that in *Nora*: simply making that journey a figment of the imagination of the dying Borkman, with the final moments taking place, like the rest of the production, on the centre-stage sofa which was the major furnishing. The *mise en scène* of *Ghosts* came much closer to the lively and shocking updatings of *Nora* and *Hedda Gabler*, making Osvald a contemporary video artist, with video screens adding an extra dimension to the scenic background as well. The final act featured one of Ostermeier and Pappelbaum's most spectacular sequences, a kind of Götterdammerung, with the turning stage in flames, and the deranged Osvald randomly spraying everything with a fire extinguisher.

Yet, the 2012 *Enemy of the People* created the greatest stir, having been shown at many international theatres and festivals around the world.[18] Even audiences accustomed to Ostermeier's iconoclasm were largely taken by surprise by this production. It began in a familiar Ibsen-Ostermeier world, a very contemporary bourgeois setting, with the Stockmans entertaining friends at a casual band rehearsal of a 2006 pop song by neo-soul duo Gnarls Barkley. This sort of wholescale updating continued, but so did Ibsen's basic action, until the climactic scene in the town hall in the fourth act. Here, as Ibsen's Stockman departs from his topic of speaking about the contaminated baths to critique modern democracy, Ostermeier took the even more radical step to have him read from a 2008 French anarchist political manifesto, *The Coming Insurrection*. While this innovation seemed not too far from Nora shooting Torvald, or from Hedda smashing Lövborg's laptop with a hammer, the director then went further by having Stockman and his opponents directly address the actual theatre audience and draw them into a political debate. Some critics complained that Ostermeier had departed from his dedication to realism by this violation of the fourth wall. On the contrary, I would argue that in doing so, more than ever, Ostermeier insisted that the project of realism is to force audiences to recognize the true reality of their political and social system – the argument he put forward on his stage from his beginnings with the 'in-yer-face' dramas of the Royal Court, right to this very literal 'in-yer-face' *Enemy of the People* two decades later. Moreover, he has done so precisely in the spirit of the original Ibsen work, which was revolutionary not only in the open discussion of contemporary social concerns, but in the playwright's challenge to conventional dramatic expectations.

Next, Ostermeier presented another updated version of an American family drama in the Ibsen tradition, Lillian Hellman's 1939 *The Little Foxes* (2014). The work of Hellman, a dedicated leftist, provided solid anti-capitalist material for Ostermeier, who kept its Southern United States setting, yet moved it to the present, where the struggle for financial power is carried out with mobile phones and laptops. The production was a powerful, even chilling updating, with an elegant open setting by Pappelbaum. It deservedly won the Performance of the Year award for that season, but in terms of innovation or surprise, it merely carried on the now familiar Ostermeier tradition of stylish depictions of the high bourgeois world of international late capitalism already familiar from his Ibsen and US playwright revivals. *Enemy of the People* would remain his most daring offering in this tradition. Meanwhile, the second decade of Ostermeier's work at the Schaubühne was marked by work outside this realist writing tradition: his series of striking and original interpretations of Shakespeare, most of them starring his popular leading man, Lars Eidinger, who also played Dr Rank in *Nora* and Tesman in *Hedda Gabler*.[19] All of these have been very well received, and all in one way or another have been staged as contemporary dramas, with characters torn from today's headlines, down to the range and depth of Eidinger's Richard as chilling echo of the forces of populism and neo-fascism all too common in today's world. Even though moving outside the

Socialist Realism, Capitalist Realism, Ostermeier Realism   65

realistic tradition of Ibsen, and the followers of this tradition from Williams to Hellman and on to Norén and the neo-naturalists of Britain, Ostermeier has found his way to make Shakespeare also an effective tool for his programme of a realist exploration of contemporary society that defines the still expanding Ostermeier canon.

Notes

1 Thomas Ostermeier, 'Ob es so oder so oder anders geht! Ein Gespräch', *Theater Heute Jahrbuch* (1999): 76.

2 Ostermeier, quoted in Franz Wille, 'All About Eva', *Theater Heute* 38, no. 5 (May 1997): 27–8. See also Jens Hillje's chapter (Chapter 10) in the present volume.

3 Ibid., 43.

4 Barbara Burckhardt, 'Back to Normal', *Theater Heute* 39, no. 10 (October 1998): 52.

5 See Erika Fischer-Lichte's chapter (Chapter 2) in this volume.

6 In Norén's scandalous, monumental *En dramatikers dagbok*, 3 vols. (Stockholm: Bonnier, 2009–15).

7 Ostermeier, interviewed by Matthias Heine and Reinhard Wengiereck, 'Wir mussten niemand aus dem Sessel bombenä', *Die Welt*, 21 January 2000, 25.

8 Ostermeier, interviewed by Franz Wille, 'Startdeutsch?', *Theater Heute* 41, no.1 (January 2000): 2.

9 See also 'A Postscript on Directing Postdramatic Theatre', in *The Theatre of Thomas Ostermeier*, eds Peter M. Boenisch and Thomas Ostermeier (Abingdon and New York: Routledge, 2016), 179–84.

10 Ian Shuttleworth, *Financial Times*, 3 September 1999, 15.

11 See also Peter M. Boenisch, 'Marius von Mayenburg and Roland Schimmelpfennig: Dissecting European Lives under Global Capitalism', in *Contemporary European Playwrights*, eds Maria M. Delgado, Bryce Lease and Dan Rebellato (Abingdon and New York: Routledge, 2020).

12 Ostermeier, quoted in Franz Wille, 'Am Kapitalismus leiden heißt lustiger leiden', *Theater Heute* 41, no.1 (October 2001): 11.

13 Ostermeier, 'Ob es so . . .', 76.

14 Rüdiger Schaper, 'Shoppen und Fischen', *Der Tagesspiegel*, 28 November 2002, 24.

15 See Benjamin Fowler's chapter (Chapter 11) in this volume.

16 Interestingly, Wallace Shawn's 2013 film of the play, perhaps inspired by Ostermeier, utilized the same device.

17 Aureliana Sorrento, 'Ostermeier im Interview; Trauer tragen', *Frankfurter Allgemeine Zeitung*, 26 February 2006, 24.

18 See 'Ostermeier at Work: *An Enemy of the People*', in Boenisch and Ostermeier, *The Theatre of Thomas Ostermeier*, 77–131.

19 See the following chapters in this section by Jitka Goriaux Pelechova and Elisa Leroy.

6

Thomas Ostermeier's Shakespeare Productions: The *Mise en Action* of Canonical Plays

Jitka Goriaux Pelechová

Back in 1999, in one of his first public reflections on theatre, Thomas Ostermeier called for 'forms of a very contemporary epic narration' on stage.[1] It is no coincidence he made this Brechtian reference at a key moment of his career, preparing his move from the Baracke to the Schaubühne. The spatial and material limitations of the small Baracke had led him to focus on the work of and with the actors; the Schaubühne would offer him richer technical and material opportunities that would allow Ostermeier to explore more fully the possibilities of *Regietheater*: the reinterpretation of dramatic works through the means of stage directing. In this chapter, I will discuss the unique form and expression of 'directors' theatre' that can be observed in Ostermeier's Shakespeare productions. On the one hand, they offer distinctive directorial interpretations of the plays, yet on the other hand, the stage direction does not claim the dominant position characteristic for European 'directors' theatre'. Instead, it emerges from co-creation with the actors and other collaborators (such as set designers, musicians and video artists), whom Ostermeier considers equal partners during the entire process of creation. The director's dramaturgic and scenic interpretations of the dramatic situations in the plays appear as a canvas on which the actors, developing their art in a variety of styles and directions, then unfold what may even be described as a succession of acting numbers or episodes. Instead of the play's *mise en scène*, we can more appropriately speak of its *mise en action*.

In Ostermeier's Shakespeare work, a Brechtian epic process of scenic narration thus goes hand in hand with purely theatrical acting, reflecting the tradition of Elizabethan theatre, which the director studied in detail. My discussion of his six Shakespeare productions to date – *A Midsummer Night's Dream* (2006), *Hamlet* (2008), *Othello* (2010), *Measure for Measure* (2011), *Richard III* (2015) and *Twelfth Night* (2018) – will analyse the specific forms of epic stage narration deployed in these performances. I will first examine the dramaturgical and scenographical solutions before concentrating on the principles of stage directing and the work with, and of, the actors in these productions. My reflections will be guided by the interrogation of the relationship between this form of epic narration and the 'new realism for the stage' that Ostermeier has been evoking since the beginning of his work in theatre.[2]

Dramaturgy *through* scenography

Ostermeier turned to Shakespeare relatively late: in 2006, after a decade of intense work within two different theatrical institutions. Five years prior, he had still asserted: 'I have always told myself I should wait a bit more before staging Shakespeare [...] I don't feel yet I'm good enough for him'.[3] Shakespeare's entry into Ostermeier's directorial repertoire went hand in hand with his turn towards other classical authors; next to Ibsen, Shakespeare gradually became Ostermeier's second canonical author of choice, of whom he would stage a (still ongoing) series of major works. This turn within the Schaubühne's repertoire politics did not, however, change the general aesthetics and critical attitude of Ostermeier's work. Be it through *Measure for Measure, Hedda Gabler* or a contemporary drama by Herbert Achternbusch, the director's main interest was still to explore the social circumstances of the dramaturgic material, studying 'all of the hidden causes, sensations, strategies, and interests, which shape human behaviour, in all their complexity'.[4] This is the background of Ostermeier's call for a 'new realism' on stage, which he later characterized as 'sociological' theatre; it is 'based on the assumption that the conduct and behaviour of human beings with each other changes in accordance with societal transformations in their environment'.[5] Applied to classical dramatic writing from the past, this sociological focus passes through a transposition of the plays into our contemporary period, in order to bring them closer to a present-day audience. *A Midsummer Night's Dream* took place at a swingers club; in *Hamlet*, Elsinor castle mingled with the Elysée Palace and the royal couple, Gertrude and Claudius, echoed the then current presidential one, Sarkozy and Bruni; *Othello* meanwhile raised questions related to the Middle East conflict; *Measure for Measure* mocked the falsely moralizing discourse of contemporary politicians; *Richard III* confronted us with the nothing-is-true/everything-is-permitted ideology of our present 'fake' and populist societies; and *Twelfth Night* turned towards what can seem 'unnatural' in our inner, very own nature.

This principle – halfway between applied dramaturgy and stage directing – determines Ostermeier's theatre to a large extent. Yet, such a directorial practice is confronted with three important challenges. The first is to find

68   *The Schaubühne Berlin under Thomas Ostermeier*

meaningful, credible and intelligent contemporary analogies for the historical circumstances, the characters' behaviour and actions, and the dramatic situations and the conflicts, while also taking into account the difference between the period of the author (in our case, Elizabethan England) and the space and time of the play's setting (such as the Renaissance and Venice in *Othello*). The second challenge is to avoid casting a simplifying gaze on contemporary society, which would lead to a reduction of both the original text and present-day reality. The third challenge is to resist the temptation of putting in the author's mouth what comes in handy but does not really correspond to his intentions, thus making use – or abuse – of his work. We will here not discuss the question of the artistic legitimacy of such a process; yet, we will examine the objectives, the pertinence, the precision and the audacity of concrete elements of updating, which introduce an 'artificial and artistic' (in Brecht's original: *künstlich-künstlerisch*) distance between the temporal context of the original play and ours.[6]

In Ostermeier's productions, the updating goes beyond any simplistic transposition of the dramas into our contemporary age. It provides the director with an occasion to examine their supposed universality through the social behaviour they reflect on stage. As Ostermeier noted in 2009:

> For me, one of the most important truths in Shakespeare's work is the fact that we all play social roles in our lives. Shakespeare's characters act in order to find the truth, to unveil it. Hamlet pretends to be mad and this helps him both to understand what has really happened and to protect himself. In *Measure for Measure*, the characters also change their identity in order to find the truth. In Ibsen's dramas, this double play does not exist; each character has one solid and undifferentiated identity. Hedda Gabler cannot imagine playing a bored woman; she is one hundred per cent bored. If she were a Shakespeare's character, such a play would have given her a possibility to escape. This is why, at this very moment, I'm more interested in exploring Shakespeare than Ibsen, because this double play allows for the search of a new theatricality.[7]

This theatricality, the 'double, or sometimes even triple, theatrical situation'[8] in Shakespeare's plays, indeed seemed to determine Ostermeier's approach. In these plays, theatre can play a veritable role in itself; it can become a means of recognition, as in *Measure for Measure*, where the duke changes his identity and disguises himself as a monk in order to discover the actual motives and the real behaviour of his people, or as in *Hamlet*, where theatre, in the famous 'Mousetrap scene', 'manages to unmask, and [...] indict, those in power'.[9] But it can also seal the tragic fate, as in *Othello*, where 'the stage director and

Thomas Ostermeier's Shakespeare Productions 69

master of ceremony in one person, Iago, uses theatrical means in order to create an illusion'.[10] This is also true for Gloucester in *Richard III*. Ostermeier's approach to Shakespeare in highlighting the play's meta-theatrical potential may appear less original (and radical) than his materialist approach to Ibsen. His somewhat partial updating enabled the director to underline a certain timelessness of these works as well as their constant relevance, as he exemplarily claimed for *Othello*:

> The Venetian society, very imperialist at its core, has to face, on the one hand, the imminent threat coming from another important power, and on the other hand, wants to keep on making business and raising money, and to progressively take over the entire Mediterranean region. The play clearly shows that the Venetians do not want to leave and make war themselves. This is why they hire mercenaries to fight their war. [...] And it's exactly this deterioration of the Venetian society, which is not able to assure its own protection, that I found striking. [...] It made me think of the present situation, such as the war in Iraq or other conflicts elsewhere in the world.[11]

In all of these productions, the major axes of interpretation found their first and most direct expression in the sets designed by Jan Pappelbaum. In *A Midsummer Night's Dream*, the plot was removed from its original pastoral environment (the forest of Athens) and transposed into a present-day nightclub, imagined by Pappelbaum as two high walls bordering a large dance floor. A spiral staircase gave access to the upper level, where sliding doors opened to intimate spaces. The elegant harmony of the materials (chrome, frosted glass and bright wood) as well as the sparse furniture (six sofas spread on the two levels of the set) clearly evoked the milieu of urban clubs, where promiscuity, sexual liberty and carelessness reign. Through this transposition, the fairy night that the four lovers and the group of mechanicals spend in Shakespeare's enchanted forest under the influence of Oberon's magical juice and Puck's tricks, turned into a crazy party in a swingers club. The love-potion was replaced, more or less explicitly, by hallucinogenic substances, and the frantic race through the Athenian forest and the variations of the couples by the alternations between the different intimate alcoves of the club. Furthermore, in order to reinforce the atmosphere of a libertine party from the very beginning, the spectators entered the auditorium via the stage where they were welcomed and offered a drink by the actors and dancers, and even invited to participate in the revels, for example by slipping banknotes into the bras of the strippers or receiving 'souvenirs' from the performers' pubic hair. The set design thus offered a scenic expression of the general interpretation of the play and its updating, thanks to its very concrete and realist space. The performers, though, did not use the space in realistic ways only; on the contrary, they took advantage of its different parts such as the spiral staircase or the railing on the upper level, in order to allow a theatrical acting, rich in physical, even acrobatic elements.

The scenic space for *Hamlet* was concentrated on a rectangular stage of approximately ten by fifteen metres that was covered with soil. On this stage, a plateau of the same width but only three metres deep slid back and forth, on it a long banquet table and several chairs. A metal gantry carrying projectors and a curtain of thin golden chains (which also served as screen for the video projections) swept the stage in the same direction. The playing area for the actors was thus constantly transformed through the horizontal motion of the plateau and the gantry. This space was evidently less realistic than that of *A Midsummer Night's Dream*, and it did not suggest any concrete transposition of the play's original setting. But just as Pappelbaum's earlier set, its various elements such as the chain curtain and the soil on the ground invited actors the make use of them in a theatrical and physical way. A similar stage of approximately ten by twelve metres constituted the main playing area for *Othello*; this time it was covered with light brown tiles that evoked a desert land cracked with aridity. At the beginning, and again towards the end of the performance, this ground was partly flooded with a dark liquid that evoked oil as much as the ill waters of the Venetian canals. At the back of the stage, two glass panels with vertical neon bars slid from the left to the right, revealing a new curtain of thin metallic chains that closed the space to the back. On this stage, several sparse elements of furniture appeared during the performance: a king-size bed in the beginning and the end, and several chairs and seats. To the right, a small platform was reserved for the musicians who provided live accompaniment to the performance. Even though the floor suggested a desert land, and the dark liquid made us think of oil, hence situating the scene somewhere in the Middle East, the space, again, did not follow a naturalistic logic. The elements, such as the water that would rise up to their knees, allowed the performers to engage with them in a non-realistic, expressly theatrical style of acting. At its premiere, the production was performed in the Greek theatre of Epidaurus, during the Hellenic Festival. Yet, the set did not take account of the specificities of the ancient theatre space in the least; in fact, the lateral parts of the *koilon* were closed for the audience, thereby transforming the Greek *theatron* into a modern frontal stage.

In *Measure for Measure*, the rectangular stage was replaced by a cubical construction with its 'fourth wall' opening towards the audience (see Figure 4). Its imposing dimensions (approx. fifteen metres of width by fifteen of depth by ten of height) were further emphasized by an effect of forced perspective. The walls consisted of golden plates that were covered with a layer of dust and a few stencilled graffiti drawings of naked female figures. The sole objects in this empty space were a single chair and a few cushions scattered at the back. Two elements completed the set: a rubber hose coming out of the right-hand wall, with which Angelo, having taken the duke's place, 'purified' Vienna by washing down the dust and the improper drawings on the walls. Second, a monumental crystal chandelier was hanging from the middle of the ceiling, which could be lowered down to the floor. The actors used it frequently for all sorts of acrobatic exercises; at the end, a pig was hoisted on it, figuring the prisoner Barnardine. Notwithstanding these spectacular effects, the set of *Measure for Measure* remained quite minimalistic, because of the simplicity of its form, the emptiness of the space, the limited number of objects and the chromatic austerity of the construction. This impression was intensified as the entire performance solely took place in this unchanging, undivided playing area. The attention was therefore fully focused on the actors (and the musicians, who shared the same space). They had to transform the space through their action alone.

Figure 4 In contrast to the lavish realism of their Ibsen sets, Jan Pappelbaum's stage designs for Thomas Ostermeier's Shakespeare productions were characterized by their minimalistic simplicity of form in an empty, unchanging space. Here, the director's regular Shakespeare protagonists Jenny König and Lars Eidinger play Isabella and Angelo in *Mass für Mass* (*Measure for Measure*, 2011). © Arno Declair/Schaubühne.

72   *The Schaubühne Berlin under Thomas Ostermeier*

The set for *Richard III* changed the frontal perspective. Ostermeier and Pappelbaum constructed a space inspired by the characteristics of the Elizabethan theatre: an apron stage with a two-storey construction at the back, fronting a vertical semi-circular auditorium. The ground of the semi-circular apron stage was covered with sand, as in a circus ring; this reference was further underlined by the presence of a drummer, who accompanied the performance live, and by the play of Lars Eidinger in the lead role, with a microphone hanging down centre stage, which he would also use as a trapeze to climb and swing over the audience's heads. This Elizabethan-type space replaced the usual horizontal distance between actor and audience with a vertical seating and spectating arrangement, reinforcing a special impression of intimacy. It allowed Eidinger to enchant the audience just as Gloucester would charm his fellow characters in the play. As abstract and theatrical as this space might seem, it nevertheless carried a reference to a contemporary environment. Set designer Jan Pappelbaum found a present-day equivalent to the Elizabethan theatre as a space dedicated to popular entertainment in motodromes. The Schaubühne's 'Globe' replica was hence constructed from wooden planks reclaimed from one of these 'walls of death'; their patina and the specific past they carried referred to a concrete, contemporary social reality – the circle from *A Midsummer Night's Dream* to *Richard III* was thus complete.

Twelfth Night, created with the ensemble of the Comédie-Française rather than with the Schaubühne actors, addressed a different audience, and therefore seemed to step out of line. The set represented Illyria as a make-believe paradise lost (a sandy beach with cardboard palm trees) alongside a spectre of Darwin (two chimpanzees variously strolled through the set). Here, references to contemporary social realities seemed more blurry, as far as the scenography was concerned. The set however functioned similarly to the previous ones: the proscenium arch frontal perspective in the Comédie-Française was dissolved by means of a narrow bridge that crossed the entire parterre towards the back boxes, slightly above the spectators' heads. In line with the other sets, these two acting areas, on the main stage and the bridge, both remained abstract and had to be defined by the performers' actions alone. The sand on the ground as well as the bridge again allowed for a playful, physical and ostentatious theatricality of their acting.

'Directorial fabrication'

Along with these dramaturgic and scenographic transpositions, the re-interpretation of Shakespeare's plays was then further supported by particular

Thomas Ostermeier's Shakespeare Productions

means of Ostermeier's *Regie*. I will here focus on two aspects closely linked to each other: his directorial 'fabrication' and the directing of the actors. What I call here 'directorial fabrication' refers to the scenic expression of the so-called 'inductive method' of directing that Ostermeier deploys in his work.[12] Taking the play's dramatic situations as his main working material, the director sets out to clarify the characters' motives for the audience by rendering on stage concrete expressions of the dramatic circumstances that are sometimes not directly mentioned in the spoken dialogue. These 'fabricated' sequences hence become the concrete scenic expression of the director's interpretation of the dramatic material.

In many of Ostermeier's productions, we can find such 'fabricated' sequences right at the beginning of the performance, where they function as prologues or preludes. *Hamlet* opened with a sequence showing the funeral of the old king, during which a clumsy gravedigger tried in vain to lower the coffin into the ground. The other characters silently watched him as he struggled with this labour that usually should require at least two people. In order to tie a rope around the coffin, the gravedigger first got into the hole, then stepped over the casket, sat on it and repeatedly slid from it into the grave. Trying to lower it, he handled the coffin as well as he could on his own, turning it around, letting it drop into the mud. The entire sequence took place in heavy rain (one of the actors held a garden hose that abundantly sprayed water over the stage) and to a repetitive musical motif that ran ever faster, rushing the gravedigger with its increasing tempo. His comical struggle gave this scene the grotesque feel of a silent slapstick movie. The frantic rhythm calmed down once the coffin finally was eventually in the grave. Now, the characters, one by one, stepped to the grave and threw a handful of dirt onto old Hamlet's casket; the stylized gesture of each of them expressed her or his relation towards the deceased and towards the others. At the very end of this prologue, the slapstick took over again, as the actors repeatedly slipped and fell into the dirty mud.

The prologue of *Othello* equally had a clearly symbolic character. At the outset of the performance, twelve performers – actors and musicians – entered the stage and sat on chairs that were positioned in the form of a horseshoe around the main playing area, which was submerged about twenty centimetres deep with the dark water already mentioned. The performance opened as a jam session of several wind and percussion instruments, and chanting; this music would again continue until the end of the prologue. In the centre of the stage stood an oversized bed with white linen, onto which was projected the black and white image of 'TV snow'. Sebastian Nakajew as Othello slowly got up from his chair, undressed and stepped towards the bed so that the snow image was now projected onto his body. The actor's skin thus literally became the screen onto which colour – black and white – was projected, which in itself would serve as projection for the other characters' anxieties as well as fantasies. Next, Desdemona (Eva Meckbach) approached the bed and started stroking Othello: her hands left black traces on his face and his body. As she also undressed, both of them lay down in the bed, while other actors covered them with a white bed sheet and slowly pulled the bed away from the stage. Before the bed disappeared, graphics representing intercourse of a white woman and a black man with an emphasized phallus were projected in the back.

In addition to such prologues, Ostermeier's directorial fabrication seeks to offer a scenic definition of the dramatic time and space, and to identify the characters and their relationships as they constitute dramatic conflicts. In *Measure for Measure*, three musicians (a singer, a guitarist and a trumpeter) remained constantly present on stage alongside the actors. Their music not only served to rhythmically phrase the performance and to accompany the transitions between different scenes, but also helped to situate the stage action within a dramatic time and space. A couple of guitar tones evoking ecclesiastic liturgical monodies were enough to transfer the action into a nunnery, while the trumpet's timbre affected by a sordino announced the arrival of the duke's helicopter. Furthermore, the musicians were also part of the dramatic world: the singer, pregnant, clearly referred to Juliet, Claudio's beloved, a central character in the dramatic conflict, who never appears on stage in Shakespeare's play. Fabricated sequences may also conclude the performance and encourage the audience to rethink the ending. Here, *Twelfth Night* offers an example, as Ostermeier introduced an ultimate image to follow the play's final moment of recognition and reconciliation: the walls closing the space to the back parted and opened the view onto the theatre's bare backstage area. There, Malvolio was standing on a ladder with a noose on his neck, then tipped the ladder over and remained swaying on the rope until the lights went off. Through this final image, Malvolio, the comical character abused and tortured by the others, became a brother to Shylock; the comedy turned into a problem play.

A further element that determines Ostermeier's fabrications is the material reality of the stage. The space itself, the set and the props give the performers occasions to develop what Ostermeier calls with a Stanislavskian term 'psychophysical chains of action'. His actors frequently perform extremely physical, sometimes outright acrobatic, actions on stage, which reveal their characters' motifs and thereby 'tell the spectators something more about the relations of this dramatic figure, about her or his attitude and emotional state, and not least about the dramatic situation itself'.[13] *A Midsummers Night's Dream* offered a pertinent illustration, not least as this production was a joint project between Ostermeier and choreographer Constanza Macras, combining theatre and dance.[14] The performers fully exploited the possibilities of physical acting offered by the set, using the railings as a trapeze, climbing and descending from the spiral staircase, etc. In *Hamlet*, the chain curtain invited making physical use of it, as did the banquet table, and equally the moist soil that covered the ground, in which the actors could bury one another, or which they could use to smear their faces and bodies, but which also softened some dangerous looking falls. The dark water in *Othello* functioned similarly: it offered the actors opportunities for expressing their characters, allowing them to dive into the liquid and disappear, push one another into it or splash it around. In *Measure for Measure*, water contributed to the action in a different way. As noted, Lars Eidinger as Angelo, once he had taken over the reign in the duke's absence, purified Vienna with a stream of water from a rubber hose, while the other performers were running around the set, trying to evade or protect themselves from this violent gush of water, which became a material expression of Angelo's terror over the city.

In *Richard III*, Eidinger's performance was much determined by his physical work. His Richard walked around the stage in a distorted corporeal figuration, with his legs crooked, stooped so his head only reached the waist of the others, giving them the impression they could literally look down at him. However, when needed, for example in the scene where Gloucester woos Lady Anne, the actor's body would straighten up and dominate the entire space with its energy. Such a chain of psychophysical actions also concluded the performance, again offering a reinterpretation of the play's end. Here, Gloucester would not die on the battlefield surrounded by his enemies, but completely abandoned, left alone in his bed, haunted by his conscience and battling the ghosts of those he had killed. He ran around the stage, frantically waving his sword and fighting these invisible shadows, before falling exhaustedly on his bed. With his leg hooked into the rope of the microphone that was hanging from above, his body was then hoisted above the stage, where – similar to the image of Malvolio in the later *Twelfth Night* discussed above – he kept swaying head upside down liked a slaughtered pig in the abattoir, until the final black.

In correspondence with Ostermeier's own explanations, we may link these directorial fabrications to the 'attractions' in the tradition of Meyerhold and Eisenstein. For the latter, this directorial tool of scenic interpretation connected theatre and the then new medium of film, and it offered a vital political function:

> an attraction (in relation to the theatre) is any aggressive aspect of the theatre; that is, any element of the theatre that subjects the spectator to a sensual or psychological impact, experimentally regulated and

mathematically calculated to produce in him certain emotional shocks which, when placed in their proper sequence within the totality of the production, become the only means that enable the spectator to perceive the ideological side of what is being demonstrated – the ultimate ideological conclusion.[15]

The link to Ostermeier's critically engaged theatre is vital.

Storytelling

According to Ostermeier, his fabrications emerge during rehearsals, both from the dramaturgical study of the playtext and from the work with the actors, not least in the director's storytelling exercises that have characterized his rehearsal process for the past decade. 'Storytelling' is Ostermeier's original working method, derived from one of the basic Stanislavskian claims: in order to act authentically, actors need to behave within the dramatic situations of the play as if they were real life. The storytelling method draws on the actors' life experience. At the beginning of a storytelling exercise, a situation is formulated, drawn from the play, such as, '"a situation where you persuade someone to do something forbidden"; [...] "you prevent someone from making a big mistake"; "you have an idea, but everyone turns against you", and so on."'[16] Any actor may contribute their own experience, creating a brief scene with their fellow actors in very short time; the only condition is that it must be a true story. This way, as Ostermeier explains, 'the actors are completely in the present moment, in the situation, because they don't know what is coming next. The dialogues are not determined beforehand, they thus need to keep a maximum of attention, same as in the real life. This is all a stage director can dream of!'[17] While the exercise may appear similar to standard improvisation work, its purpose is different: the scenes are not meant to impress with witty inventiveness, nor are they a place to expose one's private biography (the storyteller usually will not participate in the scene and instead, his experience is performed by others and thereby 'alienated'). Their main purpose is to stimulate authentic behaviour that can be observed and analysed in rehearsal: 'particular attention is afforded to physical actions, tones of voices, ways of behaving and speaking, and equally to spatial proxemics between the actors'.[18] Gradually, elements from the play will be introduced into the scene, including parts of the dialogue, while still copying the original pattern of behaviour, actions and gestures. Storytelling exercises thus serve to encourage the actors to develop the above-mentioned 'forms of a very contemporary epic narration' on stage.

In Ostermeier's productions, the inspiration drawn from twentieth century acting technique goes hand in hand with the impulses he received from the Elizabethan theatre tradition and its non-psychological, demonstrational acting. This peculiar combination found its expression in several scenic processes characteristic of Ostermeier's Shakespeare productions. First, in each one of these productions (except for the Paris *Twelfth Night*), all actors – except for the key protagonist(s) – played several characters, eliminating any identification of the performer with his role. This was further highlighted as the change of role – by means of a costume change, and some props – would often take place in full view of the audience. Second, the audience was consistently reminded of the fictional, theatrical situation they were a part of. Eidinger as Hamlet, for example, would ask technicians to put on the house lights, while his character would explain the reactions of theatre spectators. Elsewhere, he would ask the music to be turned down before the final fencing fight, or ask fellow actors to go backstage so that he stayed alone on the stage for his monologue. Third, the actors directly addressed the spectators, as when Eidinger's Hamlet, mimicking a hip-hop DJ, would ask the audience to react to his 'yeah!', or when Urs Jucker's Claudius confessed his fratricide, wandering among the spectators and asking them for absolution. In *Othello*, Iago's numerous monologues were sung in afro-beat rhythm in the style of Fela Kuti (of whom the gestures and dances of actor Stefan Stern were reminiscent). In the play, these monologues confer to the tragedy a clear meta-theatrical dimension, as Iago explains his motives and announces his actions and deeds to come. Ostermeier intensified the theatricality of these 'asides' by giving them the form of Brechtian songs. In *Twelfth Night*, the direct address to the audience reached its climax in an improvised scene, where Laurent Stocker (Sir Toby Belch) and Christophe Montenez (Sir Andrew Aguecheek) stood with their microphones on the forestage and conversed about contemporary matters of French politics (such as the 'yellow vest' protests), linking their clown-characters to their position as engaged citizens as well as to contemporary stand-up comedy and political cabaret. In this production, it was particularly interesting to observe the differences of the Comédie-Française actors to their German Schaubühne colleagues in dealing with Ostermeier's approach. They assumed the non-psychological and presentational acting, yet did not abandon the characteristic acting tradition of the Comédie-Française. Their scenic expression combined sequences of demonstrational acting with their acting as and for the character.

Again, Ostermeier's *Richard III* was the production that went furthest in exploiting the blending between the main character and the Schaubühne's star actor, Lars Eidinger. He would switch freely, with impressive virtuosity, between the different levels: Gloucester addressing the other characters of the play; Gloucester-Eidinger addressing the audience, announcing and explaining the motives and actions of his character; Eidinger commenting on his role and on the action on stage in improvisations on the night. The spectators reacted frequently, very lively and willingly. One all the time faced the Eidinger contained in this Gloucester, but at the same time, it worked the other way round as well, in the service of the play: the Eidinger of the improvisations always kept the Gloucester in him, as when, during one performance I saw, he stepped down from the stage among the public and forced an elderly, obviously well-mannered lady to repeat dirty words after him, humiliating her similarly just as Richard would humiliate the other characters in the play.

It is important to note that the licence Eidinger and other performers are granted to act and improvise on the spot thus always emerges from a clear and concrete understanding – not so much of their character's psychology, but of her or his relations to the others, their emotional state, hierarchical position and other dimensions of the dramatic situation. This knowledge is developed further through 'family constellations' exercises, another key element of Ostermeier's rehearsal work. These exercises, adapted from psychotherapy, offer a practical, entirely non-psychologizing tool to assist the performers in experiencing these situations as a basis for their play in performance. In rehearsal, the actors would create a sort of *tableau vivant* including all characters. They are asked to position themselves in space according to the position of their character: whom they are close to, whom they prefer to stay away from. Attention is paid not only to where they stand, but also to what attitude they adopt, in which direction they look, what gestures they make etc. Ostermeier notes that just like in real life, where without having to think about it, we naturally adopt a physical and spatial attitude towards others corresponding to the situation and to our position to them within this situation, the actors will be enabled to sense when their attitude on stage is not authentic, or when their spatial or corporeal relation to another character is wrong.

Epic narration and exposed theatricality

Characterized by their explicit theatricality, the Shakespeare productions form a coherent cycle within the directorial work of Thomas Ostermeier at the Schaubühne. The process of updating found its expression in allusions to a contemporary context, while direct references to specific circumstances were blurred. The set design concentrated the playing area on one surface, frequently determined by a natural element (water, soil or sand), thereby inviting the actors to make anti-naturalistic, often very physical, use of it. In most of the productions, all performers remained present on stage during the entire performance. They often played more than one role, changing their costume or adapting their make-up in full view of the audience. The dramatic situations of the play were frequently interpreted by means of directorial fabrication, i.e. the specific scenic development of circumstances not always explicitly mentioned in the text, as well as through a specific directing of the actors that combined modern methods of non-identificatory acting (Brechtian alienation or psychophysical actions after Stanislavsky and Meyerhold, among others) with the Elizabethan tradition of presentational acting. In most of the productions, musicians were present on stage and accompanied the performance live, while also participating in the dramatic situations. All these different processes allowed for an unveiling of the mechanisms of the stage, even for their exhibition in front of the audience, yet at the same time, this exposure of the theatrical reality was always fully integrated into the play's dramatic situations. Ostermeier thus achieved what he had set out in his vision at the time he began his work at the Schaubühne:

> The actors turn directly to the audience. Forms of a very contemporary epic narration are developed, which once more take account of the most basic theatre situation: an actor stands on a stage and, through her or his character, tells a story to the audience. This is a realism which, on stage, no longer needs to be trapped behind a fourth wall, within the illusionism of naturalistic, psychological acting.[19]

This quest for a realism of the stage underlies all of Ostermeier's Shakespeare productions. The principles discussed in this chapter helped the director to go beyond conventional realism in its naturalistic sense, and to open the performances to symbolic meanings and to a pure theatricality. Notwithstanding some major aesthetic and ideological differences with the director's other productions considered as more typically 'realist' (such as his work on Ibsen, Schnitzler, Horvath and others), the Shakespearian cycle contributed in vital ways to the research of his characteristic approach to realism. Following a distinctly Brechtian logic, realism here was not considered as an image and re-presentation of the reality, but as the 'artistic and artificial' expression of its social dimension and the power relationships within it.

Notes

1 Thomas Ostermeier, 'Theatre in the Age of its Acceleration', in *The Theatre of Thomas Ostermeier*, eds Peter M. Boenisch and Thomas Ostermeier (Abingdon and New York: Routledge, 2016), 18.

80 *The Schaubühne Berlin under Thomas Ostermeier*

2 Ibid., 13.
3 In Suzanne Vogel, *Entretiens avec Thomas Ostermeier* (Rennes: Michel Archimbault, 2001), 33.
4 Thomas Ostermeier, 'Insights into the Reality of Human Community: A Defence of Realism in Theatre', in Boenisch and Ostermeier, *The Theatre of Thomas Ostermeier*, 24.
5 Ibid., 22. See also Benjamin Fowler's (Chapter 11) and Peter M. Boenisch's (Chapter 9) chapters in this volume.
6 Bertolt Brecht, '*Verfremdung* Effects in Chinese Acting', in *Brecht on Theatre* by Bertolt Brecht (London: Bloomsbury Methuen, 2014), 151–9.
7 Ostermeier at the *Atelier de la pensée* at the National Theatre Odéon in Paris, hosted by Jitka Goriaux Pelechová, 3 April 2009.
8 Thomas Ostermeier, '*Totus Mundus Agit Histrionem*: Reading and Staging Shakespeare', in Boernisch and Ostermeier, *The Theatre of Thomas Ostermeier*, 189.
9 Ostermeier, 'Insights into the Reality', 22.
10 Cited in Jitka Goriaux Pelechová, 'Le théâtre de Thomas Ostermeier : phénomène culturel ou démarche artistique ?', *Cahiers d'Études Germaniques* 64 (2013): 349.
11 Ibid., 340.
12 See Thomas Ostermeier, 'The Art of Communicating: Thomas Ostermeier's Inductive Method of *Regie*', in Boenisch and Ostermeier, *The Theatre of Thomas Ostermeier*, 132–84.
13 Ibid., 170.
14 See also Sabine Huschka's chapter (Chapter 13) in this volume.
15 Sergei Eisenstein, 'Montage of Attractions', trans. Daniel Gerould, *The Drama Review* 18, no. 1 (1974): 78.
16 Ostermeier, 'The Art of Communicating', 156.
17 'Le partenaire comme impulsion', in *Le Théâtre et la peur*, eds Georges Banu and Jitka Goriaux Pelechová (Paris: Actes Sud, 2016), 115.
18 Ostermeier, 'The Art of Communicating', 156.
19 Ostermeier, 'Theatre in the Age of its Acceleration', 18.

7

Hamlet Out of Joint: Variations on a Theme in Thomas Ostermeier's Production, 2008–20

Elisa Leroy

'*Hamlet*', says Thomas Ostermeier today, 'is like a breathing organism. It is a multivocal score, anarchical, subcultural and meandering.'[1] In this statement, the director opens up two possible perspectives on the evolution of his production since its premiere in 2008. On the one hand, it can be read as the development of a living organism: it grows, matures and mutates through its repeated performance. Changes in cast, place and context entail shifts that stabilize into a new shape over time. Contrary to the living organism, however, the life of the production need not be considered an inevitable process of decay. Ostermeier himself suggests reading the evolution of his *Hamlet* in musical terms: the many performances of *Hamlet* can equally be described as a series of improvised variations on a musical theme set by his *mise en scène*. Music is a central metaphor in the director's theoretical writing: *Mise en scène*, he writes, is 'a well-orchestrated composition in time, where each instrument – each element of the stage and each medium of theatre – contributes with its own sound to the overall multi-dimensional melody of the play.'[2] The *mise en scène* of Ostermeier's *Hamlet*, as it was developed in rehearsals and premiered in 2008, is a theme that constitutes the starting point for an infinite range of improvised variations by all elements of the stage, as Eugene Holland describes for jazz music:

> Whereas classical musicians merely reproduce the parts written for their particular instruments by the composer, and play them, moreover, at the tempo dictated by a conductor, a jazz musician is free to vary the notes, the tempo, even the key in which she is playing. Indeed, the imperative of jazz improvisation is always to 'make it new' – not just once (i.e. at the moment of composition), but every time you play.[3]

Each of these perspectives on the evolution of *Hamlet* implies a different conceptualization of their object. To consider the evolution of *Hamlet* as diachronic change, as a continuous and irreversible evolution over time, presupposes a stable frame of reference against which each performance may be measured according to its correspondence with, or deviance from, said frame. Such a perspective constructs the production or *mise en scène* as a 'particular artistic arrangement and interpretation of the text with a high degree of stability',[4] as Christopher Balme has put it; it then contrasts and compares each performance, each 'particular version of the production', with that frame.[5] *Hamlet*, such a perspective suggests, has evolved in an irreversible way, away from its allegedly original design. To consider the changes in *Hamlet* as synchronic, on the other hand, places the emphasis on the fact that each of the 326 performances of *Hamlet* that have taken place up to the day I am writing this article in autumn 2019 'is unrepeatable'[6] and therefore affords the opportunity for an unpredictable and singular variation.

As both perspectives are equally reductive, only a simultaneous consideration of both provides us with a fuller understanding of the way Ostermeier's *Hamlet* has evolved over time. In this chapter, I shall therefore argue that both types of change productively interact: the visible diachronic changes that *Hamlet* has undergone since its premiere, like an aging and maturing organism, depend upon the production's particular aptitude for synchronic variation on its own lead theme in each of its performances. Ostermeier's *Hamlet* aims to 'maximize creative difference in repetition',[7] as does the improvising jazz musician. In fact, change is its constitutive principle: the director's conception of the dramatic situation anchors the dramaturgical frame created in rehearsals in the present moment of each performance, and his conceptualization of the protagonist encourages an evolution of the production, which takes place one variation at a time. The evolution of *Hamlet* is, per definition, *out of joint*, continuous and discontinuous at the same time.

I will first give a few examples for the way in which the length of the run, changes in place, cast and in the biographies of the actors have caused Ostermeier's *Hamlet* to mature over the years. I will then investigate more closely the role of Lars Eidinger, who has been performing *Hamlet* since 2008, and who has been given leeway to improvise extensively within the arrangements defined by the *mise en scène*. The fact that these fundamentally unpredictable and instantaneous changes depend primarily on one performer has caused the dramaturgical focus of the production to shift over time in a way that has in fact transformed it with regard to its original design. I will draw on diverse elements that record visible changes or narrate the experience of such variation from different standpoints. The materials I am basing this investigation on include the translation and adaptation made by Marius von Mayenburg in 2008,[8] textbooks and productions scripts that have been reworked and actualized over the years,[9] the filmed recording of the show[10] and individual performances of *Hamlet*.[11]

Diachronic change: The time is out of joint

With regards to Ostermeier's *Hamlet*, the metaphor of the human organism is particularly alluring. Over almost twelve years, at the time of writing, the production, like a human, has matured along with its actors, into a theatrical teenager. New cast members have been grafted onto the original team, and the entire production became transplanted into different places. Changing biographical contexts, but also the respective political and societal backdrops of each performance, step by step reshape, but also reinforce the larger dramaturgical frame. They determine the way in which each participant in the production interprets, in each performance, a common dramaturgical framework that has been fixed at the beginning of rehearsals, and which Ostermeier calls the dominant dramatic situation. As Jitka Pelechová outlined in the previous chapter, one of the director's core objectives for rehearsal is to establish an overarching dramatic situation in a collective reading of the play text. Instead of prescribing a fixed score of blocking, movements and utterances on stage, Ostermeier's directing method thus attempts to create a framework within which variation becomes possible. Ideally, the more detailed the understanding of the dramatic situation is, the more wiggle room there is for the shape it takes on stage:

> I am absolutely convinced that if you unpack a dramatic situation in all its depth, in its entire dimensionality and complexity, everything will naturally and organically happen just by using the clearly defined dramatic situation as a springboard.[12]

Lars Eidinger confirms this dialectic in Ostermeier's method, with a slightly different inflection: 'When I am "acting Ostermeier" [...] there will barely be a situation that is not entirely clear. There is nothing that has not been discussed previously and clarified'.[13] But such 'deep comprehension of the material [...] triggers spontaneous creativity and playful imagination'.[14] Even though it is discussed, explored and clarified as thoroughly as possible during rehearsals, the dramatic situation remains open as to the shape it will take on stage, as performers are encouraged to create their performance with special attention to all elements of the present moment – time, place, their own state of mind – of performance.

What is, then, the dramatic situation that has been agreed upon during the rehearsals of *Hamlet*? One of the main circumstances of all characters in Ostermeier's production that the members of the cast I have spoken to remember is the profound and ubiquitous fear triggered by regime change: a fear of being divested, of being discovered, of losing their position, of being

84   *The Schaubühne Berlin under Thomas Ostermeier*

next on the kill-list, of losing loved ones or their affection. As Ostermeier himself has summed up much later, his *Hamlet* is the reflection of Shakespeare's world itself, 'a world of conspiracy, suspicion, spying, and violence. [...] A world in which you could never be sure who you were talking to – a friend, or a spy?'[15] An important directorial choice has been made accordingly: whether it is an unexpected sound, an audience member leaving to use the restroom, a technical failure – all elements of the performance situation are part of the dramatic situation and therefore impact the performers' actions and reactions. That 'the time is out of joint'[16] not only constitutes a description of *Hamlet's* universe by the play's protagonist. It is the dominant circumstance for all characters: the possibility, evoked by the ghost that claims to be Old Hamlet, that the monarchical power of Claudius, uncle to Hamlet and brother to Old Hamlet, might only be usurped, generates a situation of generalized mistrust, mutual threat and constant attentiveness. Eventually, such 'out of joint-ness' also is a central feature of Ostermeier's *mise en scène* in general: each performance of *Hamlet* reconstructs the dramatic situation of the play in terms of the present circumstances of performance. The way in which the production has evolved since its opening night is therefore interpreted very differently by all participants – director, performers, technical staff – precisely because it cannot be pinned down to differences in personnel, stage set, costume, diction or blocking.

The circumstances of performing have been diverse ever since *Hamlet's* opening nights. As a co-production with the Athens Hellenic Festival and the Festival d'Avignon, its final rehearsals and the first public performance (on 7 July 2008) took place in Athens, at Peiraios 260 theatre. It then moved to the Cour d'Honneur of the Palais des Papes at the Festival d'Avignon right after, premiering there on 16 July 2008.[17] More rehearsals preceded the Berlin opening at Lehniner Platz (on 17 September 2008). Since then, this *Hamlet* has been on a journey through time and space. Including Berlin, Ostermeier's production has been performed in thirty cities across the world. On 19 October 2019, as I am writing this chapter, it will be performed for the 326th time – and this performance will take place in Mexico City. Even in German repertory theatre, where the lifespan of a production attains a length unknown to the en suite culture of French- and English-speaking theatre, the number of seasons that *Hamlet* has been running is remarkable. Entailing longer runs – as the production, as one of many in the repertoire, shares the stage and is performed perhaps two or three times each month – this system also requires pragmatic changes, for instance in the cast. At the time of writing, only three of the six performers in Ostermeier's *Hamlet* (including Lars Eidinger in the title role) had been on stage during the premiere in 2008.[18] Additionally, and somewhat uniquely as a result of the Schaubühne's institutional ecology with its extensive international touring activity, changes in place also demand technical adaptations as well as reactions to varying cultural contexts. For touring, three versions of the set exist, of 14, 16 and 20 metres width respectively, while larger or open-air spaces require additional technical solutions such as the use of micro ports. Such apparently pragmatic and exterior changes reflect deeper modifications with regard to the larger dramaturgical framework of the production.

The ensemble has particularly vivid memories of the performances in Ramallah in 2012, and Tehran in 2016, where the actress performing Ophelia and Queen Gertrude wore a full veil while singing on stage, and physical contact with male members of the cast was forbidden. In Tehran, the requirements were even a legal necessity, as the show was closely supervised by censors according to the laws of the Islamic religious police. Jenny König (Ophelia/the Queen) was severely impaired in her performance – and, by consequence, so were her partners, as their actions react to their partner's performance. The serious discussion surrounding the question of whether to bow to censure or to cancel the tour altogether had the effect, as Urs Jucker (King Claudius) remembers, of refreshing the main circumstance that the play itself poses to all characters involved: in front of an Iranian audience, performing a play on a potentially illegitimate, but unquestionable, absolutist rule gained a new concreteness. When *Hamlet* was performed in Ramallah, Jucker recalls a similar effect. As he held Claudius's confessing monologue, asking himself whether his fratricide might ever be forgiven in the afterlife, he felt, as he says, that one could cut the air with a knife. In a place in which many spectators might have experienced the violent death of a close family member, the idea of fratricide must have had a different value for many. Jucker felt that questions of loyalty in the face of power and the menace of civil war were no abstract dramatic plot to the audience of this performance. The weight of the situation at stake in the fictional space of the stage, Jucker remembers, became crystal clear in this context. Even though the scope of such an experience is limited in time – the impression wears off, as Thomas Ostermeier deplores – it provides new impulses and a new awareness for the dramaturgical framework. The actors all agree that alternating performances elsewhere and at home enriches their performance with a new alertness towards the stakes of the dramatic situations. The changing contexts can have the effect of reconnecting the ensemble with the dramaturgical framework of the production.

While the experiences in Tehran and Ramallah contributed to a stronger awareness of the dramatic situation fixed during rehearsals, the actors' individual context is a further important factor in the evolution of the dramatic situation. As their biographies are per definition subject to irreversible change, it impacts their reading of the dramatic situation, Lars Eidinger explains: 'the actor, his or her personality, is always present, and becomes a part of what is up for discussion with the audience'.[19] Urs Jucker describes, for example, that becoming a father himself, after the premiere, changed his reading of Claudius's relationship towards Hamlet, and shed a new light on the generational conflict that structures *Hamlet*, too. Playing the dramatic situation and, thereby, keeping a continuous connection with the dramaturgical framework agreed upon during rehearsals, paradoxically comprises connecting with the present situation of each performance, its time and place, and the actors' individual situation at the same time.

While each performance of *Hamlet* repeats certain arrangements between performers, director and technicians, as much as it tells the same story of the same characters – this structure needs to be forgotten to counter the danger of repetition. How does one avoid that after more than 300 performances of, as it seems, the 'same' production, actors no longer feel the urgency of arrangements that feel fresh and unfamiliar in a new show? It takes courage and alertness, as Urs Jucker and Robert Beyer (who plays Polonius and Osric) both admit, to take risks and make changes within the boundaries of the character's situation; changes in place and evolution in time provide the opportunity for a change that is necessary to the vitality of the organism of *Hamlet*. Especially, recasting produces entirely new constellations with new sparring partners to interact with. Damir Avdic, currently performing Horatio and Guildenstern, makes ample use of opportunities for spontaneous jokes and acrobatics during the 'Mousetrap' scene, which in Ostermeier's production Hamlet and Horatio perform together. An interesting effect ensues: even Eidinger, used to varying his performance while his partners have fewer 'springboards' for improvisation, may be thrown off balance from his own routine by a partner who fills out the form of the production in a new and unexpected manner. In his performances in December 2017 and in January 2019, this was the case in the following exchange between Hamlet and Guildenstern performed by Eidinger and Avdic:

HAMLET   [. . .] To withdraw with you, why do you go about to recover the wind of me, as if you would drive me into a toil?
GUILDENSTERN   O my lord, if my duty be too bold, my love is too unmannerly.[20]

Avdic, wearing only his underwear and cowboy boots as this point, performed his lines with a frivolous sexual innuendo, thereby upsetting the usual dynamic in which Hamlet frightens and unsettles his acting partners. At the same time, he introduced a new aspect to the overall dramatic situation of

Hamlet *Out of Joint* 87

generalized suspicion. What if Guildenstern was hiding a forbidden desire for Hamlet, complicating his own involvement with Claudius's plan to spy on Hamlet even more?

Putting on an antic disposition: Synchronic change through improvisation

Like a maturing organism, *Hamlet* has moved forward in time and through changing contexts, evolving into itself precisely through the enriching connection with new experiences that interact with its original dramaturgical framework. When asked about their general impression of the production's development over the past eleven years, all participants still name one aspect that strongly determines the way in which each performance varies, and which has evolved over time: Lars Eidinger's improvisations. His Hamlet frequently interacts with the audience and adds spontaneous physical acrobatics and verbal digressions to the production's arrangements. These improvisations, I argue, are at the core of a synchronic type of change that occurs in each of the performances in an unpredictable and contingent way – and that has been driving a continuous diachronic shift in the dramaturgical focus of the play. Like a jazz piece, Ostermeier's *Hamlet* intentionally creates such spaces for digression from the score and rhythm imagined by its composer.

Shakespeare's play offers a particularly fruitful starting point for this dialectic between theme and variation to take effect. Hamlet's decision to 'put an antic disposition on'[21] can be read as one possible reaction to the uncertain atmosphere in the 'warlike state'[22] that Denmark becomes under King Claudius. The dramatic situation of the protagonist becomes a situation of performance itself. Ostermeier chose to place the existential necessity for a disguise at the centre of his interpretation:

> [I]n the original myth Claudius actually pronounces his intention to kill Hamlet, who therefore goes into hiding in a pigsty and covers himself in shit so he would smell embarrassingly, in order to give the impression that he is mad. [. . .] Hamlet thus not only puts a mask on his face, but on his whole body, pretending to be somebody else.[23]

Hamlet reacts to this fear by performing a role. Consequently, for the dramatic situation of the main protagonist, 'the spectators' presence is part and parcel of the character's situation. [. . .] It becomes my main circumstance that I am a performer, sharing a space with an audience'.[24] This interpretation entailed a major directorial decision: Eidinger was given the freedom to improvise as early as at the rehearsals, as assistant director Anne Schneider recalls. This significant amount of 'wiggle room' for the title role in particular determined the degree of openness of the arrangements found and fixed during rehearsals. As Eidinger has the opportunity to make new changes each night, so the shape of *Hamlet* has shifted over time, too, as the production's running time illustrates. The 2008 TV recording comes in at 2 hours and 26 minutes long. When current assistant director David Stöhr took over the show in 2016, it ran for 2 hours and 50 minutes, while it now usually runs, as he reports, around the 2 hours and 30 minute mark again. Such a difference can hardly be attributed to slower or faster pace; indeed, Thomas Ostermeier emphasizes that the production's rhythm was set, and musical numbers, technical arrangements and the pace of dialogue were all fixed during rehearsals. Urs Jucker and Robert Beyer confirm in conversation that the production requires them to follow a rather strict structure, as the set – involving a metal curtain and a mobile podium moving up and down the stage – demands from them that they respect the timing of technical cues.

Where, then, resides the 'wiggle room' for the performance to vary so much over time? In Scene 7 of Mayenburg's adaptation (which eliminates the traditional division into acts), Hamlet encounters his old friends Rosencrantz and Guildenstern, sent by King Claudius and Queen Gertrude to find out the reason for Hamlet's 'antic disposition': a disposition that we, the audience, know to be the pretence of madness to hide his vengeful intentions. After greeting his friends, Hamlet interrupts their conversation with a series of acrobatic stunts, all of which have been precisely scripted, as evidenced in the two director's books dated 24 January 2009 and 19 March 2010. Rosencrantz and Guildenstern participate in Hamlet's show to ingratiate themselves to him. Their reactions are precisely recorded, too. At one point, Hamlet stands on the table, looking at Rosencrantz and Guildenstern's blank faces, testing their readiness to indulge him. He yells at them though a wireless microphone: 'Party people in the house, com'on and let me hear you say: YEAH!'[25] This line, not featuring in Mayenburg's published adaptation, was however already included in the earliest of the so-called 'Spielfassungen' (the 'text as performed'), dating from 21 September 2008, a few days after the Berlin premiere. It is a product of rehearsals. At Hamlet's second attempt, Rosencrantz and Guildenstern both awkwardly utter a weak 'YEAH', also recorded in the textbook.[26] Turning around to the audience to share his disappointment and disgust with his friends' dullness, Eidinger's Hamlet then seeks to elicit a reaction from the audience. This interaction with the audience is equally scripted in all four existing versions of the textbook and director's book (noted as 'Wiederholung mit dem Publikum', 'Repeat with the audience'[27]). What may appear a spontaneous digression, therefore, has been carefully rehearsed and subsequently scripted. In the Avignon performances, as the TV recording shows, the interaction with the audience did not go beyond the call and response.[28] But by 2017, Eidinger had taken the improvisation a step further. He now tested the audience's willingness to react – and to take responsibility for their reaction – by creating situations that should, at the same time, make the audience uncomfortable about their willingness to participate. During the performances on 27 October and 12 December 2017 and on 31 January 2019, Eidinger asked all men to yell 'Yeah, we want some pussy!', and 'all the ladies: When I say gang, you say bang', leading to an explicit, hardly politically correct declamation by Eidinger and the female audience. Depending on the audience, Eidinger might add new lines to chant together, or comment on the audience's reactions. None of this, now, is recorded in the textbooks or director's books. Still, as evident from my observations in 2017 and 2019, these specific variations have become part of that which is now repeated each time *Hamlet* is performed, hence also part of the production's recurrent theme. With this improvisation, like a soloist in a band, Eidinger uses the room that the original rehearsal agreement had provided for an autonomous modification that depends on the reactions of his partners as well as on the audience in the 'here and now' of each performance. But the improvisations themselves can, over time, become part of the musical score of the production, stabilizing that which emerged as a spontaneous change through repetition.

Eidinger's improvisations have thereby been able to shift the dramaturgical emphasis of Ostermeier's *Hamlet*. His Hamlet has been less and less characterized by the ubiquitous threat of being discovered by a usurping uncle who murdered his father, but by the exuberance of a character whose main dramatic situation is performance itself. The distinction between Lars Eidinger, the performer, and Hamlet, his character, has become increasingly blurred. The performance of the 'antic disposition', which profoundly divides Hamlet from himself in Shakespeare's play, has become an opportunity for Eidinger to leave unclear whether the agent of his spontaneous digressions is Eidinger or Prince Hamlet. Eidinger makes this division a theme of his interpretation. This ambiguation is part of the design of Ostermeier's *mise en scène*; but current performances reveal that it has extended far beyond what had been recorded in the textbooks. In a later part of the already quoted Scene 7 in Mayenburg's adaptation, Hamlet announces to Horatio – in accordance with Shakespeare's *Hamlet* – that he will stage 'The Mousetrap' in order to force Claudius to confess his crime. With a quick gesture, Eidinger gives a signal to the light board operator to light up the auditorium. Eidinger points to a number of audience members and singles out one as an example:

Hm, ich hab gehört, (komm mal vor) es ist schon vorgekommen, (mach mal Licht an) daß Verbrecher, die im Theater saßen, wie der da, zum Beispiel, oder der da, dass die von einer gut gestrickten Handlung so ins Herz getroffen wurden, daß sie an Ort und Stelle all ihre Taten gestanden haben.[29]

The words in brackets – 'come here', 'turn on the lights' – have been added to Mayenburg's translation of the Shakespearean text in the textbook:

HAMLET [...] I have heard
That guilty creatures sitting at a play,
Have by the very cunning of the scene,
Been struck so to the soul that presently
They have proclaim'd their malefactions.[30]

As early as 2008, the textbook indicates that Mayenburg's translation which follows Shakespeare's text closely, has been extended during rehearsals to simulate a spontaneous inclusion of the audience into the dramatic situation. But in the textbooks and director's books, as well as in the performance in Avignon in July 2008, Hamlet and Horatio only take a closer look at the audience while continuing the dialogue of the scene. By contrast, in all performances I have been able to attend, after a short deliberation during which Eidinger points to several audience members – 'This one, for example, or this one' – one audience member was asked to stand up and turn around for everyone. This sequence, which establishes a link between the fictional character Hamlet and audience members through a sort of *metalepsis*, is by now repeated in each performance. To complicate the ambiguity between actor and character further, Eidinger often uses this moment to comment on other audience members, thereby producing interactions unique to individual performances. On 12 December 2017, for examples, he engaged in conversation with a group of school students:

EIDINGER   Where are you guys from? [*no reaction*] Hello? Can't you hear me?
PUPIL   Steglitz!
EIDINGER   Ah, Steglitz! That's where I was born, at Steglitz hospital. (*Pauses.*) Not Hamlet, of course, he was born somewhere else.

It takes a while for the audience to understand that they have become part of the dramatic situation with Hamlet/Eidinger. When they respond, they are left doubting whether they are responding to the character or the performer.

Hamlet *Out of Joint* 91

This is one of the rare instances I have witnessed in which the difference between character and performer was pointed out by Eidinger himself. It disambiguated the situation, but at the same time enhanced the ambiguity of the remaining performance – shifting the focus further away from the originally dominant dramatic situation, closely linked to the fictional universe of *Hamlet*, towards the present time and space of the performance, and Eidinger's own person.

This is not only an effect of the *mise en scène* designed during rehearsals; it is enhanced by the duration of the run of this production. Over time, the expectations that audiences bring to the performance have changed compared to those that might have been present in 2008. Marvin Carlson spoke of the audience's 'binocular vision'[31] of a performance, constantly haunted by knowledge of and expectations about the play, by memories of previous productions and, especially in the case of star performers such as Eidinger, also by other roles and performances of a particular actor, whether in theatre, the movies or TV. As an acclaimed movie actor who also stars in popular TV shows and has made his name as a DJ in Berlin and beyond, Eidinger has, over the years of the run of *Hamlet*, become a very prominent public persona. Some spectators will come specifically to see him perform, a vision that equally emphasizes the person of the performer and impacts on the perception of the character. When Eidinger repeats Hamlet's DJ-ing improvisation for his friends Rosencrantz and Guildenstern today, the audience might remember him DJ-ing in Berlin or elsewhere. When he yells the lyrics of German hip-hop group Deichkind's *Remmidemmi*, a track that had just come out in 2008, to express Hamlet's provocative and destructive attitude towards his parents – 'Schmeiß die Möbel aus dem Fenster, wir brauchen Platz zum Dancen' (throw the furniture out of the window, we need room for dancing) – a 2019 audience might think of Eidinger's appearance in the prominent rap group's video clip for *Keine Party* that came out in 2019.[32]

The haunting of Ostermeier's Hamlet by Lars Eidinger illustrates how the built-in propensity of this *mise en scène* for synchronic, instantaneous change in each of the performances intersects with the diachronic evolution of the production. In a way, the diachronic change that has shaped the production from 2008 until today can be read in terms of the changing relationship between Eidinger and his character. That the gap between both was bound to increase is, I argue, a result of the specific *mise en scène* of the play – and even the audience, who can hardly be expected to have the same awareness of the evolution of *Hamlet* as its performers, notices and comments upon the distinction. During the performance I saw on 31 January 2019, a spectator intervened in scene 9, following the performance of the 'Mousetrap': 'Oh come on, keep going now!', the clearly irritated spectator demanded of Eidinger. The spectator did not precisely explain *what* was to be continued here; they felt that something had been interrupted – presumably, their expectation of the Shakespearean dramatic plot. Eidinger's increasingly angry enquiries, repeatedly met with the same imperative from the spectator, culminated in Eidinger exclaiming: 'But it is going on! It has been going on the entire time, this is a misunderstanding!' Eidinger himself apparently perceives his performance of Hamlet today in continuity with rehearsals and all performances since. As Hamlet, 'a spoilt brat who goes off the rails, messes with everyone at court, and walks all over everyone else',[33] Eidinger's performance has, over time, walked across diverse boundaries of Ostermeier's *mise en scène*. Still, one might well claim that what has been going on since 2008 and will keep going on in the future is in fact Ostermeier's *Hamlet*. It has grown and matured through the experience of variation, but has preserved its characteristic features: like a growing organism *and* a variation on a theme.

Notes

1 All quotes not otherwise referenced are from personal conversations with director Thomas Ostermeier (26 September 2019), actors Urs Jucker (26 September 2019) and Robert Beyer (30 September 2019) and sound technician Sven Poser (23 September 2019). I also spoke to assistant director Anne Schneider (8 October 2019), who was present during rehearsals up to the premiere and oversaw the production during its first two seasons, and with David Stöhr (8 October 2019), who is currently in charge of it as assistant director. I am deeply grateful to Anne Arnz, Sören Pahl and the entire Schaubühne staff for their support in assembling and checking information, and to Robert Beyer, Urs Jucker, Thomas Ostermeier, Sven Poser, Anne Schneider and David Stöhr for taking the time to share their memories and experiences with me.

2 Peter M. Boenisch and Thomas Ostermeier (eds), *The Theatre of Thomas Ostermeier* (Abingdon and New York: Routledge, 2016), 172.

3 Eugene Holland, 'Jazz Improvisation. Music of the People to Come', in *Deleuze, Guattari and the Production of the New*, eds Simon O'Sullivan and Stephen Zepke (London: Bloomsbury, 2011), 201.

4 Christopher Balme, *The Cambridge Introduction to Theatre Studies* (Cambridge: Cambridge University Press, 2008), 127.

5 Ibid.

6 Ibid.

7 Holland, 'Jazz Improvisation', 121.

8 William Shakespeare, *Hamlet*, trans. and adapt. by Marius von Mayenburg (Berlin: Henschel, 2008). Quotes from the playtext in German refer to this translation.

9 There are two textbooks ('Spielfassung' and 'Spielfassung 1') that include changes made to Mayenburg's published version of the text: the former is

dated 21 September 2008, the latter dated 8 September 2010. There are also two director's books additionally including all movements, elements of performance and cues, one dated 24 January 2009 ('Regiebuch'), the other 19 March 2010 ('Regiebuch – Endfassung Anne'). I am deeply grateful to the Schaubühne to have been allowed access to these documents.

10 Thomas Ostermeier, *Hamlet*. Dir. Hannes Rossacher. Zweites Deutsches Fernsehen, 2008.

11 Quotes referring to performances witnessed on 27 October and 12 December 2017, and again on 31 January 2019, are indicated as such in the text.

12 Boenisch and Ostermeier, *The Theatre of Thomas Ostermeier*, 149.

13 Lars Eidinger, 'Revealing Truths about Human Existence. Lars Eidinger about "Acting Ostermeier"' in Boenisch and Ostermeier, *The Theatre of Thomas Ostermeier*, 45.

14 Ibid., 50.

15 Boenisch and Ostermeier, *The Theatre of Thomas Ostermeier*, 194.

16 William Shakespeare, *Hamlet*, ed. Ann Thompson and Neil Taylor (London: Arden, 2006), 1.5.184.

17 The TV recording bears witness to the state of the production at that moment.

18 In an ensemble theatre such as the Schaubühne am Lehniner Platz, actors and actresses join and leave the troupe, but they also take on roles in other productions, resulting in overlaps that may cause scheduling issues. In the production under discussion, Stefan Stern was sharing, then gradually passing on his role of Rosencrantz to Franz Hartwig as he took on the lead role in Ostermeier's *An Enemy of the People*. Judith Rosmair, the original Queen Gertrude and Ophelia, shared the part with Lucy Wirth until the 2013/14 season, when Jenny König took over. Most recently, Sebastian Schwarz, on leaving the Schaubühne's ensemble, passed on his roles as Horatio and Guildenstern to Damir Avdic in October 2016. Lars Eidinger (Hamlet), Urs Jucker (King Claudius) and Robert Beyer (Polonius, Osric) remain as members of the original cast.

19 Eidinger, 'Revealing Truths', 46.

20 Shakespeare, *Hamlet*, 3.2.336–41. Mayenburg translates: 'HAMLET Warum stehst du so hinter mir, als ob du mich in ein Netz treiben willst? – GÜLDENSTERN: Oh, mein Herr, wenn ich in meinem Dienst zu anmaßend bin, dann liegt das daran, daß meine Zuneigung nicht der Etikette entspricht'. (*Hamlet*, transl. Mayenburg, 37).

21 Shakespeare, *Hamlet*, 1.5.170.

22 Ibid., 1.2.9.

23 Boenisch and Ostermeier, *The Theatre of Thomas Ostermeier*, 191.

24 Ibid., 180–1.

25 'Spielfassung', 21 September 2008, 20.

26 Ibid.

94 *The Schaubühne Berlin under Thomas Ostermeier*

27 Ibid., and 'Spielfassung1', 8 September 2010, 20; 'Regiebuch', 24 January 2009, 22; 'Regiebuch – Endfassung Anne', 19 March 2010, 16.
28 See 00:49:54 in the recording.
29 'Spielfassung', 21 September 2008, 22–3.
30 Shakespeare, *Hamlet*, 2.2.523–7.
31 Marvin A. Carlson, *The Haunted Stage. The Theatre as Memory Machine* (Ann Arbor: University of Michigan Press, 2003), 27.
32 Deichkind, 'Remmidemmi (Yippieh Yippieh Yeah)', in *Aufstand im Schlaraffenland* (Island Records, 2006); Deichkind, 'Keine Party', in *Wer Sagt Denn Das?* (Sultan Günther Music, 2019); Video: *Auge Altona*, dir. Timo Schierhorn and UWE, www.youtube.com/watch?v=vH1poPSIvOk (accessed 4 February 2020).
33 Boenisch and Ostermeier, *The Theatre of Thomas Ostermeier*, 169.

8

Sensing the North: Thomas Ostermeier and the Schaubühne in Brazil

Igor de Almeida Silva

Schaubühne Berlin first visited Brazil in September 2013 with Thomas Ostermeier's production of Ibsen's *An Enemy of the People*, which was performed at Teatro Paulo Autran in São Paulo. The visit was supported by a partnership between SESC (Serviço Social do Comércio/Commerce Social Service) and the Brazilian Goethe Institute. Ostermeier also visited Brazil on other two occasions without his ensemble: in May 2012, to participate in the *Revista Cult* 4th Congress of Cultural Journalism as a speaker sponsored by the Brazilian Goethe Institute, and in January 2017, when he taught a workshop and spoke at SESC Copacabana in Rio de Janeiro. Two other Schaubühne productions were also shown in Brazil. In March 2015, Strindberg's *Miss Julie*, directed by Katie Mitchell and Leo Warner, was shown at the Second International Theater Festival in São Paulo. In 2019, the same festival then brought Milo Rau's *Compassion: The History of the Machine Gun*, to São Paulo. All these occasions enjoyed significant press coverage in the Brazilian media, disseminating Ostermeier's stagings and his comments on his work and on contemporary theatre. Not surprisingly, even before his first visit, the German director had attracted some attention in the local theatre scene. Reports and reviews about his work as the Schaubühne's artistic director had led to a sound interest in his work: in particular, the Schaubühne's staging procedures and the actors' ensemble work; Ostermeier's own contemporary approach to classical texts as well as his outspoken opinions on contemporary theatre; and lastly also the defence of 'directors' theatre' and his outline of a new approach to realism in theatre were all noted from a distance in the global south.

Yet, the relationship between the Berlin Schaubühne and Brazil dates back even further, to 1962, the inaugural year of the theatre company. As mentioned by Erika Fischer-Lichte in Chapter 2, the newly founded student theatre company debuted in September of that year with *Das Testament des Hundes* (*Auto da Compadecida*) by Brazilian playwright Ariano Suassuna

(1927–2014). It was directed by Polish Konrad Swinarski (1929–75), who was working for the first time in the West, after having been Brecht's assistant at the Berliner Ensemble in the 1950s. Suassuna's renowned play was written in 1955 and premiered in Recife a year later, directed by Clênio Wanderley (1929–76), at the Teatro Adolescente do Recife. Inspired by medieval records and by north-eastern Brazilian popular culture, *Das Testament des Hundes* tells João Grilo and Chicó's quixotic adventures in a small countryside town. The play gained notoriety in 1957 during its presentation at the First Festival of National Amateurs in Rio de Janeiro. In Berlin, this meeting of a Latin American dramatist and an Eastern European theatre director facilitated an encounter of two languages and two nationalities outside the mainstream of European theatre – right in the inaugural production of the new company that had given itself the explicit subtitle of 'Contemporary Theatre', in the spirit of the legacy of the 1920s traditions of the Weimar Republic (to whose central magazine, Siegfried Jacobson's weekly *Schaubühne*, the theatre owed its name). It revealed right from the beginning the theatre's characteristic political as well as international engagement, and its aspiration to present contemporary international authors from beyond the established canonical circle to its German audience. This approach would continue to characterize the later tenures of both Peter Stein and Thomas Ostermeier as artistic directors.

Despite language barriers preventing the immediate understanding of German theatre, Brazilian audiences over the years had had opportunities to see the works of Pina Bausch, Johann Kresnik, Frank Castorf, Heiner Goebbels and Christoph Marthaler. More recently, emerging stars in the German-language theatre and performance scene such as Susanne Kennedy, Boris Nikitin and Milo Rau also visited with their productions. The Brazilian audience's interest in German theatre has had a long tradition, based on a sustained reception of modern theatre playwrights and directors such as Georg Büchner, Bertolt Brecht and Erwin Piscator, as well as Heiner Müller, Peter Handke and Thomas Bernhard. Published in 1984 as one of the first publications on German theatre, Henry Thorau's *Perspectivas do moderno teatro alemão: estruturas e funcionamento* (*Perspectives of Modern German Theater: Structure and Operation*) brought together a number of lectures he had presented in various Latin American countries. Thorau, Professor for Brazilian and Portuguese culture, was the head dramaturg at the West Berlin Freie Volksbühne at the time, and German translator of Augusto Boal's books, such as the seminal *Theatre of the Oppressed*. In this publication, commissioned by the Brazilian Goethe Institute, Thorau outlined the structure and operation of the German state and city theatre system, and he introduced the work of playwrights and theatre directors of the 1960s and

1970s such as Botho Strauss, Franz Xaver Kroetz, Klaus-Michael Grüber and Peter Stein.

A dedicated chapter on Stein's Schaubühne was, as far as I am aware, the first study on the company in a Brazilian publication. Thorau began his chapter noting that 'anyone speaking about the German theatre cannot ignore the Schaubühne in Berlin'. He introduced their work as a 'decisive chapter in the history of the German theatre in the last fifteen years, and possibly in the history of the post-war theatre or even of contemporary theatre and of Germany in general'.[1] Thorau's enthusiasm for the Schaubühne referred not only to the legendary aesthetic quality of the productions presented under Stein's tenure, but also to the system of co-management he introduced, which has already been explained in earlier chapters of the present volume. A further aspect of the Schaubühne under Peter Stein that he specifically pointed out was the theatre's cultural and political engagement with and for the working class. This established the Schaubühne's reputation in Brazil as a critical and socially committed theatre.

To a certain extent, the company's artistic and political ambitions echoed Brazilian experiments with processes of shared artistic creation, as well as the activities of politically committed theatre companies before the military coup of 1964. In the 1970s, companies such as Asdrúbal Trouxe o Trambone, Teatro Ventoforte and Teatro do Ornintorrico, among others, had introduced new practices of collective creation. In the mid-1990s, another new mode of creation and a less hierarchical theatre organization began to emerge, known as *processo colaborativo* (collaborative process). Unlike collective creation, the *processo colaborativo* still preserves artistic functions, such as the dramatist, the actor and the director. It appears close to the 'devised theatre' approach of artistic collectives in the Anglophone world.[2] With regard to a politically engaged theatre, two theatre groups of the 1960s in particular ought to be noted: Teatro de Cultura Popular, an arm of Movimento de Cultura Popular,[3] who worked in the Brazilian province of Pernambuco, and Centro Popular de Cultura, of União Nacional de Estudantes,[4] in Rio de Janeiro. Both groups were engaged in political associations and movements that, in different ways, associated popular culture and working-class politicization with the theatre of that time.

These activities informed the ongoing Brazilian interested in the Schaubühne's work, which seemed to echo as well as inspire the quest in our country for a theatre that is socially critical as well as democratic in the manner in which it creates and produces work. The translation of Thomas Ostermeier's interview by German critic Uta Atzpodien, published in *Folha de S.Paulo* in May 2000, was the first reference to the Schaubühne's new artistic director in the Brazilian press. In the same issue, a profile on

98   *The Schaubühne Berlin under Thomas Ostermeier*

Ostermeier in the section 'Quem é ... [Who is ...]' presented more information about Ostermeier's background, his productions and his theatre career so far. This served as a first, brief introduction of the German director to a Brazilian public. Atzpodien described not least the director's introduction of a new co-management structure as 'consciously going back to Schaubühne's tradition of social criticism, and foretelling – after many years of an art almost always indulged in navel gazing – the advent of a new German theatrical generation'.[5] A good deal of the interview concentrated on the challenges of assuming the direction of such a renowned theatre, following from Ostermeier's earlier experience at the small Baracke stage of the Deutsches Theater. Echoing the Schaubühne's 1999 manifesto and other writing at the time, Ostermeier once more reiterated in this interview his understanding of theatre as a place for 'awakening consciousness', and for a 're-politicization', emphasizing the function of theatre to 'speak of today, of today's conflicts. It is our duty to give life to both personal and social conflicts'.[6] In the following year, Fabio Cypriano, a *Folha de S.Paulo* special reporter for the Avignon Festival, interviewed the director alongside reviewing his production of Büchner's *Danton's Death*. In the introduction to the interview, Cypriano presented Ostermeier as an 'innovative' and 'radical' director, referring also back to his work at the Baracke, and describing him as a necessary infusion of 'fresh blood' for the Schaubühne in order to regain vitality and attract a young audience following a period of stagnation.[7] These two interviews introduced Ostermeier as a young, innovative and daring director, representing a generation of artists capable of renewing German theatre, while at the same time reinvigorating the tradition of critical theatre-making that was associated with the origins of the Schaubühne and Stein's leadership – of which a Brazilian theatre public would have been aware.

Even before their later visits to Brazil, referred to at the start of this chapter, Ostermeier and the Schaubühne continued to reappear in Brazilian theatre reviews and journals, through a number of interviews, reports and reviews, and also reports published by Brazilian journalists and artists who visited Berlin or other cities in Europe where Ostermeier's shows were being performed. Over time, Ostermeier was presented as a consolidated director, internationally renowned for his stagings not least of Ibsen and Shakespeare. In April 2011, Antonio Araújo, director of Teatro da Vertigem, an important contemporary theatre group known for using non-theatrical spaces, saw Ostermeier's production of Ibsen's *Ghosts*, which he had directed not at the Schaubühne but with Ivo van Hove's ensemble at Toneelgroep Amsterdam. Araújo wrote about it in *Teatrojornal*, a theatre review and news journal on the web, dedicated to disseminating and analysing contemporary theatre. Araújo was impressed by Ostermeier's ability in 'making Ibsen sound like a

Thomas Ostermeier and the Schaubühne in Brazil   99

21st Century dramatist', and in ignoring aspects (such as the motif of syphilis) that would date Ibsen's work for a contemporary audience, thereby 'causing discomfort in the audience'. In fact, the spectators' response was what impressed Araújo the most:

> It has been quite some time since I witnessed such an impact on the audience. It was interesting: the play reached the end – you could clearly understand it had finished. However, the public remained in silence for more than three minutes, in complete darkness and stillness. It was only when an actor clapped his hands in the backstage that the audience reacted by applauding the play. The discomfort was evident. Ostermeier managed to revive in the 21st century the same uneasiness Ibsen caused with his taboo-themes in the end of the 19th century.[8]

Other aspects that caught the Brazilian theatre-maker's attention were the directorial strategies and scenic effects Ostermeier used to fragment the realist effect on the scene. Here, this effect was achieved by using black and white projections and a revolving stage where actors appeared in a way that seemed to dematerialize their presence on the scene.

It was with the production of another Ibsen play that Ostermeier eventually debuted in Brazil. On 27 September 2013, *An Enemy of the People* visited São Paulo. Coincidently, the show opened on a day of protests in the city. Residents of a slum area in the central region of the city had blocked the *Marginal Tietê*, one of the main access roads in São Paulo, as a protest against the threat of eviction by the City Hall. The impact of the protest caused more than 200 kilometres of traffic jams, stopping the flow of people in a city of 12 million – including the Schaubühne's performers and team, who had to walk to Teatro Paulo Autran, and half of the audience, who arrived late.[9]

This interruption in the day-to-day life of a city was not an isolated event in Brazil at that time. It was in fact an episode in the Brazilian social reality, experienced by the actors in *An Enemy of the People* and that, in a certain manner, was also reflected in their performance itself. Earlier that year, numerous protests had taken place in various Brazilian cities, São Paulo being one of its main focus. These events were named by the press and public 'Manifestações de Junho' (June Protests) or 'Jornadas de Junho' (June Campaigns), certainly in reference to the 1848 Revolution, when the proletariat in Paris rose in rebellion against the monarchy and was violently repressed. In Brazil, these protests were kindled by an increase in the fare of public transportation. They rapidly gained popular support, not least after strong police repression against protesters. They eventually became the largest popular insurgency in Brazil since President Fernando Collor de Mello's impeachment in 1992. At the climax of these protests, millions of Brazilians took to the streets in protest not only against the public transport fare rise and police violence, but also against various other issues such as public expenditure in international sports events, property speculation, the poor quality of public services and corruption. The protests in June gathered a wide range of participants from the left, right and centre of the political spectrum, but at the same time they sought independence from political parties and from traditional political representations. According to André Singer, a Brazilian political scientist, these events in June 2013 were supported mainly by the middle class and by those whom he describes as 'new proletariat': 'workers, generally youngsters, who were regularly employed during the Lula years [the former Brazilian president, 2003–11], but who now endure low wages, high turnover and poor working conditions'.[10]

These June Protests expressed the deep dissatisfaction of the people with traditional political structures. Traditional political parties such as Partido dos Trabalhadores[11] and Partido da Social Democracia Brasileira[12] were discredited by a significant part of the population, and lost their voters to 'outsiders' in the following elections, culminating in the election of Jair Messias Bolsonaro as president. He benefitted from the rising anti-establishment reaction and presented himself as a candidate from outside the political system, despite his rather meagre performance as a congressman for the previous twenty years. This was the social and political climate around the performances of *An Enemy of the People* in Brazil. Many of the issues echoing on the streets of Brazil in 2013 were also found in Ostermeier's production, such as the role of financial and personal interests to the detriment of public interest and welfare, regardless of the political orientation of those in power, the manipulation of public opinion by the media and, consequently, the crisis of narratives. The vertiginous manner in which public opinion was shown as easily manipulated in the production was, perhaps, one of the aspects that resonated most with contemporary Brazilian reality. Certainly, the Brazilian media had been a major contributor to the polarization of society since the very first operations of *Lava Jato* against corruption. In that sense, characters such as Peter Stockmann, the city mayor, or newspaper editor Hovstad were easily associated with the Brazilian political and media universe. Also, Ostermeier's approach to Ibsen's original nineteenth-century bourgeois environment, short-circuiting it with the new idealist middle-class generations who were at the same time aware of their status quo, reflected elements of the protesters from 2013, many of whom were from the Brazilian middle class. Despite crying out against corruption, their protests also aimed at preserving their own social standing, which they had acquired only recently during Luís Inácio Lula da Silva's government, and which was threatened by the economic crisis that now menaced the country.

Thomas Ostermeier and the Schaubühne in Brazil   101

Yet, strikingly, all of these possible associations with the current Brazilian society, or more generally the political dimension of the Schaubühne's theatre work, were ignored by the press and in discussions of the performances. What instead piqued the interest of a few critics who wrote about them were Ostermeier's technical expertise and his approach to realism. For Márcio Aquiles, the director's production of *An Enemy of the People* 'is a glimpse in the sophisticated techniques of dramatization and acting of the group. The public attending the presentations on the weekend could see an unusual representation style in Brazilian theatre'.[13] Rui Filho, theatre critic and editor of *Antropositivo*, a culture magazine, rejected Ostermeier's 'sociological realism': 'we walk the opposite path [to that of realism]. Because the last decades have witnessed an affirmation of texts increasingly realist in day-to-day scenes, by arguing social representation, we decided to oppose them by using the deconstruction of drama and of realism'.[14] In both comments, both the admiration and rejection of Ostermeier's approach present his new realism almost as an exotic element. This limited perspective among critical observers diverted attention from the multiple political dimensions in the production, and from possible resonances with the political and social scenario in Brazil at that time. Perhaps, the reviews revealed much more about theatre in Brazil than about the production itself. Indeed, only a few Brazilian directors currently work in ways that would come in dialogue with Ostermeier's aesthetics. The Brazilian director Eduardo Tolentino de Araújo and his theatrical group TAPA are a notable exception. Originally from Rio de Janeiro and now based in São Paulo, Tolentino de Araújo and his company pursue a realist aesthetic. In a similar manner to Ostermeier, his main characteristic is his appreciation of the actor's work and for dramaturgy, focusing on Brazilian playwrights as well as classic and modern drama.

Presumably due to the serious problems of social inequality and urban violence that plague most large Brazilian cities, a considerable number of the significant theatre groups in Brazil now act in an increasingly distant manner from traditional models of theatrical creation. These groups in fact place themselves deliberately outside, even against, the very field of theatre, and instead establish an interface with performance, activism and documentary theatre, among other hybrid scenic forms. Their activities are not restricted to creating a text and a show, or any marketable 'product' for the art market. They instead seek direct intervention in the social reality by means of a series of specific actions and events that go beyond an exclusive aesthetic scope. Therefore, many of these contemporary collectives organize their work through artistic and pedagogical residencies in neighbourhoods in the outskirts of the large Brazilian cities; they establish a form of coexistence in drug and prostitution areas, in shelters for the homeless, in psychiatric hospitals, in prisons and similar sites. In these 'coexistence spaces', they then offer workshops, debates and public rehearsals that are open to the audience. The show, therefore, becomes a set of activities that makes the process in itself more significant than any product. The aesthetic outcome does not often respond to the whole artistic, political and human process involved; in fact the shows are often unfinished and temporary. The work of Teatro da Vertigem, the most significant Brazilian group representing this contemporary trend, is a major example. Their production *BR-3*, directed by Antônio Araújo, which premiered in 2006, was awarded the Golden Medal of Best Realization of a Production at the 2011 Prague Quadrennial. It narrates the saga of a family in the period between the late 1950s and the 1990s, investigating, at the same time, the Brazilian identity. As field research, the group visited Brasiléia, in the state of Acre, Brasília, the Brazilian capital, and Brasilândia, a neighbourhood on the outskirts of São Paulo, looking for material for the show in these places whose names contains the word 'Brasil'. Their investigation took two years, and the show was staged for two months on the Tietê riverbed in São Paulo. In an errant manner, the audience sailed on the dirt and bad smell of the river throughout the show.[15]

This rapid overview of contemporary Brazilian theatre evidences an urgent need for artistic practices outside the exclusive scope of stage representation and of artistic production, to insert themselves in the social reality of the country. This perspective has possibly generated lightened perceptions restricted to Ostermeier's realistic aesthetics, limiting the understanding of the political connotations of his theatre. In *The Enemy of the People* there are clearly elements of performativity in the actors' performances and insertions into actual reality, particularly in the now famous fourth act, as the character of Dr Thomas Stockmann reads passages from the political pamphlet *The Coming Insurrection*, and the audience is invited to debate, thereby abandoning the sphere of theatrical representation and invading the space of each spectator's political and personal reality. However, what prevailed in the critics' views was the overall realistic language of representation, even if in its scene design the production sought to transcend realism through Katharina Ziemke's drawings, giving an abstract and symbolic character to the scenography.

Unlike the Schaubühne's trajectory at the time of Peter Stein, where perspectives and practices could be resonate more clearly and links were commonly established between the global south and north, there is currently no such parallel between contemporary Brazilian theatre and the Schaubühne's work from an aesthetic point of view. However, one cannot speak specifically of either influence or rejection of *The Enemy of the People* in Brazil, but perhaps of a silent resonance. One should also consider that, despite having enjoyed positive press reception since his first year at the Schaubühne, the director only briefly visited Brazil and staged only one show.

All that contributes to a very limited perception and understanding of his theatre work in Brazil today. The antagonistic perspectives in the reception of his production in Brazil make him, at the same time, both close and distant from our horizon of expectation. On one hand, his theatre seduces by the power of the images he creates and by the quality of acting. On the other hand, his 'materialistic realism' disconcerts because of his appreciation for narrative and his position against postmodern deconstruction.[16]

Translated by Rômulo Arraes Belém de Alencar

Notes

1 Henry Thorau, *Perspectivas do moderno teatro alemão: estrutura e funcionamento*, trans. Elsmarie Pape (São Paulo: Brasiliense, 1984), 33. All translations from the Brazilian by the author.

2 On Brazilian theatre of the past fifty years, see Eva Paulino Bueno and Robson Corrêa de Camargo (eds), *Brazilian Theater 1970–2010: Essays on History, Politics and Artistic Experimentation* (Jefferson, NC: McFarland, 2015); Aleksandar Dundjerovic and Luiz Fernando Ramos (eds), *Brazilian Collaborative Theatre: Interviews with Directors, Performers and Choreographers* (Jefferson, NC: McFarland, 2017); and Aleksandar Dundjerovic and Luiz Fernando Ramos (eds), *Performing Arts in Brazil* (Madrid: Abada Editores, 2019).

3 Founded on 13 May 1960, the Movimento de Cultura Popular ('Popular Culture Movement') is a non-profit group maintained by the Municipality of Recife (1960–1), then by the government of the State of Pernambuco (1962–4), during the administrations of Miguel Arraes, whose projects aimed at raising people's awareness of their oppressive situation through community action of popular education, with an emphasis on popular culture.

4 The União Nacional dos Estudantes (National Union of Students) is a student organization, founded in 1937. It played an active role at important moments in the history of Brazil in the twentieth century, particularly during the military dictatorship (1964–85).

5 Uta Atzpodien, 'Gerações Substituídas', *Folha de S. Paulo*, 28 May 2000.

6 Ibid.

7 Fábio Cypriano, '*A morte de Danton*: Viver é nada mais que teatro' (*Danton's Death*: Living is nothing but theatre), and interview, 'Ostermeier dialoga com o tempo' ('Ostermeier dialogues with time'). *Folha de S.Paulo*, 21 July 2001.

8 Antônio Araújo, 'Ostermeier traz Ibsen ao século XXI' ('Ostermeier brings Ibsen to the 21st century'), *Teatrojornal*, 20 April 2011, http://teatrojornal. com.br/blog/2011/04/para-antonio-araujo-ostermeier-traz-ibsen-ao-seculo-xxi/#more-3920 (accessed 5 June 2011).

9 See also Boenisch and Ostermeier, *The Theatre of Thomas Ostermeier*, 108–9.
10 André Singer, 'Brasil junho de 2013: classes e ideologias cruzadas', *Novos Estudos CEBRAP* 97 (2013): 27.
11 A Brazilian political party founded in 1980 and linked to left and centre-left movements. Its origin was the merger between the union movements of the state of São Paulo and former left-wing militants in Brazil.
12 A centre-right Brazilian political party, founded in 1988 by former São Paulo state governor Mario Covas. It emerged from the combination of social democracy, Christian democracy and economic and social liberalism.
13 Marcio Aquiles, 'Companhia teatral alemã Schaubühne enfatiza tom político de Ibsen' ('German theatre company Schaubühne emphasizes Ibsen's political tone'), *Folha de S.Paulo*, 30 September 2013.
14 Ruy Filho, 'Thomas Ostermeier: a face de um teatro do presente, pelo encontro com a manifestação real' ('The face of a theatre of the present, by the encounter with the manifestation of real'), *Revista Antro Positivo* 8 (2013): 11 and 14.
15 See Dundjerovic and Ramos (eds), *Performing Arts in Brazil*.
16 This article was supported by a research grant from the Capes-Humboldt Research Fellowship Program, which allowed me to carry out research on Thomas Ostermeier's theatre at the Universität Hildesheim during 2019 and 2020.

9

Confronting the Present:
Thomas Ostermeier's Post-conceptual
Regietheater

Peter M. Boenisch

Thomas Ostermeier's work as a theatre director is not characterized by a readily identifiable signature, comparable to the stage aesthetics of directors such as Robert Wilson, Katie Mitchell or Frank Castorf. Instead, he finds individual approaches for each play he directs, all of which, however, disclose a distinctly Brechtian demand for 'realism', prompted by Ostermeier's expressly political impetus: his attempt to use theatre as a means to disclose political complexities, and thereby to demonstrate that these political conditions can be changed. Following the trajectory of Ostermeier's directing work over the past two decades, this chapter argues that one can detect a parallel development of both his practical working methodology and the continuing refinement of an original aesthetic form of 'contemporary realism'. I will identify three distinct phases of what Marvin Carlson in his chapter in this volume (Chapter 5) calls 'Ostermeier realism': it developed from the 'in yer face-realism' of the director's early years, via the 'neo(n)-realism' of his initial Ibsen-productions such as *Nora* and *Hedda Gabler*, to then culminate in what I shall describe as the 'reflexive realism' of his more recent work. I will align this development with the notion of a contemporary 'post-conceptual theatre',[1] bringing together its characteristic 'return to the social' with the legacy of performative, postdramatic *mise en scène*.

Towards a reflexive interpretation of society through theatre

In accordance with the characteristics of postdramatic theatre as outlined by Hans-Thies Lehmann, Ostermeier's productions open up the closed fictional world of the drama.[2] Even the director's most realist work acknowledges the theatral frame, never pretending to be anything else but a theatre performance that happens in front of the audience's eyes. His *Regie* thereby produces a dialectic effect, which perforates the fictional framework by simultaneously emphasizing the ontological reality of the theatre production itself and amplifying present realities outside the theatre.[3] Hence, Ostermeier does not intervene, in the tradition of postmodern deconstruction, from *outside* the world of the play, but on the contrary, right from its very immanent core. Whereas continental European *Regietheater*, even in its postmodern, deconstructive mode that dominated the Western stages of the 1990s and earlier 2000s, had still remained situated within a hermeneutic paradigm that concentrated on the content of the play, even if only to critique or subvert it, Ostermeier's theatre stands paradigmatic for a contemporary generation of such post-conceptual theatre directors, who do not renounce the value of fictional dramatic play. They engage with playtexts and take their narrative seriously again, doing away with postmodern irony and the attitude of a superior standpoint of bohemian rejection. These directors hence use the formal language of *post*-postmodern, and also *post*-postdramatic theatre for an earnest interrogation both of the dramatic canon and, more widely, of the place of theatre as a cultural institution within our current globalized society of the twenty-first century.

As I suggested, writing back in 2008, for Ostermeier, theatre had always been, above all, a means to scrutinize the 'structures of feeling' of the society around him, in accordance with the productive term from Raymond Williams's cultural materialism:

> Ostermeier was never after a 'modern' interpretation of a classic but, first and foremost, after an interpretation of the society around him. [...] Instead of infusing a given text with present-day material, that contemporary context in fact became the main text, and the scripted characters and narratives essentially served as the context in which to articulate an urgent analysis of contemporary moral and mental situations.[4]

This impetus of attempting to comprehend our contemporary world through the stage worlds of classical playtexts – something very different from the clichéd *Regietheater* approach of 'putting a Shakespearean character in modern clothes' – remains a central driving force behind Ostermeier's theatre to the present day. In fact, it has become even more prominent in his productions since 2008, from his signature *Hamlet* to the 2015 *Richard III*, from *An Enemy of the People* in 2012 to Schnitzler's *Professor Bernhardi* from 2016, on to his stage adaptations of Didier Eribon's autoethnographic study *Returning to Reims* and of Édouard Louis's novel *A History of Violence*, which he directed in 2017 and 2018 respectively.

Yet, as variously noted in other chapters, already in his early years as leader of the Baracke, Ostermeier had used the term 'sociological theatre' to explain

Confronting the Present 107

his aim to make theatre in order to 'observe the reality that surrounds us – the reality of human behaviour, in all its ambiguity and contradictions – and to find forms of expressing it on stage'.[5] This neo-Brechtian quest for theatral realism initially manifested itself as what might be termed the 'in yer face'-realism of Ostermeier's work at the Baracke between 1996 and 1999, and in the early years of his Schaubühne tenure. It is exemplified by his productions of Mark Ravenhill's *Shopping and Fucking* at the Baracke, his debut production at Schaubühne, Lars Norén's *Personenkreis 3.1* (*Human Circle 3.1*), right to the gritty realism of his *Woyzeck* (2003). This first phase of the director's work towards a new theatral realism was largely predicated on staging new playwriting. His subsequent move to Ibsen, the paradigmatic playwright of nineteenth-century middle-class realism, followed the same logic of a 'sociological realism'. Where, with a genuinely leftist attitude, his earlier work had focused on the disprivileged, on the 'working class' and underdogs of society, and sought to give those who lack representation a presence on stage, his work then shifted, as he himself expressed it, speaking in 2006, more towards 'the reality of people of this age, of this class, and it's maybe much more interesting than the realism of the outcast because it is a realism that directly speaks to the people in the audience'.[6] This middle-class 'neo(n)realism' blended fictional realities with recognizable resonances of the every-day present in Berlin of the early 2000s.[7] Ostermeier sought to show that distinct times and spaces may resonate with each other: that the drama of Ibsen's bourgeois protagonists still takes place in living-rooms in present-day Berlin, and that equally Shakespeare's tragedies may function as an 'outside eye' whose perspective may offer a distancing otherness to our everyday experience, and thereby may contribute to our insight, recognition and understanding of contemporary society.

With his neorealist period, Ostermeier thus turned to his own generation, and that of his new audiences – the generation of those who had come to success during the dynamic post-unification years in 1990s Germany. Even before the 2008 financial crisis, though, their energetic hedonism had begun to give way to feelings of loss, of a new *Angst*, of stagnation. Germany found itself paralysed by an economic crisis and an empty public purse, resulting in the infamous 'Agenda 2010' of social-democrat chancellor Gerhard Schröder: a fundamental reform, if not the end of the welfare state and social-security systems that used to define West German society since 1945. It was this climate of depression that underpinned his resonant reworkings of middle-class classics, in particular the (still ongoing) series of Ibsen and Shakespeare productions, and his productions of US classics of the twentieth century, from O'Neill's *Mourning Becomes Electra* (2006) and Williams's *Cat on a Hot Tin Roof* (2007) to Lillian Hellman's *Little Foxes* (2014). Over the years of

108   *The Schaubühne Berlin under Thomas Ostermeier*

global crisis and austerity, the political resonances of Ostermeier's exploration of these middle-class realities would expand far beyond the Berlin-Mitte living rooms, now reflecting global problems and the effects of a global crisis of the dominant capitalist world order.

Intensified games with exposed theatrality

At this point, signified by his production of *Hamlet* (2008), a third phase of his work had already become tangible: precisely that of his 'reflexive realism'. For Ostermeier, theatre became a key opportunity to stage essays revolving around this crisis, society's discontents, and its effect on people. Rather than observing an experiment – the 'laboratory' metaphor that had applied to the 'neo(n)realist' productions such as *Hedda Gabler* and *Cat on a Hot Tin Roof* – and even the initial articulation of *Hamlet* back in 2008[8] – Ostermeier now further elaborated his use, within the singular space of the stage, of configurations of different realities, which in their dialectical collision invited various layers of recognition – something I have elsewhere explained drawing on Slavoj Zizek's concept of the 'parallax perspective':[9] a constant shift in our perception between unsynchronizable, incompatible points of view, in this case that of everyday reality on the one hand, and the fictional world of the play on the other hand, between which the spectators' attention constantly switches, without either of the two being afforded a hierarchical privilege. This intensified play with a more prominently exposed theatrality (which had been underpinning Ostermeier's work from the outset, even during his 'Baracke' time), his play with a fluid shifting between the worlds of representation (fiction), of theatral presentation (performance) and the present (the time of the theatre event/audience/everyday life) had found its initial manifestation already a year before *Hamlet*, in the director's 2007 stage adaptation of Rainer Werner Fassbinder's 1979 movie *Die Ehe der Maria Braun* (*The Marriage of Maria Braun*), which he originally created away from the Schaubühne at Kammerspiele Munich, and which Ostermeier himself considers a significant milestone production in the development of his aesthetics.

Over a number of years, Ostermeier directed a series of productions at Munich – including Herbert Achternbusch's *Susn* (2009, still in the Kammerspiele repertoire at the time of writing in spring 2020) – which had shown a more experimental, more postdramatic approach to his *mise en scène*. It was here where he also met new collaborators who would eventually become key members of his Schaubühne production team, such as designer Nina Wetzel and video artist Sebastien Dupouey, both of whom had originally worked at the Kammerspiele. *Maria Braun* became the blueprint for the

Confronting the Present 109

more pronounced, playful theatrality that fully constituted Ostermeier's new critical, 'negative' realism, as one may term it, with both Hegelian and Adornoan echoes. Designer Nina Wetzel had created a 1950s-style interior, with groups of distinct period chairs, sofas and coffee-tables spread across the room, surrounded by curtains on all sides. Brigitte Hobmeier and, in the 2014 revival, Ursina Lardi in the role of Maria Braun remained the only constant character, and the production's singular focal point. Four male actors shared among them the more than twenty other roles from the movie, including female characters such as Maria's mother, as well as Maria's black US Army lover, whom she murders after her husband, who was believed dead, returns from wartime captivity. A simple sign – a periwig, a pair of glasses or a jumper – indicated their various characters, allowing quick switches between the roles they played, while the performers never renounced an attitude of playful 'borrowing' of the characters, performing, for instance, the female characters, not as 'drag' travesty, but in their own, male voices. They also reconfigured the space for the fast sequence of scenes, where chairs and tables served as sole props that turned the scene into a car, a restaurant, a prison or a train carriage.

This multi-roling and exposed theatricality of a singular, dynamic space prepared the ground for *Hamlet* in the following year. Compared with Jan Pappelbaum's filmic 'neo(n)-realism' of the earlier phase, which would still continue to characterize the lavish living-room realism of Lars Norén's *Demons*, staged by Ostermeier in 2010 (thereby demonstrating that these three phases overlap and display a continuous, fluid development), the sets for *Hamlet* and the following Shakespeare productions as well as later Ibsen's (not least *An Enemy of the People* from 2012), went much beyond the resonant mimetic replication of twenty-first century realities in the scenography. Whereas Ostermeier – who, as both Jitka Pelechová and Benjamin Fowler expand in their chapters (Chapters 6 and 11), had also been greatly influenced by Meyerholdian biomechanics as well as by Stanislavskian psycho-physicality – had earlier employed the kinetic energy of the performing body to insert momentary ruptures into the living-room realism of his *mises en scène*, now the otherness was introduced by the theatral frame of Pappelbaum's sets, such as *Hamlet*'s empty, soil covered playing field, or the black box set of *An Enemy of the People*. The latter was mirrored in Ostermeier's 2016 *Professor Bernhardi*, where Pappelbaum introduced the corresponding white box empty cube, resonating with the play's hospital setting. Once more, the detailed locations (a ward, or Bernhardi's office) were just written on the back of the set, and indicated by both painted and a mere handful of physical props.

I have already referred to this approach earlier as a 'negative realism': it avoids straightforward representation, semiotic efficiency and functionality.

110 *The Schaubühne Berlin under Thomas Ostermeier*

Instead, it instils an 'inefficient', and hence 'negative', excess of theatral play into the realist parameters of the stage representation. It exploits the core theatral dynamics of meaning, of corporeality and of affect, and their mutual reverberations, in order to puncture the surface of mimetic representation. At the same time, it enriches the theatral communication with the audience – and opens up the shared theatral space, precisely, towards reflection. The perceptual ambiguity, which Elisa Leroy in her chapter (Chapter 7) has outlined as a central aspect of Lars Eidinger's performance as *Hamlet*, and which was even more intensified in the later *Richard III*, outlined this dimension of reflexivity that Ostermeier's more recent productions have more and more brought to the foreground.

In contrast to a postmodern, deconstructive approach of *Regietheater*, Ostermeier did not seek to capitalize on the inherent textual openness, the gaps, ambiguities and inconsistencies within the classical texts of Shakespeare or Ibsen. The deconstructive approach to staging playtexts had emphasized an understanding of playfulness as irony, equating the challenge to the hierarchically superior status of the canonical playtext with not taking it too seriously. The self-reflexive attitude of postmodern theatre, however, led, in its most extreme cases, to an abstraction of the stage, to its closure and withdrawal from wider, non-aesthetic issues beyond the theatre world, or beyond internal art discourses. In Ostermeier's approach, once again, the perspective seems reversed: the fictional worlds themselves open up a constellation which exposes and reflects the gaps, ambiguities and inconsistencies – of our present, crisis-ridden reality. They, and not the interpretation of dramatic literature, are the 'ends' of Ostermeier's productions; the playtexts serve as, almost even contingent, means. The director thus exploits, exemplarily in his *Richard III*, the theatral potential of the Elizabethan convention of the Shakespearean 'vice character' to infuse the stage world around Richard Gloucester with a resonating, contemporary flavour of resentment and hatred, of politicians who appeal to low instincts, as well as having others taking over the initiative in leading on planning and ultimately executing the evil deeds. Richard's 'evilness' was here, in fact, almost more reflected onto him by the active, willing part those around him took on, not least Buckingham: it was their willing complicity, their obedience that knew no empathy, their own desire for power, which propelled Richard's rise in the first part of Ostermeier's production.[10] Just as the audience detected the echoes with contemporary populist leaders, the purpose-built, intimate theatre space of Pappelbaum's Schaubühne-'Globe' helped at reflecting the recognition back at the spectators, too: Richard's lure extended onto the audience, and their desires, their, *our* seduction and complicity with Richard, and perhaps the real life seduction and complicity with those who tempt us

Confronting the Present

with similar fascination, with similar promises. In this way, *Richard* continued, in a more refined and theatralized manner, the direct reflexive engagement of the audience we had previously witnessed in *An Enemy of the People* and its notorious audience discussion scene. With these productions, Ostermeier's *Regietheater* no longer presented itself as a primarily hermeneutic activity of literary interpretation but as a reflexive act in itself. Its function was no longer the proposition of a certain interpretation, nor the deconstruction and critical unearthing of a playtext, but the strategic deployment of the theatral dynamics in the service of insight, recognition and reflection with regard to our present societal, economic and political situation. Through the rhythmic structuring of times and spaces, the deployment of the materiality of 'heavy' bodies and objects (to use a term from Lehmann's postdramatic vocabulary), and the strategic interweaving of narration, representation and presentation, Ostermeier's reflexive *Regie* had shifted from the representation, the theatrical re-enactment of a playtext, to its re-play, and thereby its full 'actualization' in the Hegelian sense of the term.

Reflecting on the new fascism through theatre

Ostermeier continued this interrogation of contemporary 'structures of feeling', which were by now full of populism, resentment and the rejection of anything 'foreign', with his 2016 production of *Professor Bernhardi*. Arthur Schnitzler's play from 1912 portrays the anti-Semitic campaign against the eponymous doctor after he prevented a priest from performing the last rites on a dying patient who was, due to her heavy drugs, blissfully unaware of her imminent death. Ostermeier, even more clearly than in his *Richard*, emphasized the resonances – not least with the emergence and outright racist witch hunts staged by the fascist AfD party in twenty-first-century Germany. This was all the more true of his following production, in 2018, of Ödön von Horvath's *Italian Night* from 1930, where the local branch of the social-democratic party celebrates its Italian-themed summer party, downplaying the danger of the arriving fascists, who in the final moment of the play storm their party. In particular Laurenz Laufenberg as the nameless 'Fascist' gave a chilling portrait of a young, elegant and seductive follower of the nationalist movement; his seduction of Anna, actually the girlfriend of the young social-democrat Martin, resonated with the seduction of Queen Anne by Richard, as in both cases repulsion turns into the fascination of evil. Ostermeier took great care not to present clichéd caricatures of the fascist populists, and instead reserved vitriolic sarcasm for the portrayal of the social-democratic party's local officials, who ignore the warnings of their young comrade Martin. Where

112   *The Schaubühne Berlin under Thomas Ostermeier*

this ignorant complacency here still silently propels the rise to power of fascist totalitarianism, the third piece of Ostermeier's trilogy, Horvath's 1937 play *Jugend ohne Gott* (*Godless Youth*), shows the lack of empathy of the self-interested masses, who just close their eyes, once democracy has been lost. Jörg Hartmann, who had already played Bernhardi in the Schnitzler, returned as the history teacher who in vain attempts to counter the spread of racism among his pupils.

Where *Hamlet* and *Richard III*, then *Enemy of the People, Professor Bernhardi* and *Jugend ohne Gott* introduced Ostermeier's reflexive realism as two series of interlinked productions, which in many ways offered complementing mirror perspectives on shared thematic concerns while also disclosing echoes in their theatrical strategies, another pair of productions, created at the Schaubühne in 2017 and 2018, went beyond the reliance on dramatic playtexts from other periods to further examine the present rise of the new populist racist supremacy and anti-democratic nationalism. Ostermeier's stage adaptation of Didier Eribon's *Returning to Reims* and of Édouard Louis's *History of Violence* (the latter translated into German as *Im Herz der Gewalt*, echoing Conrad's *Heart of Darkness*) expressed the director's urgent need for a further theatral reflection in particular on the swing of the working classes from their traditional left-wing allegiance to the very opposite end of the political spectrum – the right-wing fascism of Marine Le Pen in France and of the German AfD.

In Eribon's book, originally published in France in 2009 but only appearing in German translation in 2016 following the rise of the new fascist parties in Germany, the French gay sociologist charts his return to his hometown of Reims following the death of his father. In an autobiographical narrative, interwoven with a sociological analysis of the situation, he remembers his 'coming out' in the provincial, homophobe environment of the 1960s, and his subsequent flight to Paris, to a bohemian world of academia, culture and opera, where he joined the circle of his mentors Michel Foucault and Pierre Bourdieu, thinking little about those he left behind in the province. The main strand of the book is then dedicated to Eribon's present confrontation with precisely the regional *milieu* he had previously abandoned and refused to return to; further, to the guilt about this flight, and the question of how his own, personal biography may contain some explanation for why the formerly largely communist regions today have become such a stronghold of the Front National. Ostermeier's scenic adaptation focused partly on the book's narrative, but engaged most of all with themes and open questions brought up in Eribon's narrative. In an ingenious ploy, the director set his production of the sociological essay in a sound studio, where an actress was shown recording the voiceover for a documentary based on Eribon's book. For most of the first

Confronting the Present

hour, the audience thus watched Nina Hoss reading the commentary to the film we watched simultaneously on the large screen above the stage – a film which Ostermeier and his video collaborator Sebastian Dupouey had shot together with Eribon, repeating with him once more the actual journey described in the book, from the TGV travel back to Reims, to the city's local neighbourhoods. Eventually, the film followed Eribon right to the afternoon coffee with his actual mother in her apartment, where we see them browsing through old photographs, just as they do in the book. Over time, this strand got more and more interspersed with the actress's discussion with the characters of the film director and the sound engineer on stage. Thereby, a fictionalized, scripted dramatic layer of actual reflection is introduced. Their conversations pointed towards some links, but they also thematized the differences to the current situation in Germany. Eventually, their discussion revolved around the question left out by Eribon's sociological perspective: what is the consequence for us? What is to be done?

In the final section of the production, Nina Hoss, the famous Schaubühne ensemble actress also known from various arthouse movies and for her role in the TV series *Homeland*, came to mirror, and extend, Eribon's narrative with her own story. She now told the story of her own (equally real) father, also born, like Eribon's father, in 1929. Willi Hoss was a factory worker at the Daimler Benz car factory, and an active union leader, who very early fought for equal rights and equal pay for the foreign *Gastarbeiter*.[11] Hoss later became one of the founders of the German Green party, for which he also became one of its first MPs, before eventually leaving Germany and emigrating to the Brazilian rain forest, where until his death in 2003 he worked with indigenous tribes on saving this ecological spine of our climate. Nina Hoss shows the fictitious film director, and by extension us in the audience, some film footage and photographs from her late father's work in the rain forest – thereby ending the production with a positive counter-narrative to Eribon's story, which had left its readers with a frustrated and frustrating analysis.[12]

With Nina and Willi Hoss's true biography, Ostermeier's production, in line with other post-conceptual contemporary theatre work, draws on real events, and 'authentic' narratives from the performers' own biographies, in order to ensure its efficacy. Yet, Ostermeier's 'reflexive realism' remains sceptical about the privilege often afforded to such almost fetishized notions of reality and authenticity. While other postconceptual directors blend the stage world and the reality beyond the theatre, or use reportage, verbatim and documentary formats – one may think of the work of Milo Rau and Yael Ronen, both of whom Ostermeier had invited to work at his Schaubühne – he himself remains committed to staging fictional narratives, albeit in his characteristically 'reflexive' way. In a world where 'reality' is precisely what is

114   *The Schaubühne Berlin under Thomas Ostermeier*

being fabricated on the basis of interpretations and manipulations of data and 'fake' facts, he continues to embrace the dialectical, speculative grasp of the seemingly more conventional and, allegedly, by its nature, 'fake' form of dramatic fiction. Hoss's narrative was therefore carefully embedded within a rigorously constructed aesthetic frame. Building on core Brechtian parameters, Ostermeier's postconceptual realism insists on the value of such a dramatic frame in producing insight and recognition, precisely in the contemporary world of mediated, 'fake' realities, and omnipresent self-performance. It is not the – in any case contestable – boundary between 'reality' and 'fiction' that is key for this understanding of realism, but its effect, resulting from the power of theatrality in provoking processes of thinking – as implied in the shared etymology of the words 'theatre' and 'theory'. The very act of 'looking on', and being focused and concentrated through the process of theatral mediation, in front of and together with a community of other spectators in the audience, produces the space for a common reflection to emerge.

Ostermeier's companion production in this pairing would once again further refine this proposition. Just as Eribon offered a personal interrogation of an exemplary regional working-class background, where a gay coming-out had resulted in a flight to the global metropolis and affiliation with the metropolitan *bohème*, Edouard Louis tells in his novels a similar autobiographic story. In *Im Herzen der Gewalt*, his protagonist is chatted up, in the early hours of Christmas day, by a foreigner on the street. They have a wild night together, yet the next morning the protagonist accidentally finds his mobile phone and iPad in the jacket of his one-night-stand lover. The accusation escalates, the foreigner threatens the protagonist with a gun, rapes him and strangles him until he blacks out. When reporting the assault at the hospital and the police station, the protagonist is confronted with institutional racism, while equally facing his own racist prejudices about his liaison with the foreigner, wondering whether the theft had been premeditated from the outset. Louis's novel reconstructs this traumatic autobiographical experience as narrated by the protagonist's sister, who had remained in the provincial hometown and who now tells this episode to her husband, with the narrator offering occasional objections against her perspective. Louis thereby introduced into the form of his narrative the disjunct between the new cosmopolitan middle-class and their disavowed roots in the provincial region.

In Ostermeier's stage version, we witnessed an entirely theatral re-telling of the event. The stage was separated into a marked out central area, reminiscent of a boxing ring, where the narrated, remembered events took place, while the narrators (such as the sister and her husband) sat in the

Confronting the Present

surrounding outside. A handful of props easily reconfigured the central area from street to living room to hospital ward, always in the same, bright neonworking light, while the sister, the policemen or a homeless tramp who passed by, added their commenting perspectives from the side-lines. Once again, except for the two central characters of the victim and the stranger, the two other actors shared all these other characters between them. They also used mobile phone cameras to produce close-up images for live projection at the back of the stages, while speaking their commentary and narrative into microphones. A drummer was sitting stage-left and accentuated the action with rhythmic percussion, as previously in *Richard III*. Occasionally, choreographed movement sequences interrupted the narration, reminiscent of a strategy Ostermeier had used especially in his early work. For the pivotal scene of the rape, Ostermeier then directly returned to his visceral 'in yer face' tactics, showing the rape acted out realistically, in full front of the audience, blood streaming down the actors' legs – thus echoing the central scene of his 1998 production of Ravenhill's *Shopping and Fucking*, exactly two decades prior to this production. There, Ostermeier had staged the moment, late in the play, where the call-boy Gary invites Mark to penetrate him with a knife. While the playtext cuts to the next scene, Ostermeier showed their deadly sex full-on, in a wordless, carefully choreographed scene that regularly led audience members to faint.

Right at this moment 'at the heart of violence', Ostermeier – after having broken down the 'fourth wall' from the beginning of the production – now also broke down the affective 'safety curtain'. Paradoxically, having being made aware of the fabricated 'as if' of theatre, the acted rape scene nevertheless affected us as spectators even more. The multiple simultaneous layers of narrative representation and theatral presentation made the audience observe the events, and follow the story, while being directly involved in the theatrical situation as an acknowledged audience, and therefore less able to distantiate their perception from what they were witnessing right in front of them. The implicit or explicit monologic nature of most of the scenes, their exposed narration rather than the dramatic representation of the story, foregrounded the processing, the drama of making sense, the tragedy of coming to terms – thus the reflection, instead of presence, absorption, identification. If at all, the spectatorial position directly identified with the narrative's intent to comment, to try and understand, to reflect and come to terms. The exposed intimacy of the pivotal scene, and not least also its symbolic value standing in for a trauma pointing towards a much wider deadlock in our contemporary society, gave this entirely mediated form of a 'negative' realism its cruel, brutal efficacy. As Ostermeier's exploration of realism had come full circle here, and he combined reflection with the 'in yer face' shock of the *punctum*,

116   *The Schaubühne Berlin under Thomas Ostermeier*

the affective impact intensified the urge for reflection. Ostermeier's reflective realism may thus in fact unlock a level of insight into contemporary social realities, including psychic realities, which a mere imitation, a spectacular rather than speculative attempt at replicating reality through conventional stage-realism, would be unable to tap into.

These two strands characterize Ostermeier's most recent directorial work at the Schaubühne; in 2020, he staged, with Edouard Louis himself performing, the solo *Qui a tué mon père*, about the narrator's mixed feelings towards his proletarian, right-wing, but now terminally ill father, who never accepted the narrator's homosexuality – thus another variant of the *Returning to Reims* scenario. On the one hand, Ostermeier deploys canonical playtexts – with all their baggage and burden – as an opportunity to stimulate common reflection, a shared 'theatral thinking' that may initiate an 'interpretation of the world'. As suggested earlier, playtexts are thereby actualized; they become an 'actual' signifying practice, and even more so, a concrete social practice, where they may serve as a first step for the audience to recognize, reflect on and take action in other situations, too. On the other hand, as the productions of Eribon's and Louis's writings demonstrate, such an 'interpretation of the world' may in the face of the crisis of European humanism and democracy aim not for finding answers, but for insisting on the right to ask questions about this world we are living in, at all.

Insisting on the common of theatre in a disjunctive society

Across the three phases in the development of his reflexive, political realist theatre aesthetic, Ostermeier's theatre has displayed the 'return to the social' characteristic for contemporary, post-conceptual theatre; hence the theatre after the dominant paradigm of postmodernism. His work as a director – and, as Ramona Mosse's chapter (Chapter 3) has suggested, also his tenure as the Schaubühne's artistic director – ought to be read as an attempt at situating theatre within the contemporary socio-political and cultural-economic context as a practice, and as an institution, which engenders direct practical and thereby political agency by addressing and challenging the audience's attitude. Ostermeier's enquiry has extended from his original intention of understanding contemporary society at large to a reflection on the role, and the potential, of contemporary theatre in the present global and, for European theatre, post-bourgeois context of theatre-making.[13] Both the stage, in his work as theatre director, and also the institution of the Schaubühne at large, have offered Ostermeier a rich medium for a persistent interrogation and renegotiation of the place of theatre in an ever more disjunctive society that

Confronting the Present 117

no longer maintains its strong 'middle' core, where participation still was possible for 'the many', albeit at the expense of the exclusion of minorities from the hegemonic centre of enlightened middle-class bourgeois culture. Instead, our globalized societies pitch various social milieus and subsystems ruthlessly against each other, so that – despite what the term 'globalization' may suggest on its surface – no experience of a shared world, of a 'common community', is possible anymore. The dominant neoliberalized life-experience has become one of a 'society of singularities', as German sociologist Andreas Reckwitz has suggested in his important study.[14] The idea of 'community' itself, meanwhile, has become fully reified, not least in certain brand names, or behavioural formats of cosmopolitan 'hipster'-dom.

It is this context to which the contemporary reflexive realism of Thomas Ostermeier's theatre responds. When, still during his Baracke time, Ostermeier proclaimed in an interview that 'I believe that one's view of the world may change after a good night at the theatre',[15] he was never as naïve as to assume that theatre, that his own productions, would directly intervene in politics and change the world. Instead, his work at the Schaubühne has shown his trajectory of using the stage as a laboratory to observe human behaviour in the society around us, as if under the magnifying perspective of a microscope. His sociological – and hence expressly not psychological theatre – seeks to trigger not identification but recognition, in an Althusserian sense, and hence a reflexive mode of spectating, which – as Brecht would not tire of emphasizing – is not at all the opposite of entertainment, but on the contrary true entertainment: the joy and pleasure of insight, of recognition and of a reflection of those opportunities for action, even if this insight may become painful and almost unbearable, as in the culminating moment of *Im Herzen der Gewalt*. Ostermeier's theatre aims for such insight, for the persistent quest to understand by asking questions and for communication about these questions. He thus counters the present singularization with his unfaltering insistence on a societal 'common', and on the ability of 'communication', as they are embodied in the very medium of theatre itself. The artistic approach of his stage work with actors, as much as his offering, as artistic director, of the theatre institution as a public forum to ask such questions and thereby position itself at the core of a contemporary public sphere, resists, above all, the commodification of theatrical experience in individualized, singularized, 'interactive' performance.

Ostermeier's reflexive realism thus repositions the operation of the theatral 'as if': it no longer seeks to assert a fictional dramatic reality, but employs dramatic and narrative prompts to act, in the act of theatre as an event, as if there were still some form of a relational totality, as if there were still a 'common' ground of community in the contemporary, singularized

118 *The Schaubühne Berlin under Thomas Ostermeier*

world. The stage becomes the very place on which to project an utopia that claims such a relation in the act of coming together in order to think and reflect in common, sharing our affective involvement. Ostermeier's theatre claims such a horizon of commonality and communication as key ingredients of a post-Habermasian 'public sphere' of the twenty-first century. The post-conceptual reflexivity of his political theatre work reflects, in a post-bourgeois cultural context, on the original radical impulses and on the actual achievements of this 'bourgeois' European cultural institution within the present context of global complexity, including its legacy of the dramatic canon. In his biographical as much as his artistic trajectory over the past decades, Ostermeier has come from rejection to reflection, while avoiding the dead ends of ironic subversion. The texts he stages – whether Ibsen's, Shakespeare's or Schnitzler's playtexts, or Louis's novels and Eribon's sociological writing – are no longer objects to be staged, but they become projects that open up spaces for critical reflection and for shared public understanding – or, perhaps phrased more modestly: for shared public communication – at the very moment where they meet, in performance, the present of the audience.

Notes

1 I am adapting the terms of 'the contemporary' and 'the post-conceptual' from Peter Osborne, *The Postconceptual Condition* (London and New York: Verso), 2018.

2 Hans-Thies Lehmann, *Postdramatic Theatre* (Abingdon and New York: Routledge, 2006), 31.

3 See Peter M. Boenisch, *Directing Scenes and Senses: The Thinking of Regie* (Manchester: Manchester University Press, 2015), 176–88.

4 Peter M. Boenisch, 'Thomas Ostermeier: Mission Neo(n)realism and a Theatre of Actors and Authors', in *Contemporary European Theatre Directors*, eds Maria M. Delgado and Dan Rebellato (Abingdon and New York: Routledge, 2010), 346f.

5 Peter M. Boenisch and Thomas Ostermeier (eds), *The Theatre of Thomas Ostermeier* (Abingdon and New York: Routledge, 2016), 22f.

6 Ibid., 69.

7 I introduced this term in Boenisch, 'Mission Neo(n)realism'.

8 See Elisa Leroy's chapter in this volume (Chapter 7).

9 See Boenisch, *Directing Scenes and Senses*, chapters 7 and 8.

10 For me, it was more the second half of the production that focused, as Benjamin Fowler suggests in the discussion in his chapter, on a somewhat problematic interrogation of 'the masculinist project of self-definition and self-exploration' (see Chapter 11, p. 155).

Confronting the Present 119

11 The migrants invited to come and work in post-war Germany – despite making with their factory labour a huge contribution to West Germany's *Wirtschaftswunder* economy – and even their children and grandchildren who were born and raised in Germany, were refused citizen rights until 2002, leading to their exclusion from education as well as their ghettoization in the country.

12 This section was adapted for the French version of this production, which premiered at Théâtre de la Ville, with Irène Jacob playing this role, and for the Italian version, created at Piccolo Teatro Milano, with Sonia Bergamasco (both in 2019).

13 I suggest that this specific 'post-bourgeois' context of his theatre-making results in the differences to the context in the global south, which Igor de Almeida Silva described from a Brazilian perspective in the preceding chapter in this volume.

14 Andreas Reckwitz, *The Society of Singularities* (Cambridge: Polity, 2020).

15 Thomas Ostermeier, 'Ob es so oder so oder anders geht! Ein Gespräch', *Theater Heute* Yearbook (1999), 76.

Part Three

The Schaubühne's Experiments Across Forms and Borders: Towards a New Realism

10

Theatre Towards the Liberation of Thinking: Experimenting with Realism(s) at the Schaubühne, 2000–10

Jens Hillje

Both Thomas Ostermeier and I come from Bavaria, as did Bertolt Brecht. I believe that this is the reason why we both have felt, from our earliest youth when we went to school together, a strong connection with Brecht's theatre, and with the specific humanist ideal his theatre was based on: the idea that human beings want to change, themselves as well as the society in which they live. Art, and not least theatre, is a means of a shared experience of life as it is, in order to reflect on and critique the existing conditions, and to see how one may change them to enable everyone to live a better life. This is certainly a very political and progressive idea of theatre, which takes the ideal of the equality of all human beings seriously, and uses the stage as a medium to explore how this promise may be realized. When we then got the chance to start and make our own theatre, first at the Baracke from 1996, then at the Schaubühne from 2000, we took this Brechtian imperative to heart. We understood 'the mission' of our theatre (as we expressed it back then in our manifesto, reprinted in this book) to be in showing how things really are. Therefore, our aim, and at times our struggle, has been to arrive at a correct analysis of the political, social, economic and cultural situation of our society, as an integral part of our theatre-making. This persistent discourse about the society we live in went hand in hand with interrogating the artistic means most suitable to tell stories about our society, in order to achieve, in the Brechtian sense, an effect of insight that we would arrive at together with our audiences. Our theatre thus followed Brecht in conceiving theatre as a medium that, at any moment, addresses its spectators as citizens of our society. In this chapter, I shall reflect on some key stages of these interwoven discourses on political analysis and aesthetic development as they drove our work at the Schaubühne between 2000 and 2010, while I was head dramaturg and a member of the theatre's artistic direction, alongside Thomas Ostermeier and, until 2005, Sasha Waltz and Jochen Sandig.

An active dramaturgic politics of making theatre

Coming to the Schaubühne in the autumn of 1999, Thomas Ostermeier and I brought along this idea, and also the concrete practice, of making theatre that takes its political mission seriously, which we had tested for three years at the Baracke. This included not least our exhilarating discovery of contemporary British drama, with Sarah Kane and Mark Ravenhill being the two playwrights who had been particularly important for us up to this point. As we had become engaged more deeply with their work, we made the for us quite surprising discovery that, for Sarah Kane, Georg Büchner had been an important inspiration, while for Mark Ravenhill indeed Brecht himself was a key influence; his *Shopping and Fucking* had emerged from a close dialogue with *The Threepenny Opera*, and in addition with the fairy tales of the German Brothers Grimm. Through our work at the Baracke we had furthermore come to establish a link to the Royal Court Theatre in London; there, we discovered that the theatre's founder George Devine had travelled to Berlin, seen the work of the Berliner Ensemble and met Brecht and Helene Weigel, just a short time before Brecht's death. He was then instrumental in facilitating a first, very influential visit of the Berliner Ensemble to London, in 1956. Moreover, Brecht's theatre served Devine as a model to renew the English theatre with his own work at the Royal Court, thereby integrating a Brechtian approach to theatre-making in England. Kane and Ravenhill were the great-great-grandchildren of this Brechtian English approach to make contemporary, critical political theatre, based on new plays and new writing. As we staged their plays at the Baracke, this impulse of Brecht had come back to Berlin, in a new form and with the completely different energy of these playwrights' powerful 'in yer face' writing. We sought to continue and develop this tradition further as we moved to the Schaubühne, where we were the first and only theatre to have all of Sarah Kane's plays in our repertoire at the same time, for a number of years.

We were fascinated to see how both Kane and Ravenhill, in particular, had used German impulses to free themselves from the dominant English tradition of stage naturalism, as they began to rethink the aesthetic means of realist playwriting, while at the same time offering a sharp new political attitude and resistant artistic practice. The post-Thatcher UK these authors and their British peers wrote about, which they experienced in their daily lives, had been far ahead at the time in implementing a thorough neoliberal economy and a corresponding neoliberal way of life. We therefore found in their plays a critique of capitalism that was impossible to articulate in Germany at that moment, since any such critique would be immediately linked to (and thereby discredited by) the failed East German attempt to overcome capitalism. Any

Meanwhile, those German authors who still made an effort all tended to sound like Heiner Müller, which was the aesthetic impasse to overcome in German writing. One of the major achievements of our work at the Baracke therefore was to make it possible again to have a critical discussion about capitalism. In addition to the work we staged, I had initiated the 'Streitraum' ('space for dispute'), a regular public discussion at the Baracke with key political, sociological and philosophical thinkers. At the time, it was one of the first such formats for live critical debate that have since proliferated at many German theatres. The Streitraum still continues, after almost twenty-five years, once a month in front of a mostly sold out Schaubühne auditorium, now also streamed online.[1]

Meanwhile, from our strong connection to contemporary British theatre, not only Kane and Ravenhill came with us to the Lehniner Platz: there were also colleagues such as, in particular, Maja Zade, who joined the Schaubühne as a dramaturg directly from the Royal Court Theatre. She has continued in this vital position to the present day, and meanwhile her own plays have also been premiered there. From her, and hence, from the Royal Court way of making theatre, we learnt many important lessons: about reading plays, about discussing them, about editing them, about finding plays and authors in the first place and about coaching them – and doing all this as part of an active dramaturgic politics of theatre-making. This active dramaturgy also included the annual FIND – 'Festival for International New Drama' – which continued the 'New Drama Weeks' ('Wochen der neuen Dramatik') we had launched at the Baracke. Ever since, the festival has remained a powerful engine to steer on the continuous development of the Schaubühne's programmatic artistic development; we will keep returning to its crucial impulses throughout this chapter.

In the initial period following our move from the Baracke to the Schaubühne, however, it turned out to be very difficult to present such new realistic plays. This, in fact, became quite a serious problem, especially for Thomas Ostermeier, who had become successful directing this kind of work. Yet now, our theatre was criticized for presenting and debating social classes other than the middle-class bourgeoisie, who made up the core audience in the affluent Western district of Berlin Charlottenburg, where the Schaubühne is located. We thus needed to come to terms with realizing that the context of the Schaubühne seemed to be stronger than the content, the plays and the ways of playing we had brought with us. Between these two parameters, a strong conflict emerged, which would determine our internal discussions, as well as the public debate, especially in the reviews, for a number of years.

While a good part of the audience had followed us from the Baracke to the Schaubühne, we still had to fight really hard for audiences in our new, much bigger venue. The great success of the early years was the choreographic works of Sasha Waltz, following on from her Schaubühne debut piece *Körper* (*Bodies*), which – alongside Thomas Ostermeier's production of Lars Norén's *Personenkreis 3.1* (*Human Circle 3.1*) – had opened our joint artistic direction in January 2000. *Körper* was a fantastic choreographic piece, which not least resulted from the productive relationship that Sasha had found with the architectural space of the Schaubühne, right from this first attempt (see Figure 5). It showed individual human beings with their bodies, in front of the gigantic concrete walls, and thereby generated an enormous visceral power and effect.[2] We owe it to the historical truth to admit that Sasha Waltz and the success of her dance works helped our joint project to survive over its first years; she provided us who were working with plays the time to develop and grow into the new situation.

Our own struggle and its gradual resolution manifested itself in the trajectory of productions from the initial *Personenkreis* in 2000 to Thomas Ostermeier's successful Ibsen productions, with which his approach of examining new pieces and experimenting with a new realist aesthetic came to its culmination. Ibsen's plays allowed us to portray and dissect, in our realistic approach, the German middle class of the time: by rewriting, over-

Figure 5 Showing dance bodies against the Schaubühne's gigantic concrete walls, Sasha Waltz's *Körper* (2000) found a productive relationship with the theatre's architectural space. © Bernd Uhlig.

Theatre Towards the Liberation of Thinking 127

writing and modernizing the canonical plays. With *Hedda Gabler*, our work at the Schaubühne eventually reached its first peak. Looking back, it still fascinates me to see how we had managed to challenge, with our work up to that point, the at the time still persisting white lie of the reunited post-1989 Germany: that we had become a classless society, where everyone formed part of an all-encompassing middle class, free of class struggle – hence the idea of an 'end of class society', similar to the proposed 'end of history'. At the time, the public debate showed an unwavering belief in the perfect functioning of liberal democracy, as it had teamed up with the new neoliberal economic policy and philosophy after 1989. To criticize this hegemonic attitude with our work felt, for a long time, like trying to drill through the steel walls of a heavy fortress. Yet, a curious turn occurred around 2003, following a major crisis within the German newspaper market. All of a sudden, a lot of journalists and critics were personally confronted with the social questions we had persistently raised, as they found themselves made redundant and their well-established newspaper with a tradition of more than a century shut down. The critics at once wrote very differently about plays that dealt with unemployment. Eventually, in the wake of the great global economic crisis of 2008/9, the public debate shifted entirely into such a critical direction.

In addition to the initial discursive rejection of our work, our specific critical approach also presented us with a major aesthetic challenge. The representation of social issues on stage has remained one of the major challenges in the German-speaking theatre to this day, despite Hauptmann, Brecht and their dramatic legacy. The British playwrights had presented us with an initial direction from which to confront this problem. Our first seasons at the Schaubühne were characterized by our trying out a number of other attempts to conquer, redefine, reuse and turn the theatre into a truly political place for contemporary theatre, as we had expressed in our 'Mission' manifesto. These ongoing attempts to develop new forms and new plays received continuous input from the annual FIND festivals, and their predecessor at the Baracke. Among the big discoveries was Lars Norén; then there was Jon Fosse: we were the first theatre to stage his plays in Germany. In the early years at the Schaubühne, their plays further extended the strong international influence in our work, while also helping us to expand our horizon, adding to the plays and aesthetics of Kane, Ravenhill and the English tradition with which we of course also remained engaged. The Scandinavian perspective of Norén and Fosse allowed us to explore another, quite different tradition of realism in European theatre as well, which came from the lineage of Ibsen and Strindberg, and which these contemporary playwrights carried into the present. For this reason, it was a conclusive step *forward* to eventually go *back* to Ibsen himself.

128 *The Schaubühne Berlin under Thomas Ostermeier*

At the same time, we also pursued the development of original, new German playwriting, taking a lot of inspiration from the play development work at London's Royal Court, as noted above. Roland Schimmelpfennig and Marius von Mayenburg joined us as members of the dramaturgy department from the very beginning. We commissioned them to develop plays – Mayenburg straight away as our in-house playwright, Schimmelpfennig as dramaturg. They created their work for the Schaubühne as an ensemble theatre, which the Royal Court is not: they wrote their new plays with actors from our ensemble in mind, and also responded, via their work, directly to the ongoing discourses at the theatre, in which they actively participated on a daily basis, so that their plays put forward what they considered a meaningful intervention in these ongoing aesthetic as well as thematic discussions. One of the most important original new additions to the forms, the scope and the dimensions of our development of new work then came, towards the end of our first season, with Falk Richter. As a theatre-maker, he had previously worked across dance and acting, which resonated with our experiments at the Schaubühne. His 1999 independent production *Nothing Hurts*, a collaboration between him and the Dutch choreographer Anouk van Dijk, was invited to the 2000 Theatertreffen. We then invited him to create a production at the Schaubühne – *Peace*, the final premiere of our first season in the summer of 2000.

Rather than continuing Falk's collaboration with dance (it would, in fact, be almost a decade, until *Trust*, before he once again worked with Anouk van Dijk), we made an attempt with Falk, the playwright-director, to experiment with a second, very different line of developing new German drama. At that time, Germany was waging its first war since 1945, in Kosovo. We sent Falk as an 'embedded artist' along with the embedded journalists; they did not realize that our theatre artist was writing about *them*, and not about the soldiers, as they did. *Peace* became a work about the German way of dealing with this war, and the role of the media in the public debate about it. The production made it evident that the young, enlarged 'Berlin republic' had no form of political discourse at its disposal to debate such a war mission. The German language about this topic was completely contaminated by its use and abuse during the Nazi regime. So one could not speak about an 'invasion' but called it a 'transfer of troops'; 'comradeship' between soldiers was termed 'social competence' and their 'contact with enemy troops' described as 'intercultural competence'. Vocabulary from academic socio-cultural analysis was transferred into the public discussion of this war in the German media and the country's public sphere. This utter insecurity around how to speak about war, and the conflicts that this very dilemma disclosed, became the main subject of Falk Richter's production. When his *Peace* led us straight into the

Theatre Towards the Liberation of Thinking 129

first of several court trials that his work with the Schaubühne would cause over the years – here, we were charged with presenting too malicious, open and personal criticism of the war journalists – this response confirmed to us, against our own doubts and the widespread rejection we had received from the critics and some parts of the audience in this early period, that we were indeed following the right strategy to arrive at a theatre of real societal relevance. It showed us that our critique was in fact perceived as so painful, but also so relevant, that it warranted being taken to court.

Peace marked the beginning of the Schaubühne's long cooperation with Falk Richter, which lasted until *The Complexity of Belonging*, a co-production with the Melbourne Festival in 2014, and *Fear*, a piece about the right-wing AfD party that eventually concluded his work for this theatre with another prominent court case. In the beginning, though, following *Peace*, his next big project took its prompt from a statement by then German chancellor Gerhard Schröder. In an infamous line from an important speech he delivered in the autumn of 2001, he declared that the Iraq war in response to 9/11, and the German army's new engagement in places like Afghanistan, would 'defend our way of life'. So we set ourselves the task to explore this way of life in a four-part project called *Das System* (*The System*), attempting to initiate a critical debate about this 'way of life' through the means of contemporary drama. We brought in relevant plays from abroad, following our by then established strategy, but we now were also able to add our own plays and to create new material. The project lasted over several months in the Schaubühne's Saal C, consisting of productions of texts by Falk Richter by other directors, a new text by Falk he directed himself and a production, also directed by Falk, of a text by Martin Crimp, another British author who was very important for us. A major starting point for our work on this project was the realization that the neoliberal principles, which initially had organized the economy and the work place, had begun to creep into other sectors of society – not least the arts and culture sector. Moreover, we all seemed more and more to internalize them, beginning to organize, and also evaluate, very private aspects of our daily lives according to the criteria dictated by 'the market' and an alleged 'free choice'. This thematic interrogation started with *Das System* in 2004, but it would in fact remain the focus of much of the political research we attempted at the Schaubühne for years to come.

The best known text and production to emerge from the *System* project is, in fact, still in the Schaubühne's repertoire today and regularly performed there, but it has also been produced at many other theatres: *Unter Eis* (*Under Ice*), which premiered in April 2004. By the time that, a year later, *Hedda Gabler* and *Unter Eis* ran in parallel in the Schaubühne repertoire, we had arrived, after a problematic start, at a first climax, having found and invented

130 *The Schaubühne Berlin under Thomas Ostermeier*

new, original aesthetic strategies for our project and our intentions: on the one hand, we took classics and modernized them according to what we had learnt from contemporary playwrights. On the other hand, our second strategy was to commission and develop plays and new work that very directly dealt with societal and political topics, as exemplified by *The System*. We thereby also developed new forms of playwriting in German theatre. The work with Falk Richter, in particular, led us to adapt the approach to play development we had initially taken over from the Royal Court Theatre as our role model. Over a number of years, we kept developing an approach that not only allowed the playwrights to write with specific actors from our ensemble in mind, but which also more clearly reflected the varied models of authorship and forms of playwriting that characterize German theatre. We went more and more beyond a form of play development where the theatre would commission a play from a playwright, which a director would then read and stage (or decide not to), towards commissioning the development and production in one, by a playwright-director like Falk, and we would also send the author into a situation to undertake research to develop this production. Yet, in contrast to other forms of 'devising' performance, this remained clearly an approach to 'devising plays': Falk Richter's texts that were developed from such research and which he created as part of his production processes were all published as playtexts, staged elsewhere by other directors, as well as being translated into other languages and produced abroad. This model became a blueprint for creating new play-productions, at the Schaubühne, and beyond. This approach, after all, emerged within a new, postdramatic context that was very different from the 'well-made play' tradition of the Royal Court.

After four theatre seasons, we had thus arrived at creating a small 'canon' of new, contemporary realism(s) in the plays we showed side by side in our repertoire, ranging from Kane and Ravenhill, via Norén and Fosse on to the new German plays of Mayenburg, Schimmelpfennig and Richter. Looking back, this was a crucial period, where – very literally – piece by piece we built and developed a new audience for these new plays. It certainly took a number of years for this new audience, who would go and see a new play, not just a classic, to come together – yet eventually it had a transformative impact, especially within the Berlin theatre landscape that I still see in my current work at the Gorki theatre: here, today, new plays and productions do far better than productions of classics. We thus have seen a complete reversal in the audience's expectations over the past two decades – and I have good reason to suggest that the Schaubühne with its, at the time, pioneering and unrivalled approach and commitment was instrumental for this fundamental transformation of the audience's spectating habits.

From new plays to new theatre languages

The new aesthetic impulses that the work at the Schaubühne generated not only concerned the playwriting, though. Productions, such as, in particular, *Unter Eis*, had begun to set in motion some hugely fascinating encounters between actors whom we had brought with us from the Baracke, such as André Szymanski and Mark Waschke, and Thomas Thieme, who in the 1990s had been in the ensemble of the 'old', post-Peter Stein Schaubühne. In these works, different styles and traditions of acting and performing met, came together and, in their confrontation with each other, produced a new vitality of play. This repeated an important impulse that had already energized our work at the Baracke, where productions such as *Shopping and Fucking* brought together the approaches of the Deutsches Theater, of which we were a part, with the radical non-conformism of the Volksbühne and the aesthetics of the independent scene elsewhere in the city. Over the years, such productive frictions and aesthetic dialogues between very different ways of being on and using the stage had planted the seeds for the characteristic style of acting, which in particular Thomas Ostermeier continued to develop further in his own theatre work.[3] It generated a new style defined by a very personal, and personally invested, approach to acting, and furthermore by its direct and, if you like, 'in your face' mode of performing. But beyond stylistic aspects, this osmosis between different stage languages was fundamental in order to experiment with a new realism, where both the fictional level of the text, and the performance level of the theatre event itself, were equally filled with an absolute being, a presence in the world, while still being guided, at all times, by impulses and an interrogation of the thematic and political dimensions of the respective plays.

One should imagine our work at the Schaubühne, especially in the initial decade, as driven by these evolving internal discourses, which were kept so fertile and productive because the artistic direction, the dramaturgs, the performers and the entire artistic team constantly confronted itself with the exploration and interrogation of something new. In the beginning, we had worked our way from one geographical region to another, from English-speaking theatre to the French-speaking theatre, which already had begun to play an important role during our time at the Baracke, through invitations and cooperations, then on to impulses from Scandinavian theatre. In a further, decisive next step (once more facilitated through FIND), the Dutch and Belgian theatre appeared on our map, as directors Johan Simons and Luk Perceval brought their work to our festival. Eventually, this was the ignition of the second constellation at the Schaubühne, after Sasha Waltz and Jochen Sandig had decided to go back into independence in 2005: the constellation with three in-house directors, where Thomas Ostermeier was joined by Falk

Richter and Luk Perceval as permanent associate directors. For the next several seasons, the work of this trio, alongside the choreographic work of Constanza Macras, with its – compared to Sasha Waltz – much more pronouncedly political and realistic approach to dance, marked the further development of the characteristic Schaubühne approach from its earlier focus purely on playwriting, authors and texts, to a more comprehensive exploration of, and search for, new ways of theatre direction, and also new theatre languages. As a liberation, as further development, as a new experience and as further differentiation, the tripartite constellation of very different directors was enormously fortunate for our progression, and a great influence for everyone in the entire theatre. The fact that after overcoming the difficulties of the first few years and reaching our first successes with dramatic productions, there was still so much more to happen at the Schaubühne, was owed entirely to the simultaneously competing and cooperating work of these three directors. The impact of this constellation was in its result similar to the discovery of the British new playwriting some years earlier.

Following the first peak of our work, which I described above with *Unter Eis* and *Hedda Gabler*, our strategies therefore shifted from plays to productions. In this next phase, Luk Perceval, for instance, premiered a text Marius von Mayenburg had written for him, *Turista* (2005). At the same time, both Luk and Falk Richter developed further the engagement with the classics, which Thomas Ostermeier had initiated through his Ibsen productions. A particularly important moment in this line of our work was Falk Richter's confrontation with Chekhov, as he modernized and revised, between 2004 and 2008, *The Seagull*, *The Three Sisters* and *The Cherry Orchard*. These two constellations – the direction of new playtexts written for specific directors, alongside author-directors rewriting and re-staging classics – became paradigmatic for the most significant work we created during this second phase. Our exploration of a different conception of realism now extended beyond writing, to include different ways of performing, of directing and a different mode of directing actors and texts.

Luk Perceval's work, in particular, significantly expanded our ensemble's capability. With him, a performative dimension entered the actors' approaches to playing, and equally the thinking of all artists who worked at the Schaubühne at the time. Not only the actors, but everyone working at the theatre owed a lot to Luk, as he introduced us to the specific contemporaneity – in the sense of getting close to the present times – precisely by making productive the immediate effectiveness of the actors with the spectators in the shared theatre event. This was an aspect that the Flemish and Dutch theatre had particularly developed. Whereas Thomas Ostermeier's work developed by focusing on dramatic processes and situations and the idea of acting-playing as an act and

Theatre Towards the Liberation of Thinking   133

action, and while Falk Richter considered acting as a form of thinking, characterized by language and the act of speaking a text, and also in its difference from and tension with the speaker, Luk Perceval pursued something entirely different and new for us: *non-acting* as a way of acting. 'Please don't act' was an instruction consistently to be heard in his rehearsals. He and also Johan Simons, who had both begun to regularly work and direct at a number of German theatres after 2000, introduced completely new lessons to German-language theatre, which the Flemish-Dutch tradition they came from had been developing since the 1960s.[4] There, directing plays and creating a performance, the aesthetics of dramatic theatre and the independent fringe, had productively merged. Seeing acting and performing therefore not as different approaches between which one needed to decide, Luk Perceval invited the actors to think about the situation on stage differently. Instead of inventing fictional situations, they were to take the concrete situation of standing on stage as an actor as the very basis of their acting performance – while, none the less, telling dramatic stories in a mode of 'playing' on stage that no longer claimed to invent a fictional character and a dramatic situation. Following the highlight of Mayenburg's *Turista*, Luk's work at the Schaubühne reached its peak with his *Molière* (2007), a tremendous work, where Thomas Thieme in the lead role raged over hours, while in Katrin Brack's scenography snow kept falling onto the stage, without a pause (see Figure 6). Luk's work at the Schaubühne gained its force from his struggle with and against the empty concrete space of the theatre and its architecture, which led to his most interesting works, such as *Molière*. They were based on an absolute economy and reduction of means in order to work within this very powerful and mighty space. It was a strategy that worked, for me in fact it was the only strategy the three directing colleagues developed that ever managed to fill and come to terms with this bare, brutal space. Both Thomas and Falk (perhaps with the exception of some of Falk's later dance collaborations) always had to build rooms into this space so that their theatre could function; the creation and fixed division of the Schaubühne space into the three permanent stages in their present form was eventually a decision to hide the concrete brutality.

In Falk Richter's case, the same period resulted in an enormous gain not least in the political pluri-dimensionality of his writing, and the multiplicity of worlds and life experiences that his texts came to encompass and articulate. His interrogation of Chekhov took up some of the thematic prompts from the earlier *System* plays, in order to lead him towards *Trust* (2009), which would bring together the crisis of the economy (fresh in the wake of the financial crisis of 2008), with the crisis of an entire way of life that his earlier work had interrogated, as reflected in the personal, unsettled trepidation of trying to live one's life, just from one day to the next.[5] Ten years after *Nothing*

Figure 6 As the Schaubühne's associate director, Flemish Luk Perceval introduced a new aesthetic where acting and performing were no longer considered as different approaches between which one needed to decide. His work at the theatre peaked with *Molière* (2007), featuring Thomas Thieme (in the middle), amid Katrin Brack's economic scenography that gradually filled the stage with snow. © Matthias Horn/Schaubühne.

Hurts, Trust completed a journey in Falk's oeuvre; it was once again a choreographic work in collaboration with Anouk van Dijk, in which the bodies made visible in their behaviour the inner state of this utter loss of trust into our dominant way of life and of organizing our economy. Their perturbed and confused search for something, something else and different, became a visceral experience. Interestingly, this way back to dance, and to his cooperation with Anouk van Dijk, had led via Chekhov – and I would suggest that it was the specific constellations and constructions that the Schaubühne allowed and facilitated, which made such a trajectory possible.[6]

One of the most interesting aspects that Falk's work on Chekhov revealed was that in the work of the Russian playwright, usually considered the author of melancholic longing and yearning, the chains of desire, as one might describe them, are entirely oriented alongside social and economic status. No one loves downwards. Falk Richter found – and emphasized in his productions – Chekhov's (for its period) remarkably perceptive insight into the social and economic dimensions of love. He found already in Chekhov's

Theatre Towards the Liberation of Thinking 135

plays an expression of the impact of both the economy and of ideology on everyday life, on our most private and personal desires, which his own earlier work had thematized in the lives under the 'system' of the twenty-first century. We became acutely aware of this much wider, historical dimension of the key political problems we were interested in, as we worked on *The Seagull* (2004), and then we discovered these issues again in *Three Sisters* (2006). For *The Cherry Orchard* (2008), we decided to produce our own translation. We had commissioned a literal translation from the Russian, which revealed that Chekhov's characters in fact speak very different languages. They use different tones and registers that set them and their social status apart, far more than any psychology. We felt that this had not sufficiently come across in existing translations, and therefore aimed at translating this linguistic determination of the characters – which resonated so well with the way Falk had conceived his own characters in his *System* trilogy – in a different way into German. From *The Cherry Orchard* – this primordial play on capitalism, on the rise of a new capitalist class and the capitalization of nature, but also on love in times of a financial crisis – and the many insights we had gained from working on it, the path led, in the following year, directly to *Trust*. Both plays discuss how love functions, how people engage in love relationships or not, and how such decisions are based on market-driven considerations – in short, how love and interpersonal relationships have been entirely colonized by the neoliberal economy, as sociologist Eva Illouz has also charted in her writings.[7] In *Trust*, Falk Richter's exploration of *The System* and his work on Chekhov culminated in a much more complex cosmos of characters. In contrast to the earlier *Unter Eis*, for example, the world of work and the neoliberal economy were no longer separated from personal, private relations as a somewhat external condition that the characters more or less struggled with. Instead, the economy, work, war and society are all debated through the personal relations we engage in.

The actors in the ensemble, who had first performed with Thomas Ostermeier, then with Falk Richter, would in the new constellation now also work with Luk Perceval, and then come back again to work with Ostermeier, and so on – this period was therefore a phase in the development of the theatre where the entire ensemble gained a lot. It resulted in an ever clearer distinctive style of Schaubühne-acting. All of us in the artistic direction and the dramaturgy were very aware of how the confrontation with a variety of directors noticeably developed the actors' capabilities, and how it pushed every single actor into new territory. I believe that this awareness resulted in the further development of the Schaubühne towards a theatre no longer so much driven by innovation through authors and their texts alone, but by new directors, who brought with them different ways of working, different modes of presentation and different approaches to acting and to narrating stories, and who thereby further extended the stage language of our ensemble. Following from the Flemish impulse (Ivo van Hove also staged two productions at the Schaubühne), the Spanish-language theatre became a further important source for this development, when Rodrigo García, Álex Rigola and Angélica Liddell first came to the FIND festival, and then also created new works with the ensemble. From the wider European context, Katie Mitchell, Alvis Hermanis, Romeo Castellucci and Simon McBurney would also over the years come here and expand this focus further.

In this context, I should also mention Yael Ronen, who first joined us around the time of *Trust*, and who brought an altogether different form of play development with her, where the actors themselves become authors. Her *Third Generation* (2009) introduced this genuinely new principle. She would work together with the actors in long phases of workshops, developing her production over several months, where workshop periods, breaks during which she wrote up text, and further improvisations where the director and the actors came together to continue developing the situation, the characters and the texts, followed each other. The performers contributed in this work with their personal stories, and also their own political perspectives and viewpoints, and this personal investment itself then became one of the topics within the performance on stage, too. As the era of 'the three directors' drew to a close, Yael Ronen's impulse brought a further development in our old quest to redefine authorship in a contemporary way, which now also came to include the actor – and this further challenged and developed our ensemble, as it required yet again a completely different approach to acting. Her work seemed like a very logical continuation, if not conclusion, of several years of interdisciplinary encounters between various forms of writing, performing and dancing, that had characterized these first nine years of our working at the Schaubühne. Looking back at the intentions we expressed at the outset, in *The Mission*, we had thus achieved quite a bit in this big task we had set for ourselves: to find and develop contemporary narrations and forms of artistic expression on stage that eventually helped us at the Schaubühne, and maybe the German theatre at large, to overcome the 'Heiner Müller impasse' I mentioned in the beginning, and which also tackled the other big aesthetic blockade – of a political directors' theatre that more often than not tended to get stuck in Frank Castorf-epigonism.

Finding European theatre in a transnational world

Throughout these developments, the FIND festival had consistently been an important catalyst, and not only because it was an important means in our cooperation and exchange with artists across European theatre (and eventually beyond). I therefore want to turn to some aspects of the festival more fully in this concluding section, not least because it also reflected another important intention we already had referred to in *The Mission*: namely, our aim to establish an expressly European theatre. For us, even as we started out at the Baracke, as a small venue of the Deutsches Theater, the unofficial German National Theatre, our intention had been to create international theatre. This meant for us to see ourselves very clearly situated as a Berlin theatre, but one that is also simultaneously a European theatre, opening outwards, hence not as an exclusively German theatre. Over the years, FIND mirrored our own development in this respect: from the initial focus on specific countries, on specific languages and hence on specific other nations, on to a more widely international way of thinking, and of making theatre, which eventually culminated in an approach that we considered transnational.

An important step forward in this trajectory was prompted by our ongoing discussion about the current state of society and our attention to the historical dimension of contemporary developments, as had been revealed, for instance, by Falk Richter's work on Chekhov. The neoliberal discourse tends to spread an obliviousness of history in its focus on the here and now as the only thing that counts – and we noted that much criticism of neoliberalism equally tended to do so. From our perspective as a theatre that intended to communicate the potential to change people as well as society, an engagement with the fact that things had been different once, and also that what is, has become so through history, seemed an important statement to make – as it of course suggested that, within the foreseeable future, we can become different yet again. As a result, a series of FIND festivals, in 2007, 2008 and 2009, dealt in various ways with history. For us, the complex situation of our own German history with Israel, but then also the current situation between Israel and Palestine, became the obvious starting point for such an exploration. We thus entered this exploration still very much driven by our attempts to understand the specific German situation that had characterized our work so far. I had travelled to the region and seen a production by Yael Ronen, which we invited to Berlin, and which then led to our further collaboration. After some deliberation and intense debate, we decided to separate themes and issues, and instead of one combined festival, to dedicate one entire edition of FIND to Israel, and another in the following year to Palestine. This extensive debate encompassed a complex political interrogation, which not only opened up our own attention beyond the focus on the German situation, but which eventually also positioned our artistic work and creative strategies into much wider political contexts, of historical conditions and trajectories, not least of postcolonial dynamics. Questions of who directs, who has the power, who narrates, who speaks and who does not, and to whom, appeared more and more at the forefront of our thinking, and eventually extended our previous concentration on social questions and issues, mainly prompted by the German context, considerably. Questions such as, what is your history that defines you, as an artist, whether as director or performer? Is it ethical at all, for an actor at a large German theatre, to portray on stage and speak for the homeless on the street, as we had done for instance in *Human Circle 3.1*? We realized more and more that historical and national narratives, in which our own biographies and also our artistic thinking are, to a degree, inscribed, more often than not also disclose political confrontations about access to social and economic opportunities that are granted, or perhaps taken for granted, or refused.

The fight about who has what, and who gets what and who does not, manifests itself in an official hegemonic politics of history as well – and this became the point where we sought to enter into the criticism of such narratives through this series of festivals. The debates on identity and history were first initiated through the 2007 and 2008 FIND festivals on Israel and Palestine, then culminating in the 2009 edition, which we entitled 'Digging deep and getting dirty'. This focus on history, and disavowed histories, took as its horizon the various historical anniversaries that year: 1919, 1929, 1939, 1949, 1989. While these years all mark dates with specific significance for German history, we wanted to hear from other European theatre-makers, and explicitly also from international theatre artists from other traditions beyond Europe, how they envisaged that theatre, and their theatre, may deal with history, with historical material and with historical events. It seemed particularly pertinent for us at that time to explore the role and potential of theatre in this context, as we noted that film and television had begun to develop a rather odd, very uncritical way of telling us who we are, and of presenting certain dominant narratives of history. Yael Ronen's *Third Generation*, in which Israelis, Palestinians and Germans tell themselves and each other about their and each other's history, opened this festival edition.

On occasions, the transnational dynamic of this debate hit us somewhat unexpectedly. After a trip to Asia and the far East, I had invited some productions from this region to FIND. All of a sudden, during our festival, a vocal conflict broke out behind the scenes between theatre artists from Singapore and Japan over the appropriate handling of their own respective national histories, and the relations of their countries. The colleagues from Singapore demanded from the Japanese artists a similar confrontation of their national history as we had initiated with *Third Generation* and this FIND edition, and the Japanese artists were entirely caught out by this sudden demand to express this directly in their own work. Experiences like

Theatre Towards the Liberation of Thinking 139

this made us more and more aware of how such aesthetical and artistic conflicts about the form and contents of theatre work – of what we tell in what way to whom – emerge from a similar political impulse, as artists across the world have by now become dominated by the effects of the same economic world order, and affected by the same wars that are fought out in distant places but whose aftermath directly affects all of us, everywhere.

The interrogation of history, which brought with it a confrontation with new discourses that also define the contemporary political situation, made a debate of the global issues of the present far more challenging, both politically and aesthetically. The final FIND edition that I curated, 'The Three Americas' (2010), sought to understand and analyse our European situation in the world, and how to translate it into the narratives and the form of a play, against the background of three different stories of the colonization of the world by Europeans, and what today returns back to Europe as a result of this colonization. Such an exploration led us into a completely different discursive and artistic territory, where we – who understood the Schaubühne as a 'European theatre' – had to critically confront the 'Europeanization', the long history of the colonization of the rest of the world by European culture (and equally the mutual colonization in Europe that seemed to be the preferred, specifically German strategy). Making transnational theatre and fostering international artistic exchange, we encounter colleagues who come from a theatrical tradition that is part of this colonization, of decolonization and also of new neo-colonial strategies under the banner of globalization. At the 200th anniversary of the struggle for independence in the former Spanish colonies of the Americas, we wanted to explore these dynamics through the lens of the continents' various English, Spanish and French theatre traditions, and what their approaches to articulating the social, economic and cultural conflicts of the globalized present may tell about present and future possibilities of political theatre-making in a globalized world.[8]

Of course, part of this debate, also in the theatre work we invited, was how the global power relations were still structured by Europe, and the legacy of Europe in the world. This exploration further opened up the debate of intersectional problems of class, race and gender, in all their manifold aspects and dimensions, including racism as part of the history of colonization, the sexism behind a certain understanding of man and woman, and the history of the persecution of homosexuality in the colonies, which emanated from Europe. Once again, the artists we invited to FIND worked, piece by piece, on the various dimensions of these massive questions, and through their performances passed this reflection on to the actors, the artists and the entire team at the theatre, influencing thereby also other, future productions of texts, plays and performances at the Schaubühne.

What had thus started off as research into the state of new playwriting in specific geographic areas across Europe, had eventually turned into a much more complicated examination of how we live today in a networked, global world – how power is structured, how oppression is structured, and how mechanisms of exploitation and discrimination are structured, relying strongly on categories of class, gender and race. We were in the end surprised (and also relieved) to realize that theatre as a medium felt anything but outmoded or incapable of confronting such global problems at the heart of the crisis of the twenty-first century. On the contrary, the transnational encounters of our own work with work by artists from around the globe via the FIND festival showed us that theatre has the unique ability to constantly keep developing its aesthetic tools and means further, in order to keep unsettling any rigid and entrenched perspectives by offering, in a critical spirit, different perspectives and new insights, and thereby facilitating a liberation of thinking.[9]

Translated by Peter M. Boenisch

Notes

1 Since the 2004/5 season, the series has been curated by investigative journalist and writer Carolin Emcke, who in 2018 also created a lecture performance at the Schaubühne on the MeToo-debate, *Ja heißt ja und ...* ('Yes means yes/so what ...').
2 See Sabine Huschka's chapter in this volume (Chapter 13).
3 See Peter M. Boenisch and Thomas Ostermeier (eds), *The Theatre of Thomas Ostermeier* (Abingdon and New York: Routledge, 2016).
4 See also Lourdes Orozco and Peter M. Boenisch, eds, 'Border Collisions: Contemporary Flemish Theatre', *Contemporary Theatre Review* 20, no. 4 (2010).
5 See Hans-Thies Lehmann's chapter in this book (Chapter 14).
6 We see a similar path in the work of Thomas Ostermeier, where the engagement with dance and choreography in *A Midsummer Night's Dream*, which he created with Constanza Macras (2006), enabled the later *Hamlet* (2008), by expanding his conception and use of space, and also the way actors and texts would interact in other ways than 'speaking the line'.
7 See Eva Illouz, *Cold Intimacies: The Making of Emotional Capitalism* (Cambridge: Polity, 2007), which was at the time much discussed at theatre. See also her more recent *The End of Love: A Sociology of Negative Relations* (Oxford: Oxford University Press, 2019).
8 See also Marina Ceppi's chapter in this book (Chapter 12).
9 This text originated from a conversation between Jens Hillje and Peter M. Boenisch, which took place on 8 January 2020 at the Maxim Gorki Theater Berlin.

11

Re-scripting Realism: Katie Mitchell and Thomas Ostermeier at the Schaubühne

Benjamin Fowler

Thomas Ostermeier has raised the international profile of the Schaubühne over the last two decades as a centre for experiments in a new, contemporary theatrical realism. Since 2010, he has invited the British director Katie Mitchell (b. 1964) to contribute seven productions that bite back against the gendered biases of the conventional realist form.[1] Mitchell adapts dramatic and literary texts into realist scenarios that she then *re*-frames using technology – often, but not always, involving cameras. This chapter argues that Mitchell and Ostermeier are linked in their (certainly distinct) directorial attempts to measure texts anew in contemporary circumstances, using them to craft highly tangible dramatic worlds while harnessing the materiality of those worlds to convey immaterial forces. In this, their work rehabilitates a much maligned genre of theatrical production. Although what passes as theatrical 'realism' has varied over time, contemporary theatre theorists (and some reviewers, too) tend to align it with simple mimesis to signify forces that entrench, rather than challenge, a determinist world-view and naturalize essentialist notions of identity. Realism has come to figure as the antagonist of experiment and innovation that characterize properly politicized forms of theatre-making.

Offering an antidote to this prevailing view, I connect the work of Ostermeier and Mitchell as cultural materialists who insist upon the political relevance of dramatic theatre and realism as a theatrical genre in a highly complex twenty-first century setting. I first examine their separate productions of the same play, Franz Xaver Kroetz's *Wunschkonzert*, to demonstrate how each director retools the century-old work of Russian pedagogues (Stanislavsky or Meyerhold) for contemporary sensibilities and socio-political circumstances. The chapter then concentrates on Mitchell's work at the Schaubühne, before contrasting her *Ophelias Zimmer* (*Ophelia's Room*) with Ostermeier's *Hamlet*, showing how Mitchell's perspective has exposed significant blindspots in Ostermeier's work on Shakespeare. Nevertheless, both directors create work

142   *The Schaubühne Berlin under Thomas Ostermeier*

that arrays itself against any complacent acceptance of the world 'as it is', as they test the critical purchase of a commitment to texts and to fictive totalities as a potent artistic response to the political crises of our times.

Lessons from Russia: 'Doing rather than feeling'

The polarized and inconsistent reception of both Katie Mitchell's and Thomas Ostermeier's work exposes contradictory forces shaping ideas about what it means to stage plays. It might even seem surprising to place them in a bracket with a dramatic tradition of character-based realism, especially as British reviewers habitually describe both directors as 'auteurs' whose distinctive styles draw acolytes over the lure of a particular writer or play. Michael Billington, in his book surveying post-war British theatre, called Mitchell a 'controlling figure' belonging to a 'continental European tradition' in which directorial auteur-ship trumps the playwright's authorship.[2] Reviewers responding to Ostermeier's London visits have paid him similar regard. Lyn Gardner, unusual in celebrating rather than deriding *auteurs* as vital figures who prolong the life of classic texts, linked Mitchell and Ostermeier as figures for whom plays are 'simply a suggestion for a performance'.[3] Nevertheless, both directors have insisted that they do not promote their director's version over the writer's vision. Although (in Mitchell's words) her handling of text is often misconstrued 'as an aggressive sabotaging act', she styles herself as a 'secondary artist not a primary artist' whose careful research into an author's milieu informs her directorial labour.[4] Ostermeier also refuses to identify as 'a comprehensive artist' working on a blank canvas: 'For me, the most important part of my job is to find the best way to bring out the core of the playwright's work.'[5]

These might sound like disingenuous statements from directors who frequently cut, reshape and add to the dramas they stage (often in collaboration with a living writer), but they speak of the inadequacies of a constructed binary between directorial disobedience and fidelity to a writer's vision. Rather than consider plays as transhistorical expressions of our shared humanity, Mitchell and Ostermeier understand that writers produce scripts within particular circumstances that shape a particular view of reality. Sometimes this leads them to discover traces of hidden scripts within scripts – brought to light, for instance, when Mitchell explores plays through the eyes of single protagonists, as in *Fräulein Julie* and *Ophelias Zimmer* – or, to nest new scripts inside existing ones, such as Ostermeier's interpolation of a French anarchist manifesto in Ibsen's *Ein Volksfeind*. They open a dialogue (or mount a challenge) from within the dramatic co-ordinates of a given fictional totality, thereby putting literary texts into *play*. Complicating matters further,

German critics often perceive less radicalism in Ostermeier's productions than their British and American counterparts. In their postdramatic zeitgeist, any whiff of dramatic totality is cause for suspicion, intimating not only problematic politics, but also – perhaps this is the worse misdemeanour – that the work producing it might actually reek of the 'conceptually boring'.[6] Meanwhile, commentators outside of Germany often perceive radicalism in Ostermeier's work, prompted by visceral aesthetic provocations that apparently upset the conventional realist machinery of Anglophone theatre, revealing a gap between international appraisals and a local German sense of Ostermeier's old-school investment in realist dramaturgies.

Mitchell has also invented theatrical forms involving cutting-edge technology that, to some eyes, disrupt realism. All but two of her Schaubühne works belong to the Live Cinema genre in which onstage actors construct a film captured by a roving camera team and live-streamed to a suspended projection screen. Although some British reviewers called Mitchell's Live Cinema 'anti-theatre' when *Fräulein Julie* visited the Barbican, performance scholars have criticized its adherence to old-fashioned theatrical values.[7] If postdramatic theatre requires directors to puncture the cohesive dramatic totality then Mitchell's work refuses to obey orders, curbing the subversive potential some view as inherent in her technological tools. To my mind, such contradictions invite us to ask why the aesthetics of these directors challenge our understanding of representation (and its relation to politics) in such disorientating ways. How might we account for Mitchell's and Ostermeier's avowed textual curiosity and their investment in sealed narrative totalities alongside their use of tools and techniques typical of deconstruction and their steadfast critical reputations for 'smashing up the classics'?

To address these questions, we need to examine how both directors in their formative years encountered the living legacies of historical practices by Stanislavsky and Meyerhold. Each would use the threads of these traditions to stitch together their new realist forms, fitted to an era shaped by different politics and with enough stretch to accommodate evolving stage technologies. Following the fall of the Berlin Wall in 1989, Mitchell used a travel grant to study directing in Poland, Russia, Georgia and Lithuania. In Russia she encountered Lev Dodin, a director who had studied under Boris Zon, one of Stanislavsky's pupils, and who now taught at the Leningrad State Institute of Theatre, Music and Cinematography. Mitchell observed his classes and his exhaustive questioning of directors learning their craft by performing actors' *études*. Dodin interrogated a class doing animal study (in role as flamingos) according to realist logics, asking: 'What is the fourth feather on the left wing doing? What is the time of day? Is your flamingo hot or cold?'[8] His diagnostic approach focused on the physical effects of time and place – even in the

144 *The Schaubühne Berlin under Thomas Ostermeier*

surreal scenario of humans playing flamingos – demonstrating a rigorous application of Stanislavsky in which the actor's full imagination of given circumstances should, as Dodin instructed one student, 'occupy your entire body from the top of your head to the tip of your toes'.[9] Mitchell found the approach powerful because its tangible, sometimes estranging, outcomes cut through theatrical approximations of 'real life' in British stage realism. Struck by the precision Dodin elicited, Mitchell in her own work came to address the actor's physicality as the main priority; Stanislavsky's later work on physical actions has proven germinal to her methods, which as she puts it engineer '"doing" rather than "feeling"'.[10]

Ostermeier meanwhile has made similarly flexible use of Russian traditions, creating modern applications for Meyerhold's biomechanics, which he learnt as a student at the Hochschule für Schauspielkunst 'Ernst Busch'. This system that (like Dodin's direction) prioritizes the body over the spoken word appealed to Ostermeier as he was frustrated with the clichés of psychological realism in the German *Regietheater* of the time, where directors sought to stage 'the landscape of the soul' by stressing the 'psychoanalytical' dimensions of plays they perceived as a 'pre-dramatization' of Freud.[11] For him, this ossified tradition fixed character in the false, romantic coherence of 'personality', obscuring how, in much dramatic literature, a 'character starts at a certain point in the play and ends up at a completely different point'.[12] His approach would thus frustrate the actor's reliance on psychology, prioritizing the *material* processes through which (in Robert Leach's phrase) 'the body happens'.[13]

Despite drawing from separate Russian pedagogues who on the surface seem oppositional, Mitchell and Ostermeier intuitively fixed upon compatible elements. Both would use their historical precursors to help them deploy realism in politically charged ways, contesting over-simplified assessments of naturalistic 'character'. The productions they realized demonstrate their supple engagement with historical practices, revealing a complex approach to character-as-process that prompts new varieties of highly theatrical and aesthetically innovative realism. Rather than being hamstrung by a realist proclivity, then, these directors draw on tradition to perform realism's radical recuperation. A clear expression of this can be gleaned from comparing their separate treatments of the same play, *Wunschkonzert*, written in 1973 by Bavarian playwright Franz Xaver Kroetz (b. 1946).

Ostermeier's and Mitchell's *Wunschkonzert*

Illustrating that dramatic writing is not predicated on dialogue alone, Kroetz's play is composed entirely of stage directions. His short text describes the

Katie Mitchell and Thomas Ostermeier at the Schaubühne 145

routines of a middle-aged factory worker, Fräulein Rasch, on returning to her single-occupancy apartment from a shift in a stationery warehouse. She tidies, watches television, prepares her solitary supper, accomplishes some sewing and readies herself for bed, all while listening to a sentimental radio request programme. Finally, a few minutes into a restless sleep, she gets up again and takes an overdose. The play ends with this simple desperate action. According to Kroetz's preface, it 'documents one's inability to shake loose the slavery of production', culminating in the self-destructive act of an alienated individual whose 'exploitation and repression' by capitalist culture becomes, literally and tragically, privatized.[14] Although showing an individual suicide, the play represents Rasch's death as a consequence of an 'inhuman order' (capitalism) that pushes citizens to the 'point of infirmity and collapse'.[15] Herein lies *Wunschkonzert*'s appeal for Ostermeier at a time when he had started using Ibsen's nineteenth-century 'social plays' as a lens through which to examine the political textures of ostensibly private acts behind the closed doors of Berlin's 'new' bourgeoisie. He directed *Wunschkonzert* as a sequel to his internationally fêted 2002 production of Ibsen's *Nora*; Anne Tismer played the lead in both productions, which sometimes toured together. Jan Pappelbaum's sets resembled contemporary Berlin apartments at opposite ends of the socio-economic scale. Ostermeier explicitly linked Nora Helmer and Fräulein Rasch as complementary studies of figures trodden underfoot in a neoliberal political economy (see Figure 7).

Four years later, Katie Mitchell pitched a multimedia version of Kroetz's play to Karin Beier, who in 2007 had become the artistic director of Schauspiel Köln. The stage design (by Alex Eales) was a facsimile of a West German apartment in 1973 (the play's publication year), with a solid fourth-wall that flew out to let in camera operators. The apartment only used one section of the stage; media technology occupied the rest: a Foley station; a large soundproof booth containing a string quartet (playing the music Rasch listens to on the radio); small areas for filming flashbacks and close-ups with replica settings and body-doubles; and a four-by-eight-metre projection screen stretched taught above the stage. Following its 2008 premiere, Mitchell's inaugural project in Germany was invited to the 2009 Theatertreffen. No British director had previously managed an invitation to this prestigious annual showcase, indicating Mitchell's appeal in a theatrical culture that highly prizes formal experimentation. Seeing *Wunschkonzert* at the Theatertreffen, Ostermeier invited Mitchell to direct for the Schaubühne. Kroetz's play thus brought the directors into each other's professional orbit, although it had prompted them to make divergent choices. Whereas Ostermeier used the smallest Schaubühne auditorium for Fraulein Rasch's intimate apartment, Mitchell staged her production in Schauspiel Köln's main house. Whereas Ostermeier showcased a virtuoso performer engaged in a

Figure 7 In Thomas Ostermeier's 2003 production of Franz Xaver Kroetz's silent play *Wunschkonzert*, conceived as companion piece to his staging of Ibsen's *Nora*, Anne Tismer played Fräulein Rasch as a woman performed by (rather than performing) a movement score of habitual acts that structure her 'leisure' time. © Arno Declair/Schaubühne.

solo exercise, Mitchell put twelve actors, musicians and technicians onstage, exhilarating in a colossal collaborative endeavour.

Ostermeier's update illustrated his obsession with reading plays 'through the glasses of today's society'.[16] Mitchell, in contrast, has argued the importance of situating plays in historical period so that we 're-observe the world through a new pair of glasses'.[17] The similar optical metaphors establish a shared concern with the dialectical relationship between a classic text and the contemporary moment. Mitchell's multimedia treatment materialized that dialectic through technology. Although Rasch and her apartment occupied 1973, the modern digital apparatus (and its operators) very literally filtered our gaze through contemporary lenses. Revealingly, Mitchell's Schaubühne debut, *Fräulein Julie* (2010), also marked the debut of historical costume on the theatre's stages under Ostermeier's leadership. She recalls him feeling physically sick on seeing corsets in the building, but he made this allowance (as Mitchell deduced) because the live cinema apparatus signified 'a modern interpretation of an old piece'.[18]

Ostermeier: Putting flesh on the bones of a realist concept

Offering detailed descriptions of Rasch's physical routines, Kroetz shaped a politics from inarticulacy through a mute realism of the body informed by

Katie Mitchell and Thomas Ostermeier at the Schaubühne   147

meticulous social research, having gathered evidence from police reports stressing the prevalence of 'routine' in the lead-up to suicide. In Ostermeier's production, Anne Tismer played Rasch as a woman performed by (rather than performing) the repetitive acts that structure her 'leisure' time. Ostermeier accentuated her conditioned responses to demonstrate how the pressures of globalized, flexible capitalism resurface as symptoms in the bodies of its citizens. Each time Tismer's Rasch crossed the room, she extended her arm habitually to touch the radiator. Repeatedly checking faucets for drips and double-checking doors to ensure they were locked, she used her apron to polish each cherry tomato accompanying her supper. Her reflexes, rather than unfolding personality traits, drew attention to pressures and hazards both physical and financial in her risk-laden social environment. Indeed, some objects posed a literal threat: Rasch cut her finger on a knife when washing up; on entering her flat she stubbed her toe painfully on a chair; when she danced to a song on the radio (as Kroetz writes), Ostermeier had her slip on the wet bathroom lino, plunging her outstretched arm into the uncovered toilet bowl and banging her head on the underside of the sink as she stood up. In his *Nora*, the word 'Kopfschmerz' (headache) appears in the prompt-script at moments when Tismer physicalizes the wearing effects of Nora's social performance by massaging her temples. Later, her frantic dance to the Tarantella drew blood as she threw her body against the sharp angles of her sleek modernist apartment. Such choreographic realism demonstrated the thesis by German sociologist Ulrich Beck that modern capitalism demanded 'biographical solutions' to 'systemic contradictions', outsourcing responsibility for ailments generated by social problems to the individual citizen.[19]

Contrasting with Meyerhold's ideological enthusiasm for the rapid industrialization in the infant Soviet republic, Ostermeier appropriated biomechanics to facilitate a sharp critique of capitalist economy, particularly of the hedonistic materialism in the aftermath of German re-unification. This continued the priority afforded to physical, visceral acting, which had gained the director some notoriety in his 1990s Baracke productions such as Ravenhill's *Shopping and Fucking* (1998). *Wunschkonzert* modelled exemplarily Ostermeier's continued commitment to heightened physicality within a given dramaturgical framework that cut through ossified emotional realist portrayals, in what he came to call his 'movement scores': '[E]very single move, each close of a door, each turn of the back of an object, the clatter of dishes being washed – all of these sounds, which result from the movement, are constructed [...] and the actress [...] simply sticks to the framework/scaffolding of these sounds'.[20] His production effectively associated Rasch's order obsession with pathological disorder. It affirmed his

148 *The Schaubühne Berlin under Thomas Ostermeier*

conviction that 'all these physical and psychological deformations that affect people today are a direct indicator that a purely economic way of thinking has been built into even the tiniest arteries of our society'.[21] This correlated with Brecht's insistence on a form of realism that discloses hidden power structures in order to render them open to scrutiny, in contrast to his understanding of naturalism as a superficial facsimile of everyday life. In Ostermeier's theatre, such insight led to explosive visceral moments of corporeal forcefulness that punctured external naturalism to expose directly states of suffering and alienation. Some viewers experienced these moments as jolts out of realism; I read them as indicative of a critical realism that opens an enquiry into contemporary ways of living by asserting the physical and emotional costs of the devastating performances prompted by competing social, political and economic forces.

Alongside intense physicality, the materiality of objects also generated critical insight in Ostermeier's contemporary realism. Although the ordered clutter of Rasch's apartment contrasted with the sleek, expensive minimalism of Jan Pappelbaum's living room settings for the marital homes in *Nora* and *Hedda Gabler*, it performed similar critique. Rasch's sole sofa cushion featured an image of the American boy-band *N-Sync*, which she kissed goodnight before bed. She also wore a pyjama T-shirt emblazoned with the slogan 'Be My Valentine' as she battled to unfold her single-person sofa bed. Objects signalled her aspirations, while also revealing her entanglement in a kitsch materialist culture offering empty substitutes for satisfying intrapersonal relationships. Altering Kroetz's stage direction that Rasch does sewing, Ostermeier had her turn on her desktop computer and play the then ubiquitous PC game *Solitaire*. The questionable value of commodities in these productions lay in their capacity to defer emotion and introspection.

Ostermeier's *Wunschkonzert* thus modelled a sociological realism with clear political aspirations, but one that had yet to fully address its own relationship to (and involvement in) the structures it critiques. It stood problematically outside its subject, not unlike Fräulein Rasch herself, who in one of the first actions of her 'movement score' traced with her fingers the movement of a pet fish inside a glass bowl, perched on a shelf above the radio (an action not scripted by Kroetz, while the fishbowl echoed the huge fish tank that banked *Nora*'s apartment in the companion piece). Ostermeier and his audience – like Rasch – here still gazed at a figure placed on display but trapped behind a transparent wall. Symptomatically, the precise nature of Ostermeier's social critique was controversially commented upon in the reviews. For Ulrich Seidler, the director undermined Kroetz's political critique by making his protagonist 'a figure for our amusement', relegating her 'to a curiosity' and encouraging spectators to 'indulge in the consolation

Katie Mitchell and Thomas Ostermeier at the Schaubühne 149

that we are better than the daft Fräulein Rasch'.[22] Ostermeier's tendency to centre his early Schaubühne realism on the socially destitute (as well as ill women) risked manufacturing a gaze that 'othered' his protagonists, situating himself (and his audience) as onlookers distanced from the problems his theatre represents. Over time, Ostermeier has more and more reflected on his positionality and how it figures in his realism, interrogating his own contradictions as an establishment artist with political aspirations and how these intersect with narrative tensions, making personal context the generator for his most wide-reaching and provocative work.

Mitchell: Stratifying Stanislavsky

Mitchell also gave Rasch a fishbowl, but with two occupants, not one. Counterpoising Rasch's isolation – even her goldfish were paired – Mitchell emphasized Rasch's romanticism with a close-up (filmed through the water) of her dancing pupils as they tracked the feeding fish. In an indicative contrast with Ostermeier's external focus, Mitchell's production used the materiality of theatre to make manifest the character's internal, subjective perspective. Her live cinema apparatus functioned as a multisite network from which Rasch's experience of 'self' emerged through a process of coordinated display. Mitchell split Kroetz's protagonist among a range of performers in order to synthesize their activities on the projection screen: Julia Wieninger provided a consistent face for the character, and performed most of the action in the apartment set; Birgit Walter donned a series of replica costume sleeves (only her arms in shot) to duplicate Rasch's activities for close-ups at swiftly assembled sites downstage; Therese Dürrenberger produced sound effects at a foley table, conjuring the noises Rasch hears (amplified to match the perceptual logic of the editing); musician Simon Allen performed an experimental score for prepared piano, adding musical emphases to the character's encounters with a range of objects (both physical and mental); Laura Sundermann played the adolescent Rasch in a series of artfully composed 'flashbacks' on a square of artificial grass, at times joined by Stefan Nagel whose enigmatic presence evoked memories of a lover in sequences intercut with shots of the middle-aged Rasch in her apartment. Sundermann also read extracts from Anne Sexton's poetry as a voice-over, creating associations that knit together the production's disparate elements.

Mitchell thus filled the space left by the play's lack of dialogue with the words of another 1970s author whose work gave artistic expression to experiences of depression and mania (Sexton took her own life in 1974). Mitchell would mine similar themes in her later Schaubühne work, most notably in *Die Gelbe Tapete* (2013), based on Charlotte Perkins-Gilman's *The Yellow Wallpaper* (1892), which animated the novella's first-person journal entries written by a woman whose physician husband takes her to a remote mansion to recuperate from a nervous illness. Sleeping in the nursery, she comes to perceive another woman trapped inside the patterned wallpaper and scratches it off to let her escape. Dramaturg Lyndsey Turner transposed the narrative to present-day Berlin and gave the woman a newborn baby, linking the action to postnatal depression, which Mitchell had discovered in Perkins-Gilman's biography. Alex Eales designed duplicate bedroom sets, allowing the onscreen action to cross-fade between objective reality and the protagonist's hallucinations.

Ophelias Zimmer (2015) then achieved similar effects entirely without cameras. Examining *Hamlet* from the fixed perspective of Ophelia's bedroom, Alice Birch's version added several steps between Ophelia's attendance at the play-within-the-play and her 'mad scene' (both dramatized by Shakespeare, moved 'offstage' in this play). These included Hamlet dragging Polonius's mutilated body into Ophelia's bedroom before he flees for England; Ophelia's forced medication to ensure her docile compliance after she demands to see her brother (the maid, overseen by a psychiatrist, brings her water and pills and locks the bedroom door); and Ophelia's loosening grip on reality as the pills make her drowsy and she sees her bedroom flooding. The audience did too – Chloe Lamford's trough design allowed water to seep in under the stairs of Ophelia's prison-like room and rise up to her shins, but her maid and her psychiatrist moved as if unhindered by water (it both was and was not there), making the room the site of two dimensions simultaneously – 'reality' and psychosis – in a subversion of strictly naturalistic representation that materialized Ophelia's perceptual experience (see Figure 8).

Rather than *auteurist* intervention, such details reveal Mitchell's ability to plug gaps within existing narratives in ways that add texture and dimensionality to realist depictions of women *in extremis*. Her productions generate an *episteme* – a way of thinking and producing knowledge – out of what Rebecca Schneider called 'the reverberations of the overlooked, the missed, the repressed, the seemingly forgotten'.[23] In dialogue with the source texts, they force audiences to consider how the shape of our watching colludes with pre-existing narrative structures that enact sensational violence or madness (as in Ophelia's 'mad scene'), while effacing the before and after that would allow those characters to transcend masculinist projection and attain personhood. Mitchell has also contested assumptions about female characters without sensationalist performance histories, such as the marginal and mostly silent cook Kristin in *Miss Julie*, whom Strindberg described in his author's preface as 'without individuality'. In what was her first work for the

Figure 8 Katie Mitchell's *Ophelias Zimmer* (2015) examined *Hamlet* from the fixed perspective of Ophelia's bedroom. Allowing water to seep in, Chloe Lamford's set visualized Ophelia's loosening grip on reality, under forced medication in her prison-like room. © Gianmarco Bresadola/Schaubühne.

Schaubühne in 2010, Mitchell turned Kristin into the protagonist, using her technological setup to filter Strindberg's drama entirely through Kristin's eyes and ears. Mitchell also used the poetry of Scandinavian poet Inger Christensen (1935–2009) as Kristin's stream-of-consciousness, creating a counterweight to Strindberg's casual nineteenth-century misogyny and evoking a complex inner life for a character whose emotions and processes of decision-making enjoy scant attention in the original play.

The technique thus built on the apparently paradoxical use of Sexton's poetry in *Wunschkonzert* to register what Kroetz called Rasch's 'emptiness', juxtaposing the banality of her mute solitary existence with thick textures of memory and desire. Drawing on Kroetz's indication in his preface that the 'involuntary sexual abstinence' of his romantic, but isolated, protagonist followed 'one early, short, and painfully sad love affair',[24] Mitchell used flashbacks to evoke an adolescent romance expressed through poetry from Sexton: *I Remember*, an elegiac lament spoken over a close-up of Rasch crying, unable to eat her supper, harks back to a time when 'the door to your room was / the door to mine'. Concurrently, the music playing on the radio triggered an aerial image (a memory) of adolescent Rasch sat on

152   *The Schaubühne Berlin under Thomas Ostermeier*

the grass with a man beside her, their hands edging closer together: the perceptual processes communicated on screen were linked, through Sexton's poetry, to the biographical information outlined in Kroetz's script. Mitchell has long made use of textual analysis procedures derived from Stansislavsky, mining plays for information about character biographies, relationships and given circumstances. Her experimental work at the Schaubühne has made those elements conscious to spectators, using the hidden Stanislavskian preparation as a creative mechanism for forging complex realist depictions of character. Rather than using technology to frustrate realism and dramatic totality, Mitchell uses it to forge machines of consciousness, often devoted to the perceptual moment-by-moment experience of a single character.

In this, Mitchell has drawn from contemporary neuroscience, particularly the writings of Antonio Damasio. Describing consciousness as 'image-making', he echoes the director's intermedial techniques that seek to make consciousness tangible. Her *Wunschkonzert* was paradigmatic in creating, through live cinema, a spatial and temporal context that transcended linearity, generating what Damasio calls a complex multi-track experience involving, at any one time, 'several' objects 'generat[ing] more than one narrative'.[25] Mitchell herself spoke about her attraction to the 'bundle theory', which posits the self as 'a constantly changing bundle of people, always reconfiguring [itself] in response to external stimuli'.[26] Her 2019 Schaubühne production *Orlando* was perhaps the most literal expression of this approach, following with Virginia Woolf's text an ageless protagonist who lives through four centuries of social and historical 'development' and changes sex half-way through. The production's slippery temporality (an eighteenth-century cat calendar epitomized how anachronistic design elements pulled the contemporary through past worlds) drew attention to the ongoing legacies of the patriarchal and imperial regimes that underlie Western capitalist societies. In this, *Orlando* marked the ways in which historical residues – as well as contextual alterations – influence reiterations of gender hierarchies and stereotypes.

Mitchell's experiments with technology develop her exploration of the mimetic function of theatre, forging a realism that shows how identities reconfigure and respond to shifting (and sometimes unexpectedly contiguous) political, social, historical and economic circumstances. Although her interest in 'ill women' (like Ostermeier's early work) might appear to render political questions biological (attributing them to a human 'nature' that is beyond human influence and thus de-politicising them), Mitchell remains attentive to the interpenetration of the biological and the social world, connecting her realism to politics. Her work at the Schaubühne has only made these commitments more explicit as she has staged her chosen texts on the scaffolding of carefully researched and historicized scenarios in order to make manifest the social (and hence political) processes within which a protagonist's reflexes and biology – their animality – are enmeshed. Stratifying the various elements of a Stanislavskian character, Mitchell parses protagonists into a series of sounds and gestures – a collage – that brings actors into a technical relation with the work (as do Ostermeier's 'movement scores'). In doing so, her live cinema form also contests false assumptions about the essentializing tendencies of Stanislavkian realism. As Louise LePage observed, Mitchell's use of technology separates performers from 'any illusion of an essential identity or self' and causes identity to arise from 'what the body *does*, not what it *is*'.[27]

Dragging Shakespeare through time

Both directors, then, engage with historical practices to the extent that the past may offer new perspectives on the present and vice versa. Both have reached for Shakespeare as a way of marking their own positionality and to interrogate gendered patterns of cognition. Against the *auteur* claim, I again propose a different perspective, suggesting that Ostermeier and Mitchell understand Shakespeare as a cultural phenomenon, more than a repository of stories to be staged 'faithfully'; as their productions show, the culture industry surrounding Shakespeare is not easily divorced from the plays themselves.

Mitchell's already referred to *Ophelias Zimmer* (2015) drew questions of production and representation more fully into the web of her critical realism than her previous Schaubühne work. This radical collaborative re-visioning of *Hamlet* confused the hierarchical distinctions between writer (Alice Birch), designer (Chloe Lamford) and director (Mitchell) during a process that Mitchell herself described as 'three adults together working out how to do it'.[28] By nailing our attention to the narrow confines of Ophelia's 'offstage' bedroom (Mitchell's premise for the collaboration), spoken dialogue became a minor element in a performance language where space and time were the central grammar. What is 'scripted' in the fragment of Birch's text (reprinted in the Schaubühne programme) is tedium; waiting; the length of gaps between fragments; foley sound effects like owls hooting or footsteps on the gravel below Ophelia's window created by the other three actors (doubling as maid, Hamlet and state official) in a sound-proof booth to the side of Ophelia's bedroom; interactions with objects (mugs, cassette tapes, sewing, a daily delivery of flowers). Birch interweaves sounds and scenography,

154   *The Schaubühne Berlin under Thomas Ostermeier*

creating texture from the traditional redundancies of a dramatic script reliant on dialogue, perhaps most fetishized in the Shakespearean tradition. She thus writes with a consciousness of text as one component in the larger machine of a performance – which made some reviewers complain that Ophelia hardly speaks. Hamlet's tapes, which Ophelia plays and which are 'produced' live by Renato Schuch in the foley booth, give him the largest word count. Such criticisms fail to note the shift in dramatic expressivity proposed here by a realist performance language that departs intentionally from the classical logocentric tradition.

From *Fräulein Julie* onwards, Mitchell had pursued a realism that rejected the spoken word's dominance, utilizing technology to amplify the expressive qualities of non-verbal performance. Her choice to engage with Shakespeare added further dimensions to this feminist reworking of realist representation. With *Ophelias Zimmer*, she sought to counter the tendency of 'drag[ging]' plays like *Hamlet* 'through time' and bringing with them the 'toxic gender politics' of the sixteenth-century, a process she now deems to unconsciously reinforce those politics as somehow acceptable.[29] Contesting assertions that casual misogyny belongs to another era, even insisting on its renewed prevalence in contemporary Western societies, Mitchell shows it haunting theatre's *present-day* practices by shining light into the dark corners of its most popular texts. Re-framing *Hamlet* from the perspective of Ophelia's bedroom became part of a co-ordinated strategy of reinscription. It marked the dilemmas of performers and directors negotiating the classics, and the contemporary implications of their scripted narratives, by imagining marginal characters as fully as famous protagonists, while making visible the emotional labour of the actors charged with bringing them to life. *Ophelias Zimmer* thus gathers a special political force in the context of the Schaubühne's repertoire, where it was shown alongside Ostermeier's celebrated series of Shakespeare productions showcasing Lars Eidinger as the anarchic clown given licence to dominate ensemble and audience. Ostermeier has used Shakespeare to examine paradoxes and contradictions in an alienated male consciousness out-of-joint with the surrounding world. *Richard III* (2015), the Duke in *Measure for Measure* (2011), Iago in *Othello* (2010) and *Hamlet* (2008) all are characters who live through soliloquy and communicate their feelings of alienation directly to the audience. Ostermeier has given each figure special focus, ceding to them control of the spatial, technological and temporal dynamics of his respective productions. Using these protagonists to knock through the wall separating actor and character, as well as stage and auditorium, Ostermeier has made extensive textual cuts, jettisoning what follows the chosen protagonist's death and excluding the concept of political

Katie Mitchell and Thomas Ostermeier at the Schaubühne 155

resolution or collective understanding of the wider narrative. Like Mitchell's live cinema work, these productions can be viewed as studies of a character's processes of thinking and being, although this narrow perceptual focus is not so openly declared.

Shakespeare, then, has allowed Ostermeier to address his own contradictions in ways that add political nuance to his realism. Whereas his early Ibsen productions focused on female victims of gendered violence, Ostermeier has shifted to interrogate the masculinist project of self-definition and self-exploration, focusing on figures who react to their alienation by creating complex theatrical scenarios that serve to oppress and dominate those around them. As Elisa Leroy discusses in her chapter (Chapter 7) in this volume, enabling Hamlet's abusive tendencies (via Eidinger's spontaneous outbursts) was part of Ostermeier's rejection of a reading of Hamlet as a romantic 'cliché of the last pure soul in a bad world'.[30] Rather than idolize a protagonist who might release a generation from the guilt of its own political inactivity, Ostermeier wanted to analyse a consciousness that was 'as mediocre as the world around him, as corrupted, as rotten as the rest of Denmark', reflecting on the failures of the contemporary left (as well as his own theatre) in providing viable alternatives to hegemonic capitalism.[31] Similarly, Eidinger told spectators at a post-show talk for *Richard III* in London that 'Richard is evil, but we all have evil in us'.[32] In arguing that these protagonists mirror 'us', however, Ostermeier and Eidinger universalize the contradictions they depict. This risks validating criticisms of realism as a genre that reifies one view of reality, distorted through the wounded and alienated male self, as the only view. Although the charismatic anarchists Eidinger plays wield performance to create chaos, the women in Ostermeier's Shakespeares have no choice in the roles they play, certainly not to the extent that they might appropriate performance as a way of examining the female self, or to unmask the powerful 'other' who manoeuvres against *them* as Eidinger's characters are able to do. Mitchell's *Ophelias Zimmer* highlights this problem by showing us the moments before and after Ophelia's coerced performances in Shakespeare's play, doubly resonant given that she is played by Jenny König, who regularly has to submit to Eidinger in Ostermeier's Shakespeares (in *Richard III*, where she plays Lady Anne, as well as in *Hamlet* and, as Isabella, against Eidinger's Angelo in *Measure for Measure*). Mitchell's presence at the Schaubühne has made visible a systemic problem in an ensemble that privileges the male performer, who is allowed to spread anarchy across the stage and often into the auditorium. Reviewing *Richard III*, Peter von Becker referred to Eva Meckbach's Elizabeth and König's Anne as peripheral characters, 'abandoned by the director'.[33]

156 *The Schaubühne Berlin under Thomas Ostermeier*

The critical force of contradiction

Yet there are indicators that Ostermeier has become alert to this institutional problem. He brought the well-known actress Nina Hoss (her notoriety outstrips Eidinger's) to join the Schaubühne ensemble in 2014, and also programmed *Status Quo* (2019), a play by one of the theatre's dramaturgs, Maja Zade, which lambasted workplace misogyny by showing a gender-flipped rehearsal in which König wore a replica of Eidinger's Richard costume, while Jule Böwe – in Ostermeier's ensemble since the Baracke days – gave a juicy parody of the artistic director himself. As Ramona Mosse has argued in her chapter (Chapter 3), Ostermeier's artistic trajectory over the past two decades shows him capable of such critical self-reflection, and open to the transformation and renewal he discerns in dramatic characters. Similarly, Mitchell has acknowledged criticisms (not least from her daughter) that staging reiterative narrative patterns culminating in female suicide has a cumulatively wearing effect.[34] Her live cinema version of Elfriede Jelinek's *Schatten (Eurydike Sagt)* (2016) was a transitional work in this respect, beginning with a female death but following its protagonist into a liberated afterlife, where Eurydike frustrates Orpheus's rescue attempt. *Orlando* then looked like a confident assertion of a new phase of practice, surprising audiences with a gender-fluid comedy that playfully examined the historical vectors underpinning contemporary conversations around gender identity, suggesting that Mitchell is seeking new ways to widen the scope of her realism.

Both directors thus craft dramatic totalities, but these counter some of realism's most common critiques by becoming conscious (to varying degrees) of their own perspectival distortions and positional blind spots. Thereby, they connect realist theatre practice with a politics of perception grounded in twenty-first century realities. Both directors also pursue realisms that push beyond straightforward mimesis to demonstrate highly attuned compositional sensibilities in a sensitive dialogue with the texts they stage. Invariably, the results are heightened viewing experiences, where the sensual registers of theatricality evoke a density of character subjectivity. These directors do not bind dramatic character in a shroud of metaphysical coherence or unity. Rather, their striking innovations are geared at making audiences *feel* how subjectivities are constituted (and/or crushed) by material forces and interlocking socio-economic pressures in open-ended processes of becoming. With this emphasis on feeling, they both depart considerably from Brecht in seeking affective means of confronting aspects of our ideological formation (resonating with the critical writings of Lauren Berlant, Sara Ahmed and others). The intricate artistry of their productions may not reliably enact real-world change, but it makes tangible, in the shared cultural space of theatre, socio-structural forces through how they make us feel. As a result, Ostermeier and Mitchell avoid reinforcing a deterministic world view. Instead, they recast realism as an agential form that makes us confront who we think we are and how we behave: a realism that enables, rather than strangles, agency.

Notes

1 The productions were *Fräulein Julie* (2010), *Die Gelbe Tapete* (2013), *Atmen* (2013), *The Forbidden Zone* (2014), *Ophelias Zimmer* (2015), *Schatten (Euridike Sagt)* (2016), and *Orlando* (2019).
2 Michael Billington, *State of the Nation: British Theatre since 1945* (London: Faber & Faber, 2007), 405.
3 Lyn Gardner, 'Daring directors are shaking up the classics', *Guardian Theatre Blog*, 29 October 2014.
4 Interview with the author, 4 September 2012.
5 Thomas Ostermeier, 'Presenter Interview', *Performingarts.jp*, 18 August 2005.
6 Eberhard Spreng, 'Transfer eines Demokratie-Experiments', *Deutschlandfunk. de* (Kultur Heute), 9 September 2012.
7 Ian Shuttleworth, 'Prompt Corner', *Theatre Record* 33, no. 9 (2013): 387.
8 Quoted in Andy Lavender, 'Directors give instructions', a transcript of an event held at CSSD (London) on 14 October 2008, 8.
9 Quoted in Katie Mitchell, *The Director's Craft* (Abingdon: Routledge, 2009), 229.
10 Ibid., 227.
11 Quoted in James Woodall, 'Thomas Ostermeier: On Europe, Theatre, Communication and Exchange', in *Contemporary European Theatre Directors*, eds Maria Delgado and Dan Rebellato (Abingdon: Routledge, 2010), 370.
12 Quoted in Geburg Treusch-Dieter, 'Formal das Alltägliche betonen: Thomas Ostermeier gegen Theater als Angstveranstaltung', *Der Freitag*, 31 October 2003.
13 Robert Leach, *Vsevolod Meyerhold* (Cambridge: Cambridge University Press, 1989), 92.
14 Franz Xaver Kroetz, *Farmyard, and Other Plays*, trans. Peter Sander (New York: Urizen Books, 1978), 25.
15 Ibid.
16 Quoted in Magnus Florin and Hannes Meidal, 'Thomas Ostermeier besökte Stockholm', *YouTube*, 22 February 2012.
17 Quoted in Alfred Hickling, 'Choice Part for Katie', *Yorkshire Post*, 12 October 1994.
18 Interview with the author, 4 September 2012.

19 Ulrich Beck, *Risk Society: Towards a New Modernity* (Munich: SAGE Publications, 1992), 137.
20 Quoted in Treusch-Dieter, 'Formal das Alltägliche betonen'.
21 Peter M. Boenisch and Thomas Ostermeier (eds), *The Theatre of Thomas Ostermeier* (Abingdon and New York: Routledge, 2016), 244.
22 Ulrich Seidler, 'Das Hupferl ist ein Symbol', *Berliner Zeitung*, 10 February 2003.
23 Rebecca Schneider, 'Performance Remains', *Performance Research* 6, no. 2 (2001): 104.
24 Kroetz, *Farmyard*, 26.
25 Antonio Damasio, *The Feeling of What Happens: Body, Emotion and the Making of Consciousness* (London: Vintage, 2000), 176.
26 Quoted in Maria Shevtsova and Christopher Innes, *Directors/Directing: Conversations on Theatre* (Cambridge: Cambridge University Press, 2009), 200.
27 Louise LePage, 'Posthuman Perspectives and Postdramatic Theatre: The Theory and Practice of Hybrid Ontology in Katie Mitchell's *The Waves*', *Culture, Language and Representation* 6 (2008), 142.
28 Katie Mitchell and Chloe Lamford, 'Katie Mitchell and Chloe Lamford discuss Ophelias Zimmer', *YouTube*, 6 May 2016.
29 Ibid.
30 Thomas Ostermeier in conversation with Ian Rickson, Goethe-Institut (London), 13 November 2011.
31 'Interview with Thomas Ostermeier', *YouTube*, Theatro.tv, 2011.
32 Barbican Theatre, 17 February 2017.
33 Peter von Becker, 'Alles gegeben, bürgerlich geblieben', *Der Tagesspiegel*, 9 February 2015.
34 See Maddy Costa, 'Alternative point of view: The Malady of Death', 4 May 2018, https://www.barbican.org.uk/read-watch-listen/the-malady-of-death-an-alternative-point-of-view (accessed 22 June 2020).

12

Encountering the Rage from the South: Latin American Theatre at the Schaubühne's FIND Festival

Marina Ceppi

Since the beginning of the new artistic direction at the Schaubühne in 2000, the theatre's 'Festival of International New Drama' (FIND) has been an annual bridge constructed by the Schaubühne to connect with the global theatre scene. In addition to productions already part of a wider international festival circuit, by influential artists and companies such as the Wooster Group, Toneelgroep Amsterdam and others, the annual spring festival aims to present new voices, new productions and new dramaturgies from around the world. It has become not only an important facilitator for international exchange, but also a showcase for different views and perspectives on the social situation of the present. In this chapter, I will add to Ramona Mosse's and Jens Hillje's discussions, in their respective chapters in this book (Chapters 3 and 10), of the role of the festival within the Schaubühne's institutional strategy, by concentrating on FIND's link to Latin America, and especially to Chile and Mexico. Latin America has become a specific area of focus in recent festival editions. I will show how some of these invited works, in their respective ways, represent what may be described, following Jorge Dubatti, as a 'supra-national' political commitment and a social conscience, which on the one hand contributed to the festival's topics, but as 'comparative theatre' also connected with the Schaubühne's wider experimentation with contemporary forms of political theatre. This will also give me the opportunity to explore connections and synchronies between the Schaubühne and aesthetics created in Latin America, pointing to the catalyst function that the festival's unique 'supra-national' cultural space has provided for some of the companies invited to FIND.

FIND – a 'comparative' theatre festival

While FIND has undergone some changes since its initial edition, not least with regard to the festival's audience and its impact, its main aim of bringing

160   *The Schaubühne Berlin under Thomas Ostermeier*

both internationally renowned and lesser known theatre groups to the Schaubühne has remained intact. Discovering new artists, next texts and new ways of making theatre from outside the German – and for some time now, extensively from outside European – borders, the festival has been vital in contributing to the Schaubühne's internationalist outlook. While, rather uniquely for a German theatre company, the Schaubühne engages in intense international touring with its own productions, with FIND it also opens its own stages for international invitations. The festival, which in contrast to other international festivals in Berlin is organized and presented by a single theatre, represents a specific effort under Thomas Ostermeier's artistic direction, which goes beyond the expectations of the public financial support his theatre receives. Today, the festival continues the ambitions, which its former director Jens Hillje describes in his chapter for the initial years while he led the programming. Its continued place within the Schaubühne's focus on social and political engagement was evident from some of the recent festival themes, such as 'Archaeology of the present' (2019), 'The art of forgetting' (2018), and 'Democracy and tragedy' (2017). At the same time, from its outset, FIND has been important in associating many international expats living in Berlin with the venue. In 2011, the theatre then added 'FIND plus', an annual meeting of theatre students in acting, directing and dramaturgy, from several international conservatoires and universities, from the Schaubühne's partners within the European Prospero theatre network to New York's Tisch School of the Arts. While these theatre students make up a large number of the festival's audience, FIND has also become widely accepted by the theatre's regular audience; now, tickets even for festival invitations to artists and productions so far unknown by Berlin audiences sell out as quickly as they do for the Schaubühne's own successful productions.

While the festival's connections with Latin American theatre date back to 2005, these links intensified while Florian Borchmeyer, successor to Hillje and the theatre's head dramaturg until 2019, curated the festival between 2011 and 2019. He had studied in Berlin and Havana, wrote his PhD thesis on the literary history of the 'discovery' of the Americas, directed an award-winning documentary film about contemporary Cuba and has also curated for many years the international programme at the renowned Filmfest Munich. Fluent in Spanish, he had access to and connections with a number of Latin American theatre-makers and companies, so that – in contrast to work produced in Eastern Europe, Africa or Asia – the festival's engagement with this region had been particularly sustained under his curation. Productions from Latin America of course display an affinity with Western theatre culture, but they also hail from countries that are social and economic

Encountering the Rage from the South 161

victims of Western dominance over the southern hemisphere. Furthermore, they respond to conflicts resulting from specific political histories of the individual countries, not least the history of dictatorships. While encompassing different nationalities and countries, I still find the comparative designation of this theatre work as 'Latin American' strategically productive, since the term may be a way, following Jorge Dubatti, of problematizing nationalist discourses:

> Comparative theatre maintains initially that studying theatre from an international point of view implies problematizing the relationships or exchanges between two or more national theatres [...] or between a national theatre and any foreign culture (extern to the national). It is clear, internationality as well as supranationality assume the concept of the national, to which we contrast or relate more theatres (national ones), or work in its overcoming. The supranational point of view consists in attending to problems which transcend or exceed the concept of the national (because they are unable of being solved with the characteristic of the national).[1]

I suggest understanding FIND in this sense as an important effort in creating a perspective of 'comparative theatre', in order to overcome a national perspective, and to attend to fundamental problems of the present from a wider perspective. Dubatti's notion of 'supranationality' resonates particularly well with the festival's ambition, and in the following it will help us to articulate how some of the selected plays engage with such 'supranational' political problems.

To start with, it is certain to say that the issues and topics presented by companies from Chile and Mexico, to which I shall now turn as main examples, portray and refer to issues that concern the entire Latin American continent. Many of them are related to its exploitation by Western capitalism, therefore opening a wider, if not outright global supranational problematic. The topics discussed in these productions range from post-dictatorship trauma and marginality to the role of the artist in society, on to economic issues and gender oppression. These themes reflect wider international issues as well, yet the situation in Latin America in all these aspects proves to be more urgent and alarming for their tangible everyday impact on the population. With regard to gender oppression, Latin American countries feature prominently in statistics about increased violence against women, as well as in other pressing concerns such as inflation and poverty.[2] For all of the theatre-makers discussed in the following, these issues are not just theoretical arguments or ethical debates, but existential, daily life struggles.

Postdramatic frictions bridging political rage and enquiry

An important point when analysing these productions concerns the way these political topics are represented on stage. The productions show quite different aesthetic approaches, and they differ from each other in their representation of similar circumstances, reflecting the wide variety of aesthetic tendencies incumbent in this region, and furthermore the predisposition for experimentation within theatre. As Igor de Almeida Silva suggested in his discussion of the Brazilian engagement with Thomas Ostermeier's work as it toured his country (Chapter 8), I also suggest that the broad perspective offered by Hans-Thies Lehmann's notion of 'postdramatic theatre' brings these various tendencies into a mutual resonance. Each of the productions I shall turn to in this chapter tends to break the paradigms of the bourgeois modern Western European 'dramatic' theatre since the nineteenth century, following Lehmann's chronology. At the same time they share, with much postdramatic work, the ability to enhance the value and potential of theatre as a social platform that appeals to the audience's 'response-ability'.[3]

My selection of Latin American productions presented during recent FIND editions (between 2017 and 2019) not only demonstrates such a postdramatic aesthetic common ground. Each of them deals with a pertinent political and societal issue relating to its respective country; while the individual aesthetic approaches towards portraying these issues may differ in detail, these problems are still articulated on stage in each case in urgent, at times violent, ways that tend to confront the audience directly. Not taking away from these productions' metaphoric, at times poetic, dimensions, they do not allow for a passive consumption as they try to move the audience and alert them to the situation. In conversation, Alexandra von Hummel, performer and co-director of *El Hotel*,[4] from the Santiago-based theatre company Teatro La María, refers to the idea of rage as an important, constant and characteristic part of Latin American theatre that differentiates it from other theatre cultures such as the European. This reference to rage, as intense anger, indeed seems pertinent for our analysis. Driven by urgency, at times even violence, 'rage' indeed characterizes this theatre work from different Latin American countries, and points towards a central element of their discourse. This intuition is then confirmed not least in the context of (and contrast to) the other international productions presented alongside in the programme of FIND. If we consider further the motivations that Thomas Ostermeier, Jens Hillje and others expressed about their own theatre-making,[5] these productions that emerge from regional performance making disclose a match with the Schaubühne's discourse, making this meeting a productive combination of forces.

Confronting the privilege of the spectators: *Tijuana* and *Acceso*

Tijuana by the Mexican based performer collective Lagartijas tiradas al sol was presented at FIND 2017, which was themed 'Democracy and tragedy'.[6] We are informed that, for six months, the company's co-founder Gabino Rodríguez had changed his identity to become Santiago Ramírez, and lived in the city of Tijuana trying to survive on the minimum salary. In the production, Rodríguez narrated his experience. The marginal, precarious reality that he evoked in his narration confronted the theatre audience with their own distance towards people from this disprivileged social stratum. While apparently living there for this timespan, Rodríguez compromised his own body in order to become able to narrate and relate, first hand, to the guilt, frustration and, from time to time, also the tranquillity that he experienced in his adopted new identity. In sharing his journey, he made the audience part of his trip, to reflect on the price of human labour, and the implied lack of dignity. I said 'apparently', since one of the most interesting and irritating aspects of the production was the second narration that emerged in the course of the performance: that about Gabino's experience itself, which never confirmed nor denied that he had actually lived and experienced what he described. This doubt became an important dramaturgic element.

Tijuana was part of the company's larger project *La democracia en Mexico 1965–2015*. It consisted of a wider artistic exploration and analysis of the current state of the Mexican democracy, referring in particular to the expectations raised in the 1965 book *La democracia en México* by Pablo González Casanova, a key author and social investigator of Mexican society. Lagartijas tiradas al sol had begun to work together in the city of Mexico in 2003. From 2009, their productions became a regular presence in international festivals, and also in Berlin, where some of their previous shows had been presented at the HAU theatre. In 2014, they were for the first time invited to FIND with their production *Derretiré con un cerillo la nieve de un volcán*, and from there their relationship with the Schaubühne began to develop. *Tijuana*, meanwhile, had premiered in Spain and toured to a number of countries on the international theatre circuit before reaching the Berlin audience. In interview, Gabino Rodríguez noted that 'the FIND audience is different, in that they seemed to be a more local audience, close to the Schaubühne, and less the usual festival spectators used to seeing international pieces'.[7]

For Rodriguez, *Tijuana* did not intend to demonstrate anything beyond an artistic approach to the political situation, how to deal with it and the ethical problems of art-making when engaging with reality. He commented:

164   *The Schaubühne Berlin under Thomas Ostermeier*

Most politically interested artistic work does not reveal an aim of veritable change, but instead draws on reflection, intending to change the outlook from a hegemonic point of view. The play was a series of provocations to the audience and summed up a number of concerns. It presented a specific narrative in order to enhance some tensions, above all the repercussions of an artist disguising himself to go into a place which is not his and which he may leave anytime because he in fact belongs to another, more privileged social class.

Tijuana interrogated the social implications, and not least this privilege of an artist. As noted, the ambiguity of the two possibilities, that the experience presented on stage may be either true or fictional, was a central and intriguing concern of the production. Both alternatives have different aesthetic implications, and both appear valuable. Rodríguez remarked, in our interview, that 'the audience's conception of how truth on stage is linked with truth in correspondence with reality is apparently direct', and he referred to theatre productions by artists such as Lola Arias and Mariano Pensotti as examples:

> As a result, spectators were not so critical about the actual veracity of what was presented. The work by these artists is dramatical and situated within theatre, working within theatrical traditions and conventions, and hence different from the exposition of objects in a museum.

Added to that, document and fiction, rather than being two worlds apart, have always had a strong, permeable relationship, and this is where Lagartijas tiradas al sol are interested in intervening. That is why their work escapes its clear position on either side of the truth–fiction binary, and in this sense it displays its postdramatic values, while the company uses the theatre as a platform for such social and artistic enquiry, without declaring for one side.

A further interesting aspect is the audience's guilt about the social circumstances presented. It is worth citing Rodríguez in a longer passage from our email exchange:

> The play was intended to be presented to a public of financially well accommodated people who have the opportunity of sitting in a theatre seat on a Sunday, in any country. Everywhere it is the same middle class that consumes art and with a similar political tendency, leaning towards a liberal, open minded mentality. Although there are differences in each country, this social class shares a way of inhabiting the world and a way of conceiving it. The play talks about how such an 'accommodated'

Encountering the Rage from the South

audience sees an 'accommodated' artist representing a poor person and coming to tell us how they live. In that equation there is a lot to talk about.

For Rodríguez, the international, and not least northern interest, in his company's work reflects a certain need to '[get] close to these realities' from other parts of the world. Staging these issues establishes then a link between countries, which also reflects systems of exploitation within and between countries:

> The artistic bond is a bridge between these realities. What the character does in approaching poverty for five months, is what the spectator does when approaching poverty for one hour of performance. Then, they both go on with their life.

This brings us back to the topic of 'rage'. The social inequality that is directly and urgently presented on stage leaves spectators with no other chance but to be challenged for their own privileged position in society. Lagartijas tiradas al sol thus make their audience themselves an actor in this search for what is true or not, and at the same time they call on the audience's conscience about their own role in the oppression portrayed. This feeling of guilt makes the audience relate to the character as well as forcing them to rethink how far they themselves are implicated in this marginal reality presented on stage.

A similar encounter that foregrounded the position of the spectator not only as a member of the audience, but as a member of the audience, but as a member of society and someone who is able to afford to come and see this production, was staged in the Chilean production *Acceso*, directed by Pablo Larraín, the theatre and movie director of renowned films such as *NO* (2012), *Neruda* (2016) and *Jackie* (2016). The solo piece performed by Roberto Farías equally modified the spectatorial position beyond understanding or even empathy with the 'poor' protagonist portrayed on stage, a peddler called Sandokán who offered a variety of products to survive and, as he expressed it, 'to have access'. The *mise en scène* needed no more than subtle light changes; anything else, Sandokán had in his selling bag. It was his memories that the audience accessed, as tumultuous and chaotic as they turned out to be. The performer's proximity to the spectators, so near as to be able to touch them, meant that the character's panic, his fear of falling into this world, transmitted to the audience and one could not help but to feel affected. Behind Sandokán's commercial rhetoric the audience could quickly detect his personal experiences, which started as a little hint and went on to absorb his entire speech. In colloquial, working class language, he entered a maelstrom of memories. They led him to create images with his body that made the cruel reality even more tangible, as he confronted the audience with a history of abuse, excess and discrimination. Yet, this was more than just one person's story. It revealed the social difference that exists in Chile, and it exposed the history of abuse by the SENAME, the 'Servicio Nacional de Menores Chileno (National Minors Service of Chile). For this character, abuse was love, and a ticket to a dignified life.

The difficulty in seeing *Acceso* was that this world could quickly become too remote from the audience, so that it could be too readily distanced as 'other'. The long monologue eventually ended as Sandokán asked the spectators, 'What did you come to see?' Once again it was impossible not to think about one's own spectatorial position. The stakes of this kind of production are an honest portrayal of this reality, and to relate to one's audience without turning the character into an exotic animal in a human zoo of the marginalized. In order to analyse the political and social action of *Acceso*, one may understand these staged 'encounterings' along the lines of Jacques Rancière's aesthetic politics of dissensus, where those who have no voice claim their participation in speech and dialogue, or with reference to Alain Badiou's notion of the 'event', which results from the violent introduction of subjects who had previously been excluded from the field of visibility and legibility.[8] Yet, for me, this goes beyond the narrative of the play itself, which of course does precisely this: giving voice to a character representing the marginalized. Crucial, though, is that this encounter takes place in the common place of theatre, where we also encounter ourselves in our social role and position as audience members. The play's dramaturgy prevented the spectators from being able to simply watch a drama of and about the other, but instead they were implicated beyond the fiction, as an actual part of this cycle of abuse and marginalization. This was not about a negotiation between reality and fiction, but about one's own social position, and one's privilege. As a result, both of these productions were particularly interesting pieces to be shown within an international festival to audiences in the north. The gap for spectators in a country where poverty, marginalization and violence are not as present as for a Latin American audience, would be even larger. Their reflexive engagement with their own positionality, and their own privilege, became the key challenge posed by these productions.

Irruptions of past and present wounds: *El Hotel* and *Paisajes para no colorear*

Founded in Chile in 2000 by Alexandra von Hummel and Alexis Moreno, the company Teatro La María notes that 'The concepts of homeland, identity,

Encountering the Rage from the South   167

violence and failure have gotten in the way, some way or another, in all of our staging. We seek to reflect on the country, condensed, through the staging, fragments of the national reality.'[9] During the 2018 FIND, which was headlined 'The art of forgetting', they presented the already mentioned *El Hotel*. A memorable line from Alexis Moreno's script stated, 'You cannot judge the executioner if he does not remember his crime'. The audience was presented with a geriatric institution, located in Antarctica, whose old guests had all been involved in Augusto Pinochet's dictatorship. From an actress to a government minister, they had all been, in one way or another, on the side of the perpetrators while the military regime was in power. The play revolved around how these people now tried to hide behind forgetfulness. It resonated with the infamous answer of Pinochet, when questioned about his responsibility for 'Operation Colombo' that covered up 119 detainees and 'disappeared' persons: 'I don't remember, but it is not true. It is not true and if it were true, I don't remember'.

Similarly, the characters of the play did not remember, let alone regret their crimes; instead, they devoted themselves to forgetting systematically what they had done, living their last days in some superficial enjoyment. The hotel had become an escape zone for those who pretended senility and disability to make things 'not true', instead of taking responsibility for their atrocities. They stood still in time, as the audience got to see their 'golden years' again, with old music, old commercials and news reports from a time when they did not have to hide yet, and, moreover, when they were the ones who ruled. The play was full of cruel humour, as it articulated in its fictional metaphor what societies tend to do with their darkest histories: their country decided not to judge or convict them – but to forget them. The acting was filled with constant hyperbole and consistent exaggeration. There was a clear sexual undertone that according to Von Hummel was motivated by the Chilean association of the military class with insolence and superficiality.[10] The costumes, as well, were not only designed so as to turn young actors into old characters, they too disclosed a taste for the artificial. The old bodies of the characters were shown as unreal and fake. In fact, everything in *El Hotel* was outright exaggerated to mark the situation as an atrocity that cannot be represented without turning it to its extreme.

The production had already participated in the Chilean 'Santiago a Mil' festival, and had had a subsequent tour. When bringing *El Hotel* to Berlin, the company found the audience's reception similar to that they had received in Chile. Post-show talks at the Schaubühne revealed to the artists how the violence of their humour, and the types of characters and systems they portrayed in the production, had been recognized and understood by the international public, too. Von Hummel remarked in our conversation that maybe these types of plays met a demand in a European context not so much because of the topic (the details of which would only speak to a Chilean audience familiar with the references and direct context), but because as a Latin American company, they had 'this sort of passion that is so particular', because these historical pasts still affect everyday life in Latin American countries nowadays – and once more, this brings us back to what I had described earlier as characteristic 'rage'. Even the exaggerated comedy of a play discloses the tragedy of a now democratic society that cannot cure its wounds, or even at least acknowledge and remember its past. Discussing the production alongside other Chilean plays on the subject, theatre scholars Pérez Campona and Figueroa Del Campo see in *El Hotel's* 'senile flow of facts, deeds, dates, procedures and methods of torture', as they describe it, an:

> operation that bends reality to open on the scene a space for fabulation about the memories of the perpetrators. That mystery that seemed to be installed in the national imaginary about their lies and secret pacts, seems to be healed by the memories of these senile perpetrators presented on stage, imagined by the dramaturgs, as they open little fissures in their everyday life where this hidden story and their violent actions alongside their normalizations irrupt.[11]

In contrast to *Tijuana* (and *Paisajes para no colorear*, to which we will turn next), both *El Hotel* and *Acceso* were more conventional dramatic works with a 'closed' fictional word that left no doubt that actors were playing fictional characters. The directorial and aesthetic choices, however, still linked them with a postdramatic approach to theatre-making.

While *El Hotel* confronted traumatic pasts, the 2019 FIND festival, with the theme 'Archaeology of the present', put the focus onto the current social structures in post-dictatorship Chile. *Paisajes para no colorear* by the Santiago based company Teatro la Re-Sentida, directed by Marco Layera, was one of the most moving and compelling performances in the festival. Nine Chilean teenage girls narrate and act out experiences from the oppression that women (specifically teenagers) suffer in the present Chilean society. Their stories brought to light a series of instances of institutional and family violence, such as the prominent cases of Lisette Villa, Florencia Aguirre and Tania Águila, who were all murdered because they were female teenagers from a specific social class. In line with a strategy discussed earlier, the production gave speech to women who were no longer there to tell their experience. In addition, the teenagers enacted situations from their own experience of everyday abuse such as bullying, prejudice, lack of recognition or (lack of) body shaming.

Encountering the Rage from the South

Patriarchal oppression has never been greater, reaching peak numbers on gender violence and abuse of power in the whole south of the continent, while over recent years the feminist movement has become a strong voice. Again, the medium of theatre was used here to articulate the 'rage', and to discuss the urgency of a topic and of situations that are part of the audience's daily reality as well. *Paisajes para no colorear* had a crudity and force that matched its themes. The young performers were not content with expressing and explaining, but they had to yell, shout and show their rage about these injustices, addressing the audience directly as perpetrators. This desperate scream addressed to adults against patriarchy, abuse and prejudice could not be anything else but a scream, since adults normally would not listen. The audience was confronted, repeatedly, with how grown-ups tend to think of teenagers, how they dismiss them as crazy in their pain or their rebellion against injustice. Confronting this oppression would not be effective if it were not extreme. The play employed a number of staging strategies to present the situations of adult oppression and to enact the violence. Some violent scenes were re-enacted, such as Lisette Villa's death by suffocation at the hands of her guards in the SENAME, a prominently reported case of violence against a young woman. Later, a group of performers forced one of the girls to wear a doll's dress after she had been criticized about her gender-neutral clothing. Elsewhere, they asked the help of the audience to stage a cathartic scene where a daughter was finally able to express her feelings for her father, who would never listen. In yet another moment, portraying the adult establishment, we see a parodistic scene, where a group of the young performers represent upper-class ladies dressed in fur coats and jewellery who voice their derogatory opinions about 'the girls', their stories and women's liberation in general. Here, the lines were taken from a discussion of the topic in the Chilean parliament; all were actual statements by politicians.

The production came out of the company's one-year investigation, undertaken in a number of middle- and lower-class neighbourhoods of Santiago, where they held workshops with teenagers. The dramaturgy was generated between the young performers and Marco Layera and Carolina de la Maza, director and stage assistant respectively of Teatro La Re-Sentida. They worked on improvisations around topics suggested by the teenagers. Although the girls act as if the experiences they present were their own, this may not be the case (the [same] production is performed by a varying cast of twenty-five young performers with whom La Re-Sentida have worked). In their rehearsal, they worked dramatically on a topic, remembering collectively and generating a scene using their own experiences and testimony of others in a dramatical way. Similar to the earlier examples, the fact of whether the events are true or not, and of whether they have been experienced by the girl who presents them on stage, is far less important than the confrontation of the (adult) audience

170   *The Schaubühne Berlin under Thomas Ostermeier*

with this urgent social problem. The audience are forced to answer to their own position on these issues. Throughout, spectators are directly addressed. As an audience, we stand for the dominant society the girls attack. In fact, we come to recognize that we *are* this society that bears the responsibility for these woes.

Paisajes was La Re-Sentida's third invitation to FIND, after *La imaginación del futuro* in 2015, and *Tratando de hacer una obra que cambie al mundo* in the year before. In my interview with Marco Layera and Carolina de la Maza, they note that to analyse the reaction we must consider which people attend these types of shows in Chile. The production had been somewhat cathartic and met with a lot of empathy from the audience when presented in Chile, yet this audience does not represent the conservative and patriarchal parts of Chilean society that it critiques.[12] On the one hand, the theatre-makers are much concerned with the direct usefulness of making political theatre, reflecting about the challenges and contradictions involved. They believe this play unites social and artistic practice, and Layera stated that:

> This production has transformed me, and I can say the same for everyone who participated. This should be the point of every production: the change of our vision and perspective upon things. That is something which the audience can clearly grasp and perceive. The political implication gets to the audience, they cannot remain passive to such transformation, whether they find it annoying or liberating.[13]

While the play's effect is thus irrefutable, it must also be acknowledged that it was limited to an audience ready and eager to see such a show, who would likely agree with the political view expressed. One of the expressed aims of Teatro La Re-Sentida is to make a popular theatre, and a fascinating aspect of *Paisajes para no colorear* is how the production managed to address audiences of a wide range of age, gender and social make-up, including some people who had never been to the theatre before, who came to the performances at the youth centres where the company had worked with the young girls. At the same time, however, even some close relatives of the adolescent performers refused to attend, due to the sensitive topics they portrayed. But the piece was a step in the company's ongoing artistic research into making theatre that does not only belong to an elite, or to just to the people who work in it.

Conclusions

The Latin American rage staged in these productions attempts, in a Brechtian sense, to modify the audience's attitudes, preventing them from consuming a spectacle, instead at least intending to turn them into producers of a new social reality – as an effect of a violent, rabid theatre of rage, which addresses pertinent social topics with great urgency and intensity. This confrontational way of addressing the audience is a direct part of the brutal everyday reality that is here shared on stage. In this sense, the productions resonate with a core aim of the Schaubühne's attempts, in their own work, to turn theatre into a tool to catalyse a social discussion, and to reevaluate our roles as audiences, artists and as members in our society, using our agency to intervene and change things. It is obvious that the European and the Latin American social and economic situations differ. Yet, the bridge established by the FIND festival proves to be a valuable meeting point for both cultures, where the theatre stage is the very place to display artistic work and social analysis, on the European side, and thereby creating a frame for discussion and awareness, on the Latin American one. Such work of 'supranationality' enables not only the debate of questions about the relationships between continents (while establishing new platforms for perhaps a different kind of relationship), but it also produces new ways of viewing, and of reflecting both the role of the theatre audience and, eventually, the social role of theatre itself.

Notes

1 Jorge Dubatti, *Cartografía teatral: introducción al teatro comparado* (Buenos Aires: Atuel, 2008), 11. All translations from Spanish language sources are my own.
2 See for example https://data.oecd.org/inequality/violence-against-women. htm; www.statista.com/statistics/268225/countries-with-the-highest-inflation-rate/; https://worldpoverty.io/.
3 Hans-Thies Lehmann, *Postdramatic Theatre* (Abingdon and New York: Routledge, 2006), 185.
4 *El hotel* (*The hotel*). Directed by Alexis Moreno and Alexandra von Hummel. Premiere Teatro de la Palabra, Santiago de Chile, August 2016. My interview with Alexandra von Hummel took place on 5 September 2019. All citations refer to my transcript of our conversation.
5 See Peter M. Boenisch and Thomas Ostermeier (eds), *The Theatre of Thomas Ostermeier* (Abingdon and New York: Routledge, 2016), and again Hillje's chapter (Chapter 10) as well as the interview with Ostermeier (Chapter 4) in the present volume.
6 *Tijuana*. Directed by Luisa Pardo. Written and performed by Gabino Rodríguez. Premiered at Escenas do cambio, Santiago de Compostela, Spain, February 2016.

7 Gabino Rodríguez, email interview with the author, 8 July 2019. All citations in the following section are from this email conversation, with permission from the artist.

8 See also Amelia Jones, 'Encountering: The Conceptual Body, or a Theory of When, Where and How Art "Means"', *The Drama Review* 62, no. 3 (2018): 12–34.

9 See http://teatrolamaria.cl/quienes-somos/ (accessed 28 February 2020).

10 All citations in the following section are taken from my interview with von Hummel; see note 4, above.

11 D. Campona Pérez and C Del Campo Figueroa, *Figuraciones del mal: Agresores y violencia política en el teatro chileno contemporáneo* (Santiago de Chile: Fondart, 2019).

12 Marco Layera and Carolina de la Maza, interview with Marina Ceppi, July 2019.

13 Ibid.

13

Performing Bodies as a Scenic Playground of Social Realities: Choreographic Theatre at the Schaubühne Berlin

Sabine Huschka

Following the launch of the Schaubühne's new artistic direction in 2000, choreographic formats and dance-theatre productions became an important aspect of the theatre's new profile. A specific practice of theatral *mise en scène* evolved that was characterized by the interdependence of acted and danced elements; it accounted for a number of important choreographic signatures to emerge from the Schaubühne. These productions drew on, above all, the explicit confrontation with urgent socio-political concerns, but also on an active, at times experimental, interrogation of the stage's spatial and architectural dispositions. A key aspect of the profound theatre-aesthetic innovation that has characterized Thomas Ostermeier's tenure as artistic director since 2000 is his theatre's unique achievement within the German (and, perhaps, wider international) theatre landscape of the early twenty-first century: the fact that it granted dance, on an equal part with dramatic theatre, a space for aesthetic reflection. The following analysis will focus on some of the Schaubühne's most significant dance-theatre productions created between 2000 and the early 2010s. I will discuss the genealogy of characteristic modes of creation as well as some of the specific aesthetic and political enquiries, which the choreographers associated with the venue stood for. First and foremost, there was Sasha Waltz, the theatre's co-artistic director between 2000 and 2005. In her works from this period – *Körper* (*Bodies*, 2000), *S* (2001), *noBody* (2002), and her choreographic installation *insideout* (2004) – she conceived of bodies as playing grounds shaped by society and culture, which she then extended into strong scenic images, based on choreographic structures of bodies in space. Then there were two choreographers who were, after 2005, more loosely associated with the Schaubühne: Constanza Macras, whose works *Back to the Present* (2004) and *Big in Bombay* (2005) I shall focus on, and Anouk van Dijk, who created both *Trust* (2009) and *Protect Me* (2010) in collaboration with playwright-director Falk Richter. Their works, too,

174   *The Schaubühne Berlin under Thomas Ostermeier*

critically reflected social realities in choreographic arrangements of movement, speech and action. My analysis of these key dance-theatre works will concentrate on their specific aesthetic and critical positions, and their potential for political intervention.

A new start with new concepts

Taking over in late 1999, the Schaubühne's new team of artistic directors deliberately granted dance an equal share in the new aesthetic signature they envisaged for the theatre. Dance became part of a critical programming, which specifically looked at the potential of choreography and dancing performing bodies to dramatically reflect socio-political issues, in addition to, and alongside, dramatic narratives and the tactics of political theatre direction. As they are informed by societal norms, codes, images, passions, fears and desires, performing bodies have the theatral potential to express both societal conflicts and individual experiences. Stage action, steeped in this power of choreographed physicality, may gain a powerful aesthetic force and a pervasive dynamic energy that connects to the audience.

This conceptual departure resulted from Thomas Ostermeier's offer to choreographer Sasha Waltz to join the artistic direction of the Schaubühne.[1] She had become widely known during the late 1990s with the dance-theatre works she had created at the Berlin fringe-venue Sophiensäle, which she had co-founded. Together, Ostermeier and Waltz – alongside their dramaturgs Jens Hillje and Jochen Sandig – pursued in their four-year share of the venue's artistic direction a radical mission of re-politicizing theatre.[2] The four members of the Schaubühne's artistic direction at the time brought four different perspectives to the table: direction, choreography, dramaturgy, and producing. While they claimed their aesthetic and conceptual collaboration, their joint tenure never amounted to a truly collective leadership. The quartet launched its artistic direction with a publicity stunt, as they re-enacted the iconic photograph of Berlin's 'Kommune 1' of the hippie period, posing in the nude with their backs to the camera. This provocative, expressly anti-bourgeois self-image, however, in no way reflected their predominantly individual attempts to position and integrate themselves within the apparatus of a large, funded theatre institution. In an interview from 2002, Sasha Waltz commented on her position within this constellation:

> I said from the outset that I need to take my time – that primarily, this is about training together, and about an indirect, internal mutual influence. [...] For me, working with my own ensemble was, from the very

Performing Bodies as a Scenic Playground of Social Realities   175

beginning, the priority. We all agreed that neither of us envisaged a gigantic melting pot, where dance and theatre would be cooked up together. There is mutual interest to work with each others' dancers and actors, but this leads to a logistic problem. Each of us has plans – we do a lot of touring, both of us have a considerable repertoire to perform, which makes it difficult to simply borrow a dancer or an actor for one production.[3]

In the interview, Waltz also remembered the 'emotionally demanding time' of the initial seasons, noting that they had not been able to put to full use the opportunities that the large institution offered, with all its in-house workshops and departments, simply by not being familiar with such production structures, and making some false assumptions.

Effectively, therefore, the four-year period of this joint tenure saw the Schaubühne hosting two separate ensembles, which led not only to an increase in cost, but also to highly complex behind-the-scene logistics. The organizational structures of a large theatre venue with more than 200 employees countered the realization of the often spontaneous, idealistic ambitions of its four co-directors. The vision of veritable co-productions, in which drama and dance would come together in a new theatral fusion in order to offer on stage a complex critical double perspective on socio-political concerns, was, in effect, never realized. In addition, the city's cultural policy makers refused the directors' request for a raise in their annual public funding to create a separate, second in-house ensemble for dance. This decision led to Waltz and Sandig's resignation from their positions in the summer of 2003, which was initially followed by a co-operation agreement between their company, Sasha Waltz & Guests, and the Schaubühne. Yet after more disagreements over finances, Waltz and Sandig terminated this agreement as well and left the Schaubühne for good in November 2005, following a final dance production at the venue, *Gezeiten* (*tides*).

By that time, Waltz and Sandig had curated an impressive dance programme at the Schaubühne, which from today's perspective often disappears behind Thomas Ostermeier's (later) international success with his own productions. They had realized a number of projects together with Alain Platel's Les Ballets C de la B, regularly inviting choreographers, among them Christine de Smedt, Emio Greco and Pieter C Scholten, as well as Sidi Larbi Cherkaoui, who launched his international career at the Schaubühne, where he created *Foi* (2003). In addition, dancers from the company, such as Luc Dunberry, Juan Kruz Diaz de Garaio Esnaola, Laurie Young and Takako Suzuki showed their own choreographic work alongside other invited guests, such as Constanza Macras and Benoît Lachambre. In the already cited interview, Waltz described their efforts to establish a 'laboratory for new ideas, and an interface to the independent dance scene', speaking of her 'dream of the Schaubühne as a dynamic, international production centre'.[4] Such an internationally focused vision, based on cooperation with other theatres and international festivals, could not be realized within the institutional framework of the city-funded Schaubühne, while also revealing fundamental differences in the modes of productions of contemporary dance and theatre work. Far beyond international tours to other venues and festivals with their own work, their artistic self-understanding was based on a wide network of international exchange and co-operation, which as a matter of course also included an international ensemble – a structure which (also for financial necessities) is standard in contemporary dance production. In addition, Ostermeier's theatre productions and Waltz's choreographic works of that period – while embracing both the vision of politically engaged realist theatre and the challenging spatial dimensions of the gigantic venue – aesthetically pointed in rather different directions.

Transforming spaces: Sasha Waltz

Sasha Waltz opened the new Schaubühne in January 2000 with her piece *Körper* (*Bodies*, 2000), the first part of a trilogy that was complemented over the following years by *S* (2001) and *noBody* (2002). She drew in her exploration of the spatio-choreographic potential of the Schaubühne's architectural space on the experience she had gained working on her 1999 series of installation choreographic installations entitled *dialoge* (*dialogues*), one of which she had staged as part of the opening of Berlin's Jewish Museum, designed by architect Daniel Libeskind.[5] As Waltz noted in a 2008 interview:

> The Schaubühne has one of the most fascinating theatre spaces I know. The sheer dimension of the space forced me to go beyond the intimacy of my earlier work. I felt that there are such big distances here so that this approach would no longer work [...] with this gigantic height, this depth – as a matter of fact, this isn't at all a proper theatre space.[6]

Both Waltz and Ostermeier were fascinated by the enormous potential for transformation that this spatial situation offered, which could not have been more different from their own small previous respective theatres, the Baracke and the Sophiensäle.

The theatre's extraordinary variability invited scenographic and choreographic experiments. For *Körper*, Waltz emptied the huge space

Performing Bodies as a Scenic Playground of Social Realities   177

entirely and confronted her thirteen dancers with the building's massive, raw concrete shell (see Figure 5, p. 126). Against the space's bald apse, surrounded by high, grey walls, their semi-naked bodies met the full force of this bleak and sparse architectural surrounding, thereby exposing the vulnerability of their bodies. In the midst of the empty and barren space that felt reminiscent of an austere wasteland, Waltz had placed a wooden box, approximately ten metres high and six metres wide. In the beginning, the dancers climbed into its interior. In somnambulistic motion, they squeezed and heaped their semi-naked bodies behind a small window, creating a relief-like group image. In the course of the production, the wooden walls were moved and lowered, vertically as well as horizontally, thus serving as a changeable scenographic element that would define a range of scenic locations. In one moment, a skier glided down its flat surface, while in the next, it became a huge blackboard on which the performers wrote with chalk. Later, it spectacularly crashed down on the floor, becoming a new foundation for emerging physical sculptures. The audience, meanwhile, sat on a steep gallery opposite the sky-like wall of concrete, witnessing in the course of the production's ninety minutes a fast-paced series of choreographic images, formed of heterogenic scenes of dance and physical action.[7]

Thematically, the twenty-nine scenes dealt with social inscriptions of bodies, with physical biographical experiences and society's grasp on the body. The scenes thereby unfolded a multi-perspectival panorama that expressed fears, uncertainty and a fundamental feeling of unease in one's 'own' body. In the typical self-reflexive mode of dance theatre, the performers spoke about their own bodies. Claudia de Serpa Soares, for instance, had the lines:

> I didn't get the beautiful green eyes of my mother. It just didn't happen. Instead I got all these points on my skin, and a lot of hair from my father's side, I guess. Normally I don't have big problems with my body. Just sometimes I have this stupid herpes on my lips, and I really hate it. And once a month I have this horrible pain all around my stomach. I mean my breasts get bigger, my stomach gets bigger and I just feel that I am inside another body.[8]

In another scene, a similar hyper-sensitive self-observation hysterically escalated, as Luc Dunberry in a frantic rhythm pointed to parts of his body, which, however, did not correspond to the body-parts he mentioned in his simultaneous speech:

> I thought maybe it was my thyroid gland which was unstable, or my pancreas which needed stimulation. But, how can I know? My stomach

178   *The Schaubühne Berlin under Thomas Ostermeier*

is also affecting my whole digestive system. I get clogged intestines and my liver is out of place and my brain is too weak and I'm afraid I'm gonna get a cerebral accident or even a heart attack. So I finally decided to go to the doctor. I was sweating like crazy. I felt like puking and I asked: Do you think I have cancer?[9]

Such narrative sequences contrasted with a series of scenes that listed the prices for plastic surgery, showed bizarre, phantasmatic corporeal transformations, trembling and twitching bodies or body-sculptures formed through the performers' stacked, intertwined and piled up bodies, and similar moments reminiscent of some of the staples of Bauschian dance theatre.

The choreographic imagery of *Körper* combined socio-cultural perspectives, measurements and arrangements of bodies in order to reflect social realities of (un)lived contemporary corporealities, without integrating the scenes according to a single dramaturgic 'grand narrative'. Instead, Waltz relied on the theatrical power of multiple hybridity, where texts and images about the medical and surgical conditioning of the body came together with the affective physical resonance of a constant flood of overpowering stimuli in the dancers' nervously convulsing movements or their absurd physical actions. The choreographic structure thus relied on a mix of direct legibility and the sensuous impact of movements, actions, images and small narratives. This irritated some critics who, at the Schaubühne, expected a more conventionally 'dramatic' approach. Wolfgang Höbel, for example, spoke of a 'physical circus for quick, mindless enjoyment'[10], while dance critic Franz Anton Cramer aptly remarked: 'What are passionate theatre audiences making of an evening which largely consisted of composed images, delicate atmospheres, grandiose scenarios, and, as should be noted, a huge number of citations?'[11] The production still became a huge success, and was invited to the Berlin Theatertreffen, broadcast on television and even discussed in popular German women's magazines at the time. By the numbers of performances and the extent of its worldwide tours, *Körper* remains among the Schaubühne's most successful productions, standing out of this early period under Thomas Ostermeier's tenure. It returned for a short run to the Schaubühne in 2010, and was remounted in 2017 by the company still called 'Sasha Waltz & Guests' with a new cast at another Berlin venue, followed by another extensive tour.

With *Körper*, Waltz had departed from the narrative realism that had characterized her earlier breakthrough works, such as *Allee der Kosmonauten* (*Cosmonaut Alley'* named after a well-known East Berlin avenue, 1996) and *Na Zemlje (Auf Erde)* (*On Earth*, 1998), whose physical theatre realism had impressed Ostermeier. Now, Waltz's focus shifted to a genuinely corporeal exploration of emotional, physical and architectural spaces and conditions:

Performing Bodies as a Scenic Playground of Social Realities 179

Certainly [...] it would have been possible to [...] emphasize more the dancers' individualities, and to focus on the development of characters and stories. The direct proximity to the Schaubühne's dramatic theatre work should have even strengthened such an approach, had I not intended to follow a different path anyway.[12]

In common with a number of other choreographers at the time, Waltz turned to an aesthetic exploration of contemporary body images, to manifestations of psycho-physical states and to the interrogation of the social and biopolitical conditioning of physical existence in the twenty-first century (Western) world. Characteristically for her work – and in contrast to later Schaubühne productions by Constanza Macras and Anouk van Dijk that I will discuss below – Waltz discounted the aesthetic integration of acting into her dance theatre, which became even more evident in the subsequent parts of her trilogy.

With *S*, she turned to a stage space created by media. Video images projected onto the back wall of a box-shaped stage initially opened up views onto quiet seascapes. In front of the images, fully stripped dancers engaged in tender scenes of touching encounters. Thematically, the piece unfolded a somewhat random verbal kaleidoscope of words beginning with the letter 's'. Yet, the early moments of the ninety-minute production already condensed the choreographic focus onto danced moments of sensuality. Displaying sexually connoted movements, the dancers rolled across the floor to Jonathan Bepler's vibrating sound collage. While critics spoke of a 'kindergarten of desire',[13] Waltz was concerned with a serious attempt to choreograph a contemporary landscape of paradise and hell, inspired by Hieronymus Bosch's fifteenth-century painting 'The Garden of Earthly Delights':

In *S* I try to explore the full thematic range of sexuality, eroticism and sensuality, initially purely on a sensual level, via the sense of touch, simply by dancers caressing each other, for example. My task was to find an aesthetic form that tells something about sexuality while maintaining an abstract quality that keeps the situations open, and avoids any narrativity.[14]

The programme book suggested a vast associative space with a sequence of verbs, all starting with the letter 's' in German: 'salben, saugen, schämen, schaudern, schauen, schaukeln, schöpfen, schwanken, schweben, schweigen ...' (to anoint, to suck, to shame, to shudder, to stare, to swing, to scoop, to sway, to soar, to keep silent ...'). The choreography showed vague allusions, as it presented, in the second part, snapshots of human relationships, between

180   *The Schaubühne Berlin under Thomas Ostermeier*

slapstick and comic, between pose and interrupted rhythm, evoking a collage of almost arbitrary associations. The video images in the background showed interior spaces, clouds flying across the sky, birds, aeroplanes and a striding giraffe. In spite of the powerful visual and choreographic imagery, the piece failed to convey the sensuality it sought to evoke. With all its potential of the precarious and the prickling, the dangerous and the violent, it evaporated in an ever rapid rhythm of short movement sequences. Towards the end, the choreography shifted into scenes of violence and ecstasy, animating Bosch's imagery in an at times drastic theatral rendering, which soon lost its affective impact in screams, shouting and bodies immersed in milk, clawing into each other. The response of critics and audiences was reserved.[15]

Waltz completed her trilogy with *noBody*, dedicated to mourning and the transience of bodily existence. The choreography transgressed the usual liveliness of dance, seeking to make appear on stage images of dying and death through somnambulistic actions of sinking down and falling bodies, rolling across the floor, twitching, limping, lifeless bodies carried along, clad in white or black costumes. Relying on group formations evoking, as dance critic Malve Gradinger noted, 'something like a closed society' [*geschlossene Gesellschaft*, the German term for 'private function'], the company was extended from the permanent ensemble of thirteen to twenty-five, so that, in these groups, 'the individual dissolves as a "noBody". [to show] the disintegration of the human body into a "non-body".[16] Dominated by choric movement phrases, especially in the second part, in which the dancers stood closely together, walked or fell in unison, and collectively embodied moments of mourning, Waltz's choreography alone animated the stage space, which, as in *Körper*, remained completely bare and empty, with the sole difference of glaring strips of light that fell onto the movement events from without. In the programme book, Waltz noted:

> *noBody* asks questions about the material as well as spiritual existence of the body, of its presence and absence. The question of transforming matter into energy. The question of a memory of the body. What are we beyond our bodies, what is the immortal in us?

Against this thematic horizon, the lack of moments, movements and actions, over a long period of time, that conveyed moments of despair and also fear, was surprising. The unfathomable abyss of death found no aesthetic echo, only to then surface intensely in a culminating moment towards the middle of the piece, as dancers rushed across the stage, making loud animalistic cries. Next, a sole dancer found herself abandoned in the empty space, and wandered around, in utter confusion and desolation, like a ghost. But little

Performing Bodies as a Scenic Playground of Social Realities   181

more than short sequences of *Tanztheater*-inspired physical expressivity, these scenes again lost much of their intensity as the events transited into circular movement patterns evoking ritual acts, while failing to evoke affective impact. Critics remained correspondingly distant. Peter Laudenbach, for example, regretted the lacking force of the physical and scenic intensities because of 'nothing but superficial illustration that eventually made everything banal. [...] Any irritation was simply wiped away with a series of merry jokes'.[17] Andrew Jack reported from the performance at the Avignon Festival in the summer of 2002: 'The problem, perhaps, is that death is precisely far more abstract, far less visual or concerned with motion, than either of these previous two themes. But, to this viewer, much more could have been made of the idea'.[18] The quiet, and in their choreographic aesthetic very intense, scenes of mourning, which Brandon Shaw highlighted in his discussion with reference to Freud's 'Mourning and Melancholia' and Merleau-Ponty's notion of the phantom, suggested an affective intensity towards the end of the piece that remained unnoticed by most critics.[19]

In addition to extensive touring, 2003 saw Waltz reviving the space-aesthetical research of her earlier *dialogue* series, in the choreographic installation *insideout*, a coproduction of the Schaubühne with the Austrian festival Steirischer Herbst in Graz, which was the European City of Culture that year. Each of the nineteen dancers in the piece was responsible as choreographer for an individual scene, based on personal memories and biographically grounded movement research. These were then grouped together in a series of simultaneously shown scenes over almost two hours, each performed in their own place, distributed across the huge space of the Schaubühne's 'Saal A' theatre. Set designer Thomas Schenk created a course of houses, huts, pavilions and glass cabinets, arranged on two levels, which opened ever new spaces and multiple viewing axes for the spectators, to which the live video projection of the individual performances and scenes added further. A publication offered insight into the interview-based development of the scenes.[20] Waltz described her objective as 'to develop a whole gamut, a kaleidoscope of emotions and memory images, which carry through the piece like a swell of waves, taking one through a variety of states'.[21] The openness of the distributed spatial concept required the audience to adopt responsibility for an active reception, while the number and temporal density of the simultaneously performed scenes made it difficult to engage in greater depth with anything specific. Dance scholar Gerald Siegmund found that:

> the piece [...] literally runs in a void. Too early Sasha Waltz opened the individual rooms again, leaving hardly any time and concentration to

182 *The Schaubühne Berlin under Thomas Ostermeier*

really listen to several stories. The ensemble moves through the rooms, climbs up and down the stairs again, while the audience wanders along. Everywhere we see small fragments which, when they are good, disclose some surprising perspectives on the dancers.[22]

In *insideout*, Waltz once more demonstrated a dramaturgic economy of time which, based on an entertaining chain of scenes, ultimately succumbed to an all too rapid rhythmic overlapping of narrative moments and sensory impressions, preventing her thoroughly emotional and affective phrases from developing increased intensity.

Gezeiten (*Tides*, 2005) was Waltz's final work at the Schaubühne. Once more, a dramaturgy of overpowering sequences of images diluted the inventive movement aesthetics displayed within a scenic wasteland. According to the book publication that accompanied the production, the piece attempted to interrogate 'the theme of transformation in the aftermath of a catastrophe'.[23] Instead of a focused concentration on the disruption, the rift and the chasm that events of catastrophe manifest physically (often slowly, gradually and all the more tormenting), here 'catastrophe' entered the darkened atmosphere of the stage in video images of flooding, of blazing fires and earthquakes, alongside sporadic, lonesome fits of screaming and crying, and moments of oppressive distress and isolation. Scenes of futility, despair and ecstatic movement revealed a choreography that lacked a convincing dramaturgic composition. As critic Franz Anton Cramer noted, Waltz understood how to 'sketch with just a few strokes moods and atmospheres on the stage and [...] to set bombastic crescendos into motion [...]. Yet unfortunately, these skills [...] remain all too superficial, even illustrative'.[24] In the end, the stage floor burst open in an impressive way, under the force of the scenically arranged individual catastrophes. The critics interpreted the production in the context of Waltz's imminent divorce from the Schaubühne. Remarkably, though, in *Gezeiten*, as in none of her previous productions at the Schaubühne, Waltz integrated acted scenes within her choreography, which made sentences of farewell a central theme.

Pop frenzies: Constanza Macras

Following her work for the 'Choreographer's Workshops' during Sasha Waltz's time as artistic co-director in 2001 and 2002, Argentinean choreographer Constanza Macras (b. 1970, Buenos Aires) and her ensemble Dorky Park, which she founded 2003 in Berlin, presented five dance productions at the Schaubühne: *Back to the Present* (2004), *Big In Bombay*

Performing Bodies as a Scenic Playground of Social Realities   183

(2005), *Brickland* (2007), *Megalopolis* (2010) and *Berlin Elsewhere* (2011).[25] Celebrated as a shooting star of the Berlin choreography scene of the early 2000s, Macras's works were a wild pop mix of choreography, music and video, alongside fast-paced scenes crafted in a comic-strip-like aesthetic that exaggerated recognizable patterns of social behaviour and cultural codes. The choreographer noted on her approach:

> For me dance does not have to be beautiful and decoratively pleasing. I see dance as a political instrument, in the sense that it exposes the underlying problems of society. My work lives of [sic] its performers that bring their cultural input and eclectic knowledge into the concepts I choose to explore.[26]

Back to the Present, her first full-length work at the Schaubühne, was a satirical revue that exposed with great relish the disastrous excesses of capitalism, its frenzy of binge consumption, and its emotional distortions – topics that connected Macras's choreographic work directly with the theatre's drama productions. Here, the political themes were discharged in live performed rock songs, some acted scenes, acrobatic action, images of sex, synchronous group choreography, video images and eccentric, over the top solo numbers. The social and personal regression of contemporary neoliberalism was revealed in a distorting mirror of acrobatic slapstick choreography, and collective chorus-line arrangements. The piece had been originally performed as a site-specific production in the former department store Kaufhaus Jandorf, which had stood derelict since the end of the German Democratic Republic, when it used to house the East German 'House of Fashion'. The Schaubühne stage version, a light-footed hybrid of various genres, presented its serious political impetus in the form of popular entertainment, which had been hitherto rather unheard of at the Schaubühne. 'All hell was let loose at the good old Schaubühne, like never before', noted critic Peter Laudenbach.[27]

With her choreography traversing trash, satire, peep and pop show, Macras offered an approach to dance very different from that of Waltz. She presented an ecstatic physicality that lacked aestheticism and pathos, while flirting with racketeering comedy. Amid her lustful, exaggerated movement images, dance introduced itself as a cultural bodily practice of exhaustion, with which this art form is so readily identified. In fact, like no other genre of the performing arts, dance is not only able to thematize and represent the ecstatic, but to act it out energetically. Macras worked precisely with this aesthetic potentiality and the unbroken attribution of dance as a practice of sensual pleasure and erotic transgression. Her pieces provoked a lustful delight in physical-sensual escapades. They addressed a childlike joy of playful animalistic transformation, and tested the limits of libidinous transgression through their evocation of a dynamics of desire. This created, on the side of the spectators, an integrative feeling of collectivity, and an infectious lust of looking. As critic Katrin Bettina Müller suggested about *Back to the Present*, 'The images that emerge are violent, scary, funny, cruel: the world is constantly outgrowing the individual. Nevertheless, the performance creates a great "we-feeling", perhaps by drawing on the shared treasure of common memories that the production so lustfully smashed up'.[28]

These Dionysian qualities, into which the performers' bodies, dancers and actors alike, were immersed, and which were further enforced by the *mise en scène*, were at the heart of Macras's and Thomas Ostermeier's co-production, *Ein Sommernachtstraum frei nach William Shakespeare* (*A Midsummer Night's Dream loosely based on William Shakespeare*, 2006). The performance began as a big party together with the audience, as spectators were welcomed by the performers with a drink before cheerily taking their seats. Yet, the production then turned into a wild spectacle, which at times, in the guise of a peep show, radically provoked the spectator's voyeurism. Actors and dancers indulged themselves for more than two hours in a Dionysian feast of constant transformation, accompanied by pop songs and cascades of speech from Shakespeare's play, while, in particular, the dancers performed lustful artistic scenes. Confronted with such physical, energetic and erotic force, theatre critics were somewhat irritated, speaking of the production's 'brutal violence',[29] or dismissing it outright as a 'supposed orgy'.[30] Solely Christine Dössel detected in her review an aesthetic quality in the hybrid game of transgressive, lustful metamorphosis: 'Ostermeier and Macras invent some striking images for lust and frustration. The actors throw themselves into this expressive physical theatre as if they were liberated, and by no means lack behind the professional dancers, who babble on in their native languages'.[31]

Macras's *Big in Bombay*, the choreography she had created the previous year, was already challenging the audience with its two very action-intensive parts that lasted for two hours in total. Dramaturgically constructed in what became Macras's trademark approach, satirical and very touching scenes clashed with each other, coming together as a blended hybrid of Western and Eastern codes of behaviour, mixed with allusions to current politics, in order to open reflections on the experience of foreign-ness, of desire and also fear. The principal setting for the action was a transparent glass-walled waiting room, which was surrounded by acted and danced scenes. The projection of video footage, filmed during a rehearsal residency in India, offered counter shots. Thus opened a wild kaleidoscope bursting with ideas, which brought together scenes of endangered life worlds, of disturbance and destruction.

The choreography literally burst apart for its profuse abundance, eventually indulging in unconditional physical expenditure. Quiet moments created impactful intensity, in which some highly emotionalized scenes put the finger right on the thematic wounds. Yet among the plethora of scenes, they were virtually drowned.

In spite of the varied qualities of her choreographic works, Constanza Macras succeeded in establishing an original aesthetic style of choreographic dance-theatre at the Schaubühne, which integrated levels of dramatic play and physical action within her dance. With their highly expansive physicality, with corporeality always navigating the fine line between acted out lust, transgression and satirical exaggeration, her productions realized a unique choreographic art, somewhere between collage and show, between entertainment and provocation, lending themselves to debating socio-political issues, precisely by portraying them in an exaggerated 'pop' approach.

The body politics of vulnerability: Anouk van Dijk

The Schaubühne's original aesthetics of an integrated dance-theatre continued with the work of Dutch choreographer Anouk van Dijk, which she created at the Schaubühne together with playwright-director Falk Richter, before taking up, in 2012, the artistic direction of the Melbourne-based company Chunky Move in Australia. Although clearly different from Macras's approach, van Dijk created an equally urgent and tense expressive coalition of the levels of acting and dancing. Articulating the specific bodily intensities of speaking, shouting, stuttering, falling, twitching, slackening and spinning, the work of Richter and van Dijk instantiated an energetic as much as space-specific affinity of all these actions. As the choreographer noted:

Dancers are always balancing on the edge of success and failure. This vulnerability is also a strength and, as a creator, I want to show that area of tension. In dance you are constantly battling with glamour. What you see is not usually what it feels like, and there is tension between the artificial and the natural, and the cerebral and the animal. It is all about someone who is at odds, yet in harmony, with themselves. Someone who is trying to stand their ground, both literally and figuratively. This is what makes dance, in my view, more theatrical and exciting than any other art form.[32]

In contrast to Macras's exaggerated theatricality of ecstatic bodies somewhere between pop and peep show, their physicality here toyed with the frontiers of vulnerability, from which van Dijk mobilized energetic states, choreographing them as arrangements of specific moods grounded in movement-qualities. The resulting aesthetic spectrum of choreographic corporeality would not draw on the citation of social-cultural codes of physical behaviour and body images, as with Macras. Instead it was founded on the basis of a specific movement-aesthetic practice, van Dijk's original approach of 'counter technique', which she had developed with her Dutch dance company since the late 1980s.[33]

The collaboration between van Dijk and Richter put into concrete practice one of the new Schaubühne's core programmatic ideas: to bind authors and playwrights to the theatre in order to create a multifaceted repertoire of contemporary plays. While Ostermeier may not have envisaged choreography as a form of play-writing, van Dijk's contemporary dance aesthetic formed a contemporary physicality on stage, on the basis of its differentiated movement system, which in the midst of opposing dynamics and influences managed to reveal the instinctive moment of physical and emotional intensities, exhibiting them as a complex interplay of forces, hence a physicality acting from within.[34] In their two principal Schaubühne productions *Trust* (2009) and *Protect Me* (2010), dancers and actors merged into an ensemble that effortlessly interacted and communicated with each other, eventually no longer revealing the performers' original artistic discipline. The polyphony of movement and language was distributed between the performers so as to express the thematic foundation, and to unfold a physical as well as discursive space of reflection about physical states in our contemporary society (see Figure 9). Richter's auto-fictional textual surfaces[35] entirely detached themselves from the idea of representing characters. As he commented:

> when dancers are on stage, a different kind of text is required. [...] The text must be detached from a character, a place, a certain time. The text itself must become material from which the performers can work away. Performing these texts puts the actor in a certain physical state, it leads them into states of exhaustion, of anger, etc. The text becomes more of a material, it is detached from any dramatic construction.[36]

In this sense, *Trust* portrayed the dynamics of trust and the loss of trust against the background of the socially ripe states of exhaustion. Light and sound contributed to an atmosphere, which (exemplarily in the gloomy beginning) owed to the spatial configuration of choreographic arrangements.

The wide stage, furnished in a contemporary style of illusory comfort, pointed through its rear mezzanine gallery, on which was mounted a closed-off, room-like box, into a nowhere. Actors and dancers spoke, on equal terms,

Performing Bodies as a Scenic Playground of Social Realities 187

Figure 9 Bringing dance and drama together, *Trust* (2009), by Falk Richter and Anouk van Dijk, portrayed the disorientation and loneliness in contemporary society. The dancing bodies made viscerally palpable the inner state of an utter loss of trust in our dominant way of life (in the front: Stefan Stern). © Heiko Schäfer/Schaubühne.

rhythmic sentences that were interspersed by stuttering and repetition. Situations of despair and an encompassing exhaustion, as cultivated by the contemporary middle-class, unfolded, as bodies fell down, threw themselves around, clung to each other, slid to the floor, and went limp. The production gave equal space to acting and dancing scenes, thereby making tangible the physical states that hid, unspoken, behind the intense monologues, in extensive dance solos and irritating duo scenes. *Trust* created a rhythmic structure, which in its constant spatial drifting apart revealed the disorientation and loneliness that were at the heart of the narrated and acted scenes, as they told of excessive financial management, the loss of reality and hopelessness. The textual meshwork found its physical echo in dance scenes that acted out the qualities of these states, without just illustrating or doubling the spoken description in intense sections. *Trust* succeeded in creating on stage striking, intense correspondences between the physicality and the spoken texts that were permeated by horror, anger and sadness. The piece ended with an almost reconciliatory dance by van Dijk and her dancers, as they presented a rare simultaneous, elegiac sequence between the gaze of both the actors on stage and the audience. In the end, dance thus had the final

188 *The Schaubühne Berlin under Thomas Ostermeier*

word in *Trust*. Critics responded positively to the production, however only rarely discussing the dance elements. Only Simone Kaempf afforded some space to reflect on the physical intensity, which she located not least in van Dijk's own solos: 'They are driven by a force, which expresses an existential pain. This is touchingly expressed by the combination of dance and acting'.[37]

A similar choreographically closely woven interplay of movement and language also characterized *Protect Me* (2010). Here, Richter's rhythmically choreographed text-scape gained an aesthetic weight of its own, which then sprawled out into the scenic space. The piece presented fragile bodies at the verge of exhaustion. The given theatrical reality of bodies diffused into a web of changing presences, through which the areas of crises in *Protect Me* introduced a more outright political layer. The discursive spaces of reflection in Richter's texts asserted themselves in the realm of the physical, morphing into delicately sensitive perspectives of a performed physical critique of the described states. While Sasha Waltz and her dancers transformed the stage architectonics into figurative spaces and an emotionally charged dynamics, which guided the gaze towards choreographed images and exposed arrangements, the co-productions of Anouk van Dijk and Falk Richter succeeded in creating a shared inter-space of speaking and moving, which opened up, for the audience, spaces for critical reflection. The consistent merging of actors and dancers to form a joint ensemble of performers created an interactive theatre, in which textual collages transformed into performed bodies.

Notes

1   See Nina Peters and Dirk Pilz, 'Vertrauensbrücke: Thomas Ostermeier und Jürgen Schitthelm im Gespräch', *Theater der Zeit* (Dezember 2005), 6–8, here p. 7.
2   See Chapter 1 in the present volume.
3   Barbara Engelhardt, 'Subjekt und Abstraktion. Sasha Waltz im Gespräch mit Barbara Engelhardt', in *40 Jahre Schaubühne Berlin, 1962–2002*, eds Harald Müller and Jürgen Schitthelm (Berlin: Theater der Zeit, 2002), 37–44, here p. 42. All translations from German sources are by the author.
4   Ibid., 44.
5   Waltz integrated several scenes from her production *dialoge 99/2*, performed at the Jewish museum 3–10 June 1999, into *Körper*.
6   Sasha Waltz, *Sasha Waltz: Gespräche mit Michaela Schlagenwerth* (Berlin: Alexander, 2008), 59.
7   As theatre scholar Sabine Schouten, who observed the creative process, reveals, the choreography was based on twenty-nine scenes, which were given individual titles during the rehearsal process, referring to their

Performing Bodies as a Scenic Playground of Social Realities   189

protagonists or their thematic concerns. These titles, however, were never revealed to the audience. Sabine Schouten, *Sinnliches Spüren: Wahrnehmung und Erzeugung von Atmosphären im Theater* (Berlin: Theater der Zeit, 2007), 149–76.

8   Quoted from the programme notes, Schaubühne Archive.

9   Ibid.

10 Cited in Jürgen Schitthelm (ed.), *50 Jahre Schaubühne* (Berlin: Theater der Zeit, 2012), 356.

11 Franz-Anton Cramer, 'Von Engeln und Einzellern', *Frankfurter Allgemeine Zeitung*, 29 December 2001.

12 Engelhardt, 'Subjekt und Abstraktion', 41.

13 Arnd Wesemann, 'Kindergarten der Lüste', *Tip*, no. 24 (2000).

14 'Paradise Lost: *S* wie Sex, Schaubühne und Sündenfall. Sasha Waltz über ihr neues Stück', *Tip*, no. 22 (2000).

15 In contrast to most of her work, including *Körper*, Sasha Waltz never included *S* in the repertoire of her company & Guests.

16 Malve Grandinger, 'Architektonische Choreografie: Sasha Waltz, *Körper/S/noBody*', *Oper & Tanz*, no. 6, 2011, www.operundtanz.de/archiv/2011/06/rez-waltz.shtml (accessed 12 February 2020).

17 Cited in Schitthelm (ed.), *50 Jahre Schaubühne*, 392.

18 Andrew Jack, 'A Return to Innovation – 2002 Avignon Festival', www.culturekiosque.com/nouveau/review/festivald'avignon.html (accessed 12 February 2020).

19 See Brandon Shaw, 'Phantom Limbs and the Weight of Grief in Sasha Waltz's *noBody*', *Theatre Journal* 67, no. 1 (2015): 21–42, here p. 32f.

20 Karl Stocker, Nadia Cusimano and Katia Schurl (eds), *Insideout* (Vienna and New York: Springer, 2003).

21 'Das Publikum selbst wird zum Akteur: Carolin Emcke im Gespräch mit Sasha Waltz', *insideout*, programme booklet, 6–17, here p. 8.

22 Cited in Schitthelm (ed.), *50 Jahre Schaubühne*, 417.

23 Sasha Waltz, *Gezeiten* (Berlin: Henschel, 2005).

24 Franz Anton Cramer, 'Bilderflut', *Theater der Zeit* 1 (2006): 38.

25 All productions were international co-productions of her own company Dorky Park, which rarely premiered at the Schaubühne itself. See Arnd Wesemann, 'The Independent: Constanza Macras', *Ballettanz* 7–8 (2007), 52. www.kultiversum.de/Tanz-Ballet-Tanz/Choreografieren-The-Independent-Constanza-Macras.html?p=2&print=1 (accessed 12 February 2020).

26 Macras, Constanza, 'I am with you: Production Notes', http://www.dorkypark.org/site/exhibit/i-am-with-you/ (accessed 25 May 2020).

27 Cited in Schitthelm (ed.), *50 Jahre Schaubühne*, 427.

28 Cited ibid.

29 Cited ibid., 470.

30 Cited ibid.

31 Cited ibid.

190   *The Schaubühne Berlin under Thomas Ostermeier*

32 van Dijk, A., 'Anouk van Dijk – About', www.anoukvandijk.nl/en/about-us/ the-company/anouk-van-dijk (accessed 14 February 2017).

33 See www.countertechnique.com/ (accessed 7 February 2020).

34 See also Jens Hillje's chapter (Chapter 10) in this volume.

35 See also Hans-Thies Lehmann's chapter (Chapter 14) in this volume.

36 Falk Richter, Nicole Gronemeyer and Bernd Stegemann, 'Suche nach Haltung', in *Trust* (Berlin: Theater der Zeit, 2010), 11–26, here p. 13.

37 Simone Kaempf, 'Ob du gehst oder bleibst, das ändert nichts: Falk Richter und Anouk van Dijk erzählen tänzerisch überhöht vom modernen Menschen', www.nachtkritik.de/index.php?option=com_content&view=artic le&id=3349:trust-falk-richter-und-anouk-van-dijk-erzaehlen-taenzerisch-ueberhoeht-vom-modernen-menschen&catid=34:schaubuehne-berlin&Itemid=100476 (accessed 7 February 2020).

14

REST/less EXHAUSTION, SEMI-CALM: Some Notes on Falk Richter's and Anouk van Dijk's *Trust*

Hans-Thies Lehmann

The vast stage space, including a gallery to the rear, immediately signals the themes of isolation and loneliness. The few pieces of furniture make a business-like impression: reminiscent of public spaces, of the furniture characteristic for the false living in what Marc Augé termed 'non places'.[1] Cool leather sofas and armchairs, office chairs matching the impersonal design of corporate spaces, airports, urban environments. To the left and right of the stage there are silver-coloured aluminium walls, with metal boxes at the back, an aluminium ladder and guitars that are set up.[2] One feels a bit like being in a waiting room, where the performers, dancers and actors spread out and lose themselves. On top of the gallery, to the right, we see a room-like shed with a door, into which we can peek through a window. Light with no warmth, hanging lamps, a neon tube, at the front of the stage some kind of bar stool. Another home-transit-station. After a number of directorial works by Falk Richter, this environment (stage design: Katrin Hoffmann) can be identified as an objective stylistic choice. There are, mostly, wide spaces, where the gaze and orientation get lost, which make the individual at once appear isolated, and which at the same time exclude any intimistic closure of the stage space towards the audience. These spaces indicate: this is about discourse. Theatre here is part of a wider, general social field of reflection, to which it seeks to contribute with its own means: physicality, poetry, visuality, musicality.

In this space, Anouk van Dijk and Falk Richter combine drama and dance in an original way. They do not simply introduce textual elements into dance, but aim to develop a fully equal co-presence of language and dance movement. In *Trust*, text and dance come to an agreement, in that they draw gestures of questioning, of doubt, of semi-withdrawal, of breaking off and of giving up; in that together, and mutually reinforcing each other, they create an atmosphere in which something like a 'state of the world' and of life in today's society finds its expression. And they do so, no longer looking at those below us in society, and at the excluded, but focusing on the rather 'normal' world of the life, work and love of the middle classes.

Falk Richter has developed a sharp, perceptive language that shapes linguistic and scenic metaphors from the monetary, competitive reality of life under capitalism. Above all, this builds on his rather unique, crystal-clear and transparent diction, which at the same time leaves peculiar gaps that evoke the unsaid, and thereby remains enigmatic and suggestive for our imagination. It fits a certain language-sphere somewhere between the cooled off, factual debate of relationships (in colloquial German, we use the perfectly objectifying term *Beziehungskiste*: a 'relationship-box' that already aptly sounds like a 'relationship-money-box' one banks on), and the language of management, of a business world with its core parameters of efficiency and calculated speculation. This found, metaphorical speech is further mixed up with citations of a scientific, a scientifically chilled down discourse – a speaking 'under ice', as Richter's earlier play suggested: about money, banks, the economy. The language of this evening – at times monologic, at times in an exchange of words between couples – revolves around descriptions of states of crisis, abandonment, the loss of trust. The speech-scapes point towards a point zero – an in-between that in every way is exhausted, tired, helpless:

> And if I left you it wouldn't change anything
> And if I stayed it wouldn't change anything
> And if I really, really wanted you it wouldn't change anything.[3]

Even in Richter's original German text, the language again and again switches into English: 'And if I touch you it doesn't change anything . . .' Over and over again, this text-loop, which after an initial period of silent physical presence came up to then come back again and again, like a chorus, trips over its initial first clause: 'And if I trust you / *und wenn ich dir vertrauen würde* . . .'. Here, it turns, breaking off helplessly, for once not being followed by the outright statement that 'it wouldn't change anything' – as if this one, special 'as if' – trust – could still make a difference. However, eventually:

> I, I, you know, I, yeah, I, I, I, I just can't, I just cannot, I, I, I
> O my God
> I really can't do this.

All genres are mixed up in Richter's textual foundation: dialogue, diary, scientific and pseudo-scientific treatise, poetry, prose, personal reflection.

The performers, five men, four women, who casually enter the stage, wear comfortable everyday clothing – jeans and blouses, shirts, suits, too: an office world. The greatest distance discloses itself in proximity, and with it, a problem of feeling that can hardly be better articulated than through the gestures of a danced, choreographed search for encounter. Jean-Luc Nancy remarked: 'Touch is proximate distance. It makes one sense what makes one sense (what it *is* to sense): the proximity of the distant, the approximation of the intimate.'[4] This sentence could be the motto for the textual choreography of *Trust*: it is about bodies that want to cling, want to touch, about arms that want to hold, support, grab another – but there are only tiny moments before the loss – the loss of trust – is back again, and with it: turning away, sinking down. And at the same time, these are also words that look for a touch, and yet they shy away from real touch. Richter is preoccupied with the strange blurring, the disappearance, the lapse of the 'I'. A persistent theme in his notes on the play refers to the fog in which everything dissolves, blurs, and the self becomes like a 'sketch in pencil':[5] insecure and lost in an outline. Richter's text would be perfectly suitable as dramatic character speech, yet here, it is not tied to character roles, but functions as a text-scape that is used and realized by everyone – in a postdramatic restructuring of the dialogical principle. Richter comments, in his '*Trust* notes':

> After all, the text is not a prisoner who one might simply lock, on a diet of bread and water, into a character one had once found, let alone into a plot one had once found, for the text is a free body and it must come upon other free bodies, which remain mobile, which remain open, which do not get stuck into their usual hinges of rehearsed mechanics, or else it will die and just lie there, dead, and no one listens any longer to the text, no one even realizes it. Isn't that true, my dears! I think we all agree on this, don't we?[6]

What sets this production apart, is its atmosphere of lightness, and yet still one of concentration, with which the all too weightless life, feelings and words are navigated. It is difficult to pin down which elements specifically contribute to its elegance. First, there is the open approach to creating this 'project', which is tangible in the resulting production: the scenic elements were gradually found and elaborated, taking the author's writing as 'work in progress' and point of departure, rather than treating it as the sacred scripture. In this mode of production, play-writing intends to create a 'space resonant with ideas, through which we move' ('*einen Klangraum an Ideen, durch die wir uns bewegen*').[7] The author himself went in and participated in the improvisations, incorporating echoes and impulses from the rehearsal work

194   *The Schaubühne Berlin under Thomas Ostermeier*

into his writing process. And then, there is the choreography. The dance sequences reinforce, play around, comment on, and in a physical sense 'make sense' of the textual motifs, yet they gain their own autonomous quality of experience beyond illustration. The choreography, in a congenial way, runs parallel to the principal topics of proximity and distance, that distance even in the greatest closeness mentioned above, and the peculiar mood of restlessness and insomnia. The dance language expresses the perpetual, ever new attempts to come together, to trust – and their failure. Throughout, the choreographed movements remain within sight of everyday motion.

The bodies gravitate towards each other – and are yet already distracted and diverted by a different kind of motor activity, thus drifting apart again. In a series of hyperbolic scenes, 'exaggerated' and thereby no longer outright mimetic gestures and courses of action, the state of relationships between people is disclosed. The dancers regularly move in a way close to collapsing. They slide down, glide down, sink down as if into a temporary non-being: terminating, falling, spilling, in all kinds of ways. Couples move around closeness, the search for proximity, but then also sudden aversion. Energies appear to work on these bodies, to tear them away from each other – yet are these internal forces that are pulling here, or is it the impact of social, external effects? In any case, these bodies never arrive at more than a temporary semi-rest. Over and over again, we observe their masterfully slowed down, heavily tired receding, as they sink down deep into the armchair and couch. Another quote from Richter's notes reads:

> All of them are lying in the space, or somewhere isolated on their own, the bodies are restless but exhausted, they are looking for proximity but they can't get engaged with anything for longer, the bodies are in need of protection, but they do not accept any help.[8]

The gesture of the dance in *Trust* corresponds exactly to these descriptions. To add a further quote:

> their heads throw them back and forth, their bodies no longer obey their will, their feelings gush out of them and take over the control of their bodies.[9]

The striking correspondences between Richter's expressions and the impression of the dance clearly demonstrate the artistic accord between Anouk van Dijk and the playwright.

The – in every respect futile and in any case merely half-hearted – attempts to approach, catch, prop up and support the partners are answered in dance,

REST/less EXHAUSTION, SEMI-CALM 195

again and again, by the basic movements of sliding, gliding, falling down. Everyone separates very quickly again from the other, and instead aims ... somewhere. These are psychologically connoted, yet autonomously choreographic sequences. Their principal attitude differs decidedly from the analogous motifs (such as tumbling, picking up, falling, supporting) we know from Pina Bausch or Jan Fabre. These movement phrases are not 'tragic', they do not lead to fundamental despair, but rather – to a perplexed, restless exhaustion in the face of a permanent overload, to a loss of any energy, to resignation. The sociologist Alain Ehrenberg's *Weariness of the Self* is cited on stage for a reason.[10] Here, the psychological is directly social. Just as the psyche of the present is apt to malfunction and fail in the face of the demands for constant availability and strive for excellent performance in all areas, we experience here a corporeality that is at once searching and constantly stressed, afflicted by crises, exhausted, tired. Critic Simone Kaempf wrote aptly in her review:

> Van Dijk often dances alone on stage, her body writhing, as if different forces were acting on arms and legs, provoking rapid changes of direction. When couples come together in dance, an approaching, huddling and sliding off each other prevails, thereby leaving open where these forces actually come from: are they brought in from the society outside, or are they punched out from the inside?[11]

The fatigue of a life without trust, without proximity, yet always in a futile longing for it, is expressed. Perhaps the saddest moment is the chorus-like repetition of the insight that it is far too 'exhausting' to change anything in the system now, after such a long time: in the 'system' of a couple's relationship, the financial system, even the entire economic and social system at large. The momentary gesture of insurrection vanishes the moment one gets closer:

> But we'll leave it like this, right?
> We'll just leave it
> We'll just leave it there
> We'll just carry on, okay?[12]

This sounds almost like a contemporaneous response to German poet Rolf Dieter Brinkmann (1940–1975), who called his posthumously published, hitherto untranslated diary *Explorations for the Specification of the FEELING for a Revolution*,[13] or like another 'Essay on Tiredness'.[14]

But that is not all, for this state at the same time is a crisis, after all. The topic of *Trust* is, in a sense, the hidden logic of the system, its crisis, the collapse of the system, the loss of trust – and it is this latter state that is unfolded on stage, instead of a revolution. Fitting in terms of the drama, the moment was chosen when – as in the old tragedies – the truly decisive events have already happened. The separation has happened, one already has been abandoned and a helpless void has already spread. A relationship has come to an end. How can one deal with such a crisis, with this spreading emptiness? Through poetry, dance and textual discourse, the piece keeps asking this same question over and over again in manifold variations. *Trust* has a clearly analytical dramaturgic structure, even if at first sight the individual parts appear lined up like a series of 'virtuoso acts'. One could, in fact, unfold the carefully plotted dramaturgy of collapse, of helplessness, of a futile search for rage, mourning and 'keep going on' in great detail. At its heart is the thematic intertwining of the private with the public crisis – not by means of a personalization, and a storyline that would 'allegorically' stand in for the social totality, but through the very force of the form of language and dance. Moods and atmospheres change from the energetic to the melancholic, from the grotesque to the lyrical. It navigates around the key question: what exactly happens at the very moment when a private or a social system collapses?

Occasionally, the utopia of silence makes its appearance, physically in the bodies on stage, poetically in the text. In these moments, the perspective on that lack of any real proximity to the others is reverted: perhaps, finally left alone, free from the constant demands and impositions of a partnership, one may in fact finally find one's true self? Then, the dramaturgy comes close to the seemingly paradoxical propositions by philosopher Robert Pfaller. His much quoted theory of 'interpassivity' reflects on this underrated desire not to be bothered by stronger affects, to *not* live, but in perfect peace.[15] He points out the evidence that suggests that the widespread and much talked- and written-about desire for action, experience, density and abundance of events, for an actively filled time, etc., may eventually turn out to be the self-delusion of the contemporary soul. As a matter of fact, it actually prefers 'rather not to', it wants to be left alone and remain in a state of 'interpassivity', where others love for them, listen to music for them, perform an action or experience feelings for them. Strange, by the way, how this echoes, some 100-plus-years later, in a 'de-aristocratized' way, the well-known *bon mot* from Auguste Villiers de l'Isle-Adam's otherwise barely remembered 1890 *fin-de-siècle* closet drama, *Axël*, in which his aristocratic protagonist proclaims, 'Vivre? Les serviteurs feront cela pour nous' ('Living? Our servants will do that for us!').

Trust conveys, both physically and through the style of its language, which is consistently reminiscent of the reality of our everyday common communication, yet without mimetically depicting actual reality, a peculiar mental state and a psychological habitus at the same time. One is tempted to describe it as an equally crazy, yet at the same time oddly innocent numbness that appears devoid of feeling. A state of uncertainty; to deploy a term Brecht kept using, one might call it 'provisionality' (*Vorläufigkeit*) – where nothing is fixed, even the greatest desires for proximity, intimacy, dare one say: 'love', remain entirely of the moment. There is this incomprehension in talking with(out) each other, as each and every one effectively utters monologues. These set pieces of everyday conversation cover up this absence of veritable communication. This numb feeling-less-ness in our private lives corresponds to the objective cynicism of those in power. Trust is out of joint, and out of place everywhere. And still, everyone vies for trust. This may seem absurd, but it is logical, as without trust, the danger of a large-scale collapse, far beyond the financial collapse of the banks, becomes an ever more real threat.

At times energetic, at times sad and reticent, then again hilariously funny and parodistic, the production stages in a wide range of registers how systems in breakdown are being dealt with, in economy, in society, in relationships. In an impressive, long lecture, actor Stefan Stern explains with nothing short of uncanny concentration, that the financial gamblers of the present actually ought to be seen as the 'fourth generation' of the German Red Army Faction terrorists, since their speculation brought the hated 'system of pigs' (*Schweinesystem*), as the RAF had termed capitalism, much more efficiently to the brink of collapse than the bombs and terror of the 1970s. It is not merely ironic cynicism that makes him then contemplate the proposition that the present system might in fact be so wrecked that in a few years it will have been replaced by a new system. This intense discursive moment is then followed with a little song, sung by Judith Rosmair, with the motto 'you need love'. Next, three ladies in fur (the 'banks') walk up to the front of stage, one after the other, smugly touching their forehead with their hands, 'I think I'll just collapse now', and tumble theatrically to the ground. 'Me too'.[16]

And we encounter Judith Rosmair again, in her own monologue section, uttering the absurd hyperbolic infidelity of a woman who has given away quite a few of her lover's cars, who has spent 'some three or four billion' on something, but maybe she has lost the money, or just gave it away as well, as she can't quite remember exactly, and, for sure, she has also already put his home on the market. But now, she asks him to trust her, after all – because she is going to change completely, now. Or maybe from tomorrow, or perhaps, at the latest, the day after tomorrow. 'I promise! Trust me!' Her monologue tirade spirals up into ever more abstruse absurdity: she wants to squander a little more money on some other men first; she has made millions in debt; she does not even know his name. Two men then lift her up high, carry her around as if she were flying weightlessly through the room, while she unswervingly continues her speech, which is devoid of any empathy to the

198 *The Schaubühne Berlin under Thomas Ostermeier*

friend, who sits speechless on the side. Eventually, as her wonderfully insubstantial talk does not want to stop, she is dumped in a metal container, and thereby silenced. This abstruse portrayal of a financial-capitalist 'relationship-locker' makes the spectators hold their breath, since in its exaggeration, the financial crash and the public discourse about the crisis become utterly indistinguishable from the collapse of trust between us, between human beings in the early twenty-first century. There are narratives, or at least traces and fragments of narratives, but they are alienated in such a way that they will be read more as parables than as stuff of our actually existing, really lived present-day lives. The one about the abandoned man, for instance, who stares out of the window into the void, day after day. Or the girl who had been left behind by her parents in a hotel room in Shanghai, and in revenge became a fund manager – an 'explosives expert', she calls it[17] – since she hopes to bring the entire financial system to a gigantic explosion, one day. Very telling, furthermore, is the recurring motif of a separating couple, who cannot agree whether they had been together for three weeks, or for fourteen years, whether their separation took place three weeks ago, or fourteen years ago – culminating in the punch line that they perhaps have only ever seen each other for three weeks in fourteen years.

As a satirical cabaret act, we see a course in aggression management, in which the participants are instructed by their therapist to bark, yet much to his annoyance they are unable to elicit even a minimal outburst of rage. This spoken scene is then again directly followed by a dance episode, in which, at last, two of the dancers seem to engage, just for a brief moment, in gestures of rage. Yet, it becomes immediately apparent that this rage is nothing but despair. It is directed only against the self, resulting in twisting bodies, twitching convulsions and momentary explosions of limbs – not at all a revolt against those responsible for the crisis. Instead, it is once again yet another attempt to mobilize the last remaining energy in order to withstand exhaustion. But why is there no real rage? This question becomes a major topic of the production. At least, hardly coincidentally merely on the periphery, brief glimpses of a general destruction appear, wishful thinking of an encompassing systemic collapse, as in the woman who dreams of becoming the 'explosives expert'. But such anarchic fantasies never gain clearer contours; they remain in the mist, precisely as no substantial, resilient and sustained rage manages to emerge. Richter summarizes:

> So basically the whole thing is a study – or a dancing excess – about the attempt to get oneself to peak performance, to optimal high performance, while the body works against it from the inside. All these various states of exhaustion, search, fear, crisis, going on, of an utter relentlessness in

REST/less EXHAUSTION, SEMI-CALM 199

spending one's own resources, fight against each other. Attempts to escape the paralysis.[18]

In line with a number of contemporary postdramatic works, there is no boundary that separates theoretical texts, poetry, dialogues, epic narratives, language games and monologic speeches. Theory and theatre have merged – again a typical gesture of Brecht. And here, once more, theatre, text and theory. We are on the way to a fundamentally changing notion of theatre and playtext. What *Trust* indicates programmatically, even in its title, is realized quite successfully: it achieves, in the combination of choreography and language, but even at the level of language itself, a complete blending of the individual, personal life with the financial life of the present. 'Money prefers to live on without us'.[19]

Richter articulates relationship issues, the placelessness and instability of the self, in ways that consistently link these concerns back to the economy, to issues of money. Thus, one's own 'interest' changes, a new 'system of interests' becomes necessary, the other person 'withdraws' like money from a machine, relationships are 'devalued' like currency, no one is really certain about their 'value' on the market of relations. The self is egoistical. Run for your lives, even if the others are stuck, trapped – the ego sets off, regardless (or, all the more so?) towards the next 'interest', the next dancer, the audience. Both on the stock market and in relationships, an extremely exhausting vigilance prevails: don't you dare to feign tiredness! Caution, safe spaces, places of retreat – this new kind of psychology as general condition does not allow for trust. Just as investors withdraw their money ideally just before the point the maximum increase in value has been reached in order to make the most profit with their investment before anyone else, private relationships are now equally subject to a sudden shift of 'interests'. Financial capitalism has turned money into something transient, volatile, immaterial, disembodied, which can change its location at the push of a button. This has become the model for subjects and their behaviour, too, and also for their relationships with others.

The space on this stage is hence not a historical, political one. It is a mental and psychological space. Money eats up the stories. Compare this with Richter's earlier *State of Emergency*, where a certain throwaway remark in a dialogue between the couple all of a sudden reveals, almost in passing, that the wife has been in contact with her husband's employer for a good while already, as he no longer seems to perform as he used to. For this reason, she is almost eaten up by the fear that because of his failure in his job, they may lose their apartment in the utterly boring, yet hitherto 'safe' gated community. The themes in Richter's work may, at any point, flip into outright tragedy, at least melancholy. In *Trust*, this is the case, too, in a number of moments, as

200 *The Schaubühne Berlin under Thomas Ostermeier*

for instance in a monologue, spoken by Anouk van Dijk herself at the end of the play. Revolving playfully around the topic of the emptiness of a life form entirely determined from without, it culminates in the uncanny experience of being a *Doppelgänger*, and the 'security' one longs for so much eventually reveals itself as the one decisive obstacle, which separates the self from the other, from the world – from itself:

> All these years precisely mapped out for me
> Someone must have been there before me
> Someone must have been there before me doing all the research and I
> am following what they have come up with.[20]

A cue to the others follows, to resume dancing. After just a few seconds more, blackout.[21]

Translated by Peter M. Boenisch

Notes

1 Marc Augé, *Non-Places: An Introduction to Supermodernity*, new edn (London and New York: Verso, 2009).

2 I will not discuss the role of music in this production in this essay.

3 All citations from the playtext are taken from the English translation: Falk Richter, *Trust*, trans. Maja Zade (Frankfurt a.M.: S. Fischer, 2009).

4 Jean-Luc Nancy, *The Muses*, trans. Peggy Kamuf (Redwood, CA: Stanford University Press, 1996), 17.

5 Richter, *Trust*, 36. See also Falk Richter, 'Trust Material', in *Falk Richter – Trust*, ed. Nicole Gronemeyer (Berlin: Theater der Zeit, 2010), 103–34, here 105. This 'material' consists of 'diary-style writing, at times towards a possible playtext' (ibid., 103), which Richter had written ahead of the first rehearsal day, as well as his rehearsal notes.

6 Richter, 'Trust Material', 120f.

7 Ibid., 122.

8 Ibid., 107.

9 Ibid., 111.

10 Alain Ehrenberg, *The Weariness of the Self: Diagnosing the History of Depression in the Contemporary Age* (Montreal and Kingston: Mc Gill-Queen's University Press, [1998] 2010).

11 Simone Kaempf, 'Ob du gehst oder bleibst, das ändert nichts: Falk Richter und Anouk van Dijk erzählen tänzerisch überhöht vom modernen Menschen', www.nachtkritik.de/index.php?option=com_content&view=artic le&id=3349:trust-falk-richter-und-anouk-van-dijk-erzaehlen-taenzerisch-

REST/less EXHAUSTION, SEMI-CALM 201

ueberhoeht-vom-modernen-menschen&catid=34:schaubuehne-
berlin&Itemid=100476 (accessed 7 February 2020).

12 Richter, *Trust*, 11 *passim*.

13 Rolf-Dieter Brinkmann, *Erkundungen für die Präzisierung des GEFÜHLS
für einen Aufstand* (Reinbek: Rowohlt, 1987).

14 Peter Handke, 'Essay on Tiredness', in *The Jukebox and other Essays on
Storytelling* (New York: Farrar, Straus and Giroux, 1994).

15 Robert Pfaller, *Interpassivity: The Aesthetics of Delegated Enjoyment*
(Edinburgh: Edinburgh University Press, 2017).

16 Richter, *Trust*, 23.

17 Ibid., 42.

18 Richter, 'Trust Material', 126.

19 Richter, *Trust*, 49.

20 Ibid., 63.

21 This text was originally written towards a planned, more comprehensive
study on Falk Richter. It was first published, alongside Falk Richter's own
production notes and the playtext, in Gronemeyer, ed., *Falk Richter – Trust*.
Reprinted and translated with permission of Hans-Thies Lehmann and
Theater der Zeit.

Index

Productions at the Schaubühne are listed under the playwright's name, stating the German production title, followed by the play's English title and the name of the director.

Achternbusch, Herbert
    Susn (dir. Ostermeier) 67, 108
Aeschylus
    Oresteia (dir. Stein) 13, 17, 24, 43
Antiquity Project (dir. Stein/Grüber) 14, 16, 17
Attar, Ahmed El 33
Avdic, Damir 86
Avignon Festival 61, 63, 84, 90, 98, 181

Baracke (Deutsches Theater Berlin) xvi, 18, 25, 28, 39, 45, 49, 55–8, 60, 62, 66, 98, 106–8, 117, 123–7, 131, 137, 147
Bausch, Pina 96, 178, 195
Berliner Ensemble (Berlin) xiv, 24, 39, 41, 46, 96, 124
Beyer, Robert 86, 88
Bierbichler, Josef 63
biomechanics (Meyerhold) 55, 109, 144, 147
Birch, Alice
    Ophelias Zimmer (*Ophelia's Room*, dir. Mitchell) 141, 142, 150–5
    after Virginia Woolf, *Orlando* (dir. Mitchell) 31, 152, 156
Bondy, Luc 14, 25, 43, 56
Borchmeyer, Florian 160
Böwe, Jule 34, 156

Brecht, Bertolt xiii, 11, 28, 39, 41, 46, 49, 66, 68, 79, 105, 107, 114, 117, 123–4, 148, 170, 197, 199
    Man Equals Man (dir. Ostermeier) 18, 55
    after Gorky, *The Mother* (dir. Stein), 41
Breth, Andrea 25, 43, 56
Brinkmann, Rolf-Dieter 195
Brooklyn Academy of Music BAM Next Wave Festival 29
Büchner, Georg xvi, 96, 124
    Danton's Death (dir. Ostermeier), 59, 98
    Woyzeck (dir. Ostermeier) 60, 61, 107
budget (of the Schaubühne) xviii, 44, 47
Burgtheater (Vienna) 61

Castellucci, Romeo xvii, 48, 136
Castorf, Frank xv, 46, 54–5, 96, 105, 136
Chekhov, Anton 31, 43, 132–7
    The Cherry Orchard (dir. Richter) 132–5
    The Cherry Orchard (dir. Stein) 43, 54
Clever, Edith 11, 40–1
co-determination (Mitbestimmung) 4, 5, 11, 12, 43
Comédie-Française (Paris) 72, 77
The Coming Insurrection 19, 64, 102

Index

comparative theatre (Dubatti) 159-61
contemporary theatre 4, 6, 11, 95–8, 116
Crimp, Martin 129

dance theatre xiv, 4, 5, 26, 75, 128, 134, 173–5, 179, 183–8, 191, 194, 196, 198
Dead Centre 22–3, 26, 31–2
Shakespeare's Last Play 22, 32
Dene, Kirsten 63
Deutsches Theater (Berlin) xiv, 18, 24–6, 39, 56, 98, 131, 137
Devine, George 124
directors' theatre *see Regietheater*
Dodin, Lev 143–4
Dupouey, Sebastian 108, 113

Eales, Alex 145, 150
Edinburgh Festival 59
Ehrenberg, Alain
Weariness of the Self 195
Eidinger, Lars xvii, 19, 35, 64, 71–8, 82–92, 110, 154–6
Eisenstein, Sergej 19, 75
Elizabethan theatre 49, 66, 72
Emcke, Carolin 26, 35
ensemble (of actors at the Schaubühne) xvii, 4–5, 23, 24, 32, 40, 41, 46, 48, 128, 135–6, 155, 186
epic theatre (Brecht) 10, 66, 67, 76, 78, 79, 199
Eribon, Didier
Rückkehr nach Reims (Returning to Reims, dir. Ostermeier) 32, 47, 49, 106, 112–16
Ernst Busch Theatre Academy xvi, 18, 48, 144
Euripides
Bacchae (dir. Grüber) 14, 16

Fabre, Jan 195
fabrication (directorial) 72–6, 79, 115

Fassbinder, Rainer Werner
Die Ehe der Maria Braun (Maria Braun's Marriage, dir. Ostermeier) 108-9
FIND Festival of International New Drama 31–3, 125, 127, 131, 136–40, 159–63, 167–71
Fleisser, Marieluise
Fegefeuer in Ingolstadt (Purgatory in Ingolstadt, dir. Stein) 13, 41
Fosse, Jon 18, 127, 130
Der Name (The Name, dir. Ostermeier) 59
Freie Volksbühne (Berlin) 10, 42, 96
Frey, Barbara 14
Fritsch, Herbert 14

Ganz, Bruno 11, 40, 41
García, Rodrigo 31, 136
Gawenda, Christoph 32
Giehse, Therese 41
Globe (stage of the Schaubühne) 26, 32, 72, 110
González Casanova, Pablo
La democracia en México 163
Gosch, Jürgen 25, 43, 56
Gottwald, Moritz 32
Gropius, Walter 24
Grüber, Klaus Michael 11, 14, 20, 24, 40

Handke, Peter
Der Ritt über den Bodensee (The Ride Across Lake Contance, dir. Peymann), 41
Harrower, David
Knives in Hens (dir. Ostermeier) 18, 55
Hartmann, Jörg xvii, 112
HAU Hebbel am Ufer (Berlin) xvii, 30, 163
Haupt, Carolin 34

204 Index

Hauptmann, Gerhart 127
  Vor Sonnenaufgang (*Before Sunrise*,
    dir. Ostermeier) 61
Hellenic Festival (Athens) 70, 84
Hellman, Lilian
  Die kleinen Füchse (*Little Foxes*,
    dir. Ostermeier) 64, 65,
    107
Hermanis, Alvis 14, 136
Hillje, Jens xiii, xv–xvii, 25, 123–40,
    160, 174
Hobmeier, Brigitte 109
Hochhuth, Rolf
  Der Stellvertreter (*The Deputy*, dir.
    Piscator) 10
Hoffmann, Katrin 191
Hölderlin, Friedrich
  Winterreise (*Winter Journey*, dir.
    Grüber) 14, 24
Horvath, Ödön von
  Die Italienische Nacht (*Italian
    Night*, dir. Ostermeier)
    32, 111
  Jugend ohne Gott (*Youth Without
    God*, dir. Ostermeier) 32,
    112
Hoss, Nina xvii, 113, 114, 156

Ibsen, Henrik xvi, 23, 60, 62, 64, 69,
    79, 98, 107, 118, 126, 127,
    145
  Baumeister Solness (*The Master
    Builder*, dir. Ostermeier) 61
  Ein Volksfeind (*An Enemy of the
    People*, dir. Ostermeier) 19,
    28–30, 63–4, 95, 99–102,
    106, 109–12, 142
  Hedda Gabler (dir. Ostermeier)
    18, 19, 31, 62–4, 68, 105,
    108, 127, 129, 148
  John Gabriel Borkman (dir.
    Ostermeier) 63
  Nora (*A Doll's House*, dir.
    Ostermeier) 18, 30, 31,
    59–64, 105, 147, 148

Peer Gynt (dir. Stein) 41, 54
Spoken/Les Revenants (*Ghosts*, dir.
    Ostermeier) 63, 98
improvisations 19, 78, 86, 87, 89, 136,
    169, 193
'in-yer-face theatre' xvi, 45, 55, 59,
    60, 64, 105, 107, 115, 124,
    131
inductive method of *Regie*
    (Ostermeier) 73
institution (Schaubühne as a theatre)
    23–8, 32, 35, 36, 116

Jelinek, Elfriede
  Schatten (*Eurydike Sagt*) (*Shadow
    – Eurydice says*, dir.
    Mitchell) 156
Jianjun, Li 33
Jucker, Urs 77, 85–6, 88

Kammerspiele (Munich) 9, 40, 61,
    108
Kane, Sarah xvi, 18, 23, 54, 58, 124,
    125, 127, 130
  Gier (*Crave*, dir. Ostermeier)
    58
  Zerbombt (*Blasted*, dir.
    Ostermeier) 55, 59, 62
Kelling, Gerhard
  Die Auseinandersetzung (*The
    Altercation*, dir. Stein) 14
Kirchhoff, Corinna 41
Kleist, Heinrich von
  Prinz Friedrich von Homburg
    (*The Prince of Homburg*,
    dir. Stein) 13, 54
König, Jenny 34, 71, 85, 155
Kortner, Fritz 40
Kroetz, Franz Xaver 60, 97
  Wunschkonzert (*Request Concert*,
    dir. Ostermeier) 60, 61,
    144–8
  Wunschkonzert (*Request Concert*,
    dir. Mitchell) 144–6, 149,
    151, 152

Index

Lagartijas tiradas al sol
 Tijuana 163–5, 168
Lamford, Chloe 150, 153
Lampe, Jutta 11, 40, 41
Langenscheidt, Leni 39
Langhoff, Shermin xvii
Langhoff, Thomas 55
Lardi, Ursina xvii, 109
Larraín, Pablo *Acceso* 163, 165, 166,
 168
Laufenberg, Laurenz 111
Layera, Marco 168–70
Liddell, Angélica 136
Live Cinema (Mitchell) 143, 146, 149,
 152–6
Louis, Edouard
 Im Herzen der Gewalt (*A History
 of Violence*, dir. Ostermeier)
 49, 106, 112, 114, 116–18,
 153
 Qui a tué mon père (dir.
 Ostermeier) 116

Macras, Constanza 74, 132, 175,
 182–6
 Back to the Present 173, 183, 184
 Big in Bombay 173, 184
Maeterlinck, Maurice
 Der blaue Vogel (*The Blue Bird*,
 dir. Ostermeier) 56
materialist theatre 69, 103, 141
Mau, Waltraud 39
Maxim Gorki Theater (Berlin) xvii,
 130
Mayenburg, Marius von 18, 34, 58–9,
 88–90, 128, 130
 Ein Stück Plastik (*Plastic*, dir.
 Mayenburg) 59
 Feuergesicht (*Fireface*, dir.
 Ostermeier) 58
 Peng (*Bang*, dir. Mayenburg) 59
 Turista (dir. Perceval) 132, 133
McBurney, Simon xvii, 33, 48, 136
Meckbach, Eva 74, 155
Mendelssohn, Erich 23, 24

meta-theatricality 22, 35, 69, 77
Meyerhold, Vsevolod E. 55, 75, 79,
 109, 141, 143, 144, 147
mise en action 66
Mitbestimmung *see* co-
 determination
Mitchell, Katie xvii, 14, 48, 136,
 141–56
Mitrović, Sanja, 32
montage of attractions (Eisenstein)
 19, 75
Montenez, Christophe 77

Nakajew, Sebastian 73
national theatre xvi, 45, 161
Norén, Lars 18, 57, 127, 130
 Dämonen (*Demons*, dir.
 Ostermeier) 109
 Personenkreis 3.1 (*Human Circle
 3.1*, dir. Ostermeier) xiii, 6,
 57, 107, 126, 138

O'Casey, Sean
 Shadow of a Gunman 39
O'Neill, Eugene
 Trauer Muss Elektra Tragen
 (*Mourning Becomes Electra*,
 dir. Ostermeier) 62, 107

Pappelbaum, Jan 18, 25, 26, 55, 56, 58,
 60–4, 69–72, 109, 110, 145,
 148
Pearson, Joseph 31, 33, 34
Perceval, Luk xvii, 14, 131–5
 Molière (dir. Perceval) 133,
 134
Perkins-Gilman, Charlotte
 Die gelbe Tapete (*The Yellow
 Wallpaper*, dir. Mitchell)
 150
Peymann, Claus 11, 12, 14, 20, 40, 41,
 57
philosophical theatre 17, 20
Piscator, Erwin 10, 11, 24, 42, 96
Plate, Uta 15

206   *Index*

political theatre 10, 15, 41, 44, 159
postconceptual theatre 105, 106, 116
postdramatic theatre 13, 27, 105, 106, 108, 111, 130, 143, 162, 164, 168, 193, 199
postmigrant theatre xvii
processo colaborativo 97
psycho-physicality (Stainslavsky) 74, 75, 79, 109, 179
public sphere (theatre and) 26–9, 32, 33, 117, 118, 128

Rau, Milo xvii, 28, 29, 31, 48, 113 ·
   Mitleid: Die Geschichte des Maschinengewehrs (Compassion: The History of the Machine Gun, dir. Rau) 30, 31, 95
Ravenhill, Mark xvi, 23, 54, 56, 59, 124, 125, 127, 130
   Shoppen und Ficken (Shopping and Fucking, dir. Ostermeier) 18, 49, 55, 56, 107, 115, 124, 131, 147
realism xvi, 28, 42, 55, 56, 64, 79, 101, 103, 105, 108, 109, 112–17, 127, 130–2, 141–4, 146–9, 152–7, 178;
   capitalist 53, 58
   contemporary 57, 105, 130, 141, 148
   critical 148, 153
   materialistic 103
   negative 109, 115
   new 4, 18, 67, 101, 126, 131
   reflexive 105, 108, 112, 113, 117
   social xiii, 40, 58
   socialist 53, 58, 63, 65
   sociological 101, 107, 148
Regietheater (directors' theatre) xiii, 11–5, 20, 23, 36, 66, 95, 106, 110, 111, 144

repertoire (of the Schaubühne) 5, 11, 23, 26, 58, 62, 67, 84, 124, 129, 130, 154, 186
repertory theatre system (in Germany) 30, 33, 84
Reza, Yasmina 59
Richter, Falk xvii, 48, 128–35, 173, 185–8, 191–3, 198, 199
   Complexity of Belonging, 129
   Das System (The System) 129, 130, 133, 135
   Peace 128–9
   Unter Eis (Under Ice) 129, 131, 132, 135
   with Anouk van Dijk
      Protect Me 173, 186, 188
      Trust 133–6, 173, 186–8, 191–201
Rigola, Álex 31, 136
Rodríguez, Gabino 163–5
Ronen, Yael 14, 113, 136, 137
   Die Dritte Generation (The Third Generation) 136, 138
Rosmair, Judith, 197
Royal Court Theatre (London) 54–9, 64, 124–5, 128, 130

Sander, Otto 41
Sandig, Jochen xiii, xv, xvi, 25, 131, 174–5
Schaubühne am Halleschen Ufer xiv, 8, 11, 24, 30, 42, 43
Schaubühne am Lehniner Platz xiii, xviii, 22, 24–5, 43, 84, 125
Schenk, Johannes
   Transportarbeiter Jakob Kuhn (dir. Stein) 14
Schillertheater (Berlin) xiv, 11, 42
Schimmelpfennig, Roland 128, 130
Schitthelm, Jürgen xiii–xvi, 11, 39, 41
Schnitzler, Arthur 23, 79, 106, 118

Professor Bernhardi (dir. Ostermeier) 46, 106, 109, 111–12
Schuch, Renato 154
Shakespeare, William 23, 31, 64, 65, 67, 69, 72, 110, 118, 153–5
Ein Sommernachtstraum frei nach William Shakespeare (after *A Midsummer Night's Dream*, dir. Ostermeier and Macras) 67, 69, 74, 184
Hamlet (dir. Ostermeier) xiii, 19, 23, 31, 67, 68, 70, 73, 75, 77, 81–92, 106–12, 141, 151, 154–5
La Nuit des Rois (*Twelfth Night*, dir. Ostermeier) 67, 72, 74, 77
Mass für Mass (*Measure for Measure*, dir. Ostermeier) 67–71, 74, 75, 154, 155
Othello (dir. Ostermeier) 67–70, 73–7, 154
Richard III (dir. Ostermeier) 26, 30, 67, 69, 72, 75, 77, 78, 106, 110–12, 115, 154, 155
Shakespeare's Memory (after *As You Like It*, dir. Stein) 17, 24, 42
The Tempest (adapt. Dead Centre) 22
Silver, Nicky
Fette Männer im Rock (*Fat Men in Skirts*, dir. Ostermeier) 18, 55
Simons, Johan 131, 133
situation (dramatic) 66, 68, 73–9, 83–91, 132, 133
sociological theatre 5, 15, 19–20, 57, 67, 101, 106, 107, 117, 148
Sophiensäle (Berlin) xvi, 25, 174, 176
Srbljanović, Biljana 18
Stanislavsky, Konstantin S. 46, 74, 76, 79, 109, 141–4, 149, 152, 153

Stein, Peter xiii–xiv, xvi, xvii, 7–20, 24–5, 39–46, 54, 56, 63, 97, 98, 102, 131
Stern, Stefan 29, 77, 187, 197
Stocker, Laurent 77
storytelling, method of (Ostermeier) 43, 76
Streitraum 28, 33, 35, 125
Strindberg, August
Fräulein Julie (*Miss Julie*, dir. Mitchell) 95, 142, 143, 146, 150
Sturm, Dieter xiv, 11, 12, 39
Suassuna, Ariano
Das Testament des Hundes oder die Geschichte der Barmherzigkeit (*O Auto da Compadecida* / A Dog's Will, dir. Swinarski) 11, 95, 96
supra-national theatre (Dubatti) 159, 161, 171
Swinarski, Konrad 11, 96
Szymanski, André 131

Tanztheater *see* dance-theatre
Teatro da Vertigem 98, 102
Teatro La Maria
El Hotel 162, 166–8
Teatro La Re-Sentida
Paisajes para no colorear 168–70
Theatertreffen (Berlin) 10, 42, 128, 145, 178
theatrality 105–17, 173–5, 180
Thieme, Thomas 62, 131, 133, 134
Tismer, Anne 60, 61, 145–7

Vandalem, Anne Cécile 31
Van Dijk, Anouk 128, 134, 173, 179, 185–91, 194-200
Van Hove, Ivo 14, 48, 98, 136
Vishnevsky, Vsevolod
An Optimistic Tragedy (dir. Stein) 41

208 *Index*

Volksbühne (Berlin) xiv, xvii, 24, 26,
 46, 131
Voss, Gert 61

Walsh, Enda 23
 Disco Pigs (dir. Ostermeier)
  18, 61
Walter, Birgit 149
Waltz, Sasha xiii–xvi, 25, 26, 126, 131,
 173–83, 188
 Gezeiten (*Tides*) 175, 182
 insideout 173, 181, 182
 Körper (*Bodies*) xiii, xvi, 126, 173,
  176, 178, 180
 noBody 173, 176, 180
 S 173, 176, 179
 Travelogue xvi
Waschke, Mark xvii, 131
Wedekind, Frank
 Lulu (dir. Ostermeier) 61
Weiffenbach, Klaus 11, 39
Weigel, Helene 39, 124

Weiss, Peter
 Die Ermittlung (*The Investigation*,
  dir. Piscator) 10
 Vietnamdiskurs (*Vietnam
  Discourse*, dir. Stein) 10, 40
Wengenroth, Patrick 34
Wesker, Arnold
 Roots 39
Wetzel, Nina 108, 109
Williams, Tennessee, 10
 *Die Katze auf dem heissen
  Blechdach* (*Cat on a Hot
  Tin Roof*, dir. Ostermeier)
  62, 107, 108
Winkler, Angela 63

Zade, Maja 31, 34, 35, 125, 156
 Abgrund (dir. Ostermeier) 35
 Status Quo (dir. Mayenburg) 34,
  156
Zadek, Peter xiii, xiv, xvi, 11, 20
Ziemke, Katharina 102

CPSIA information can be obtained
at www.ICGtesting.com
Printed in the USA
LVHW080000150522
718802LV00014B/1078